Contributions to Finance and Accounting

The book series 'Contributions to Finance and Accounting' features the latest research from research areas like financial management, investment, capital markets, financial institutions, FinTech and financial innovation, accounting methods and standards, reporting, and corporate governance, among others. Books published in this series are primarily monographs and edited volumes that present new research results, both theoretical and empirical, on a clearly defined topic. All books are published in print and digital formats and disseminated globally. This book series is indexed in Scopus.

Michael Adelowotan • Collins Achepsah Leke
Editors

Artificial Intelligence in Accounting, Auditing and Finance

A Guide for Implementation and Use

 Springer

Editors
Michael Adelowotan
Department of Accountancy
University of Johannesburg
Johannesburg, South Africa

Collins Achepsah Leke
Department of Accountancy
University of Johannesburg
Johannesburg, South Africa

ISSN 2730-6038 ISSN 2730-6046 (electronic)
Contributions to Finance and Accounting
ISBN 978-3-031-87367-6 ISBN 978-3-031-87368-3 (eBook)
https://doi.org/10.1007/978-3-031-87368-3

This Springer imprint is published by the registered company Springer Nature Switzerland AG
The registered company address is: Gewerbestrasse 11, 6330 Cham, Switzerland

If disposing of this product, please recycle the paper.

Preface

This book provides a comprehensive examination of how Artificial Intelligence (AI) is transforming accounting, auditing, and finance. Each chapter explores a specific aspect of this transformation, offering both theoretical insights and practical guidance for professionals and organisations navigating this changing landscape.

The chapters are organised to provide a logical progression from foundational concepts to specific applications, including:

- Theoretical frameworks for understanding AI in finance
- Technical aspects of AI implementation
- Practical applications across different domains
- Future trends and emerging possibilities and
- Case studies and real-world examples

Whether you are a practicing professional, an academic researcher, or a student preparing for a career in financial services, this book will help you understand the opportunities and challenges that AI presents and how to prepare for the future of finance.

As we begin this exploration, remember that the integration of AI into financial services is not just about technology—it is about how we can use these new capabilities to create better outcomes for organisations, professionals, and society. The chapters that follow will guide you through this transformation, providing the knowledge and insights you need to succeed in an AI-enabled financial world.

This book represents a collaborative effort to capture the state of the art in AI applications across financial services while looking ahead to future possibilities. Through detailed analysis, case studies, and expert perspectives, we aim to provide a comprehensive resource for understanding and navigating this rapidly evolving landscape.

The second chapter explores the development of Artificial Intelligence and Machine Learning with emphasis on the applications in the financial services sector. The third chapter also discusses the development of Accounting as a service activity.

The fourth chapter explores the challenges of Artificial Intelligence and the Fourth Industrial Revolution to the accountancy profession. The fifth chapter also emphasises the impact of Artificial Intelligence on the role of management accountants.

The sixth chapter discusses the impact of Artificial Intelligence on Auditing and Assurance Services while the seventh chapter explores the integration of artificial intelligence into taxation processes.

The eighth chapter reflects on Artificial Intelligence and Financial Statement Analysis by using a critical management framework approach while the ninth chapter presents Artificial Intelligence Tools and Use Cases in Corporate Finance.

The tenth chapter discusses the benefits and challenges of utilising Artificial Intelligence in Enterprise Risk Management while the eleventh chapter presents Financial Time Series Forecasting in the Artificial Intelligence domain.

The twelfth and the concluding chapter reflects on the centrality of data as the new currency of our remade world.

Johannesburg, South Africa   Michael Adelowotan
                                                                              Collins Achepsah Leke

Acknowledgements

We thank all the authors and peer reviewers for contributing to the success of this book project. We also thank Dr Adesanmi Adegbayibi and Dr Mohammed Ajape, who are currently Postdoctoral Research Fellows at the Department of Accountancy of the University of Johannesburg, for administrative roles performed in the course of this book project.

Contents

Introduction: Our Remade World. 1
Michael Adelowotan and Collins Achepsah Leke

The Development of Artificial Intelligence and Machine Learning:
Applications in Financial Services. 9
Collins Achepsah Leke

The Development of Accounting as a Service Activity. 31
Michael Adelowotan

The Accountancy Profession and the Challenges of Artificial
Intelligence. 45
Nicolaas Strydom and Ahmed Mohammadali-Haji

The Impact of Artificial Intelligence on the Role of Management
Accountants. 63
Amanda F. Mhlongo

The Impact of Artificial Intelligence on Auditing and Assurance
Services. 83
Morepe Ncalo and Benjamin Marx

Integration of Artificial Intelligence into Taxation Processes. 103
Adesanmi Timothy Adegbayibi and Mohammed Kayode Ajape

Reflecting on Artificial Intelligence and Financial Statement
Analysis Using a Critical Management Framework Approach 127
Gideon Els

Artificial Intelligence Tools and Use Cases in Corporate Finance 153
Mohammed Kayode Ajape and Adesanmi Timothy Adegbayibi

**The Benefits and Challenges of Utilising Artificial Intelligence
in Enterprise Risk Management** 173
Justine Gomolemo Nkobane

**Financial Time Series Forecasting in the Artificial Intelligence Domain:
Learning Through the Lens of Time** 189
Milan De Wet and Botha Ilse

Conclusion: The Currency of Our Remade World 209
Collins Achepsah Leke and Michael Adelowotan

Contributors

Adesanmi Timothy Adegbayibi Department of Accountancy, University of Johannesburg, Johannesburg, South Africa

Michael Adelowotan Department of Accountancy, University of Johannesburg, Johannesburg, South Africa

Mohammed Kayode Ajape Department of Accountancy, University of Johannesburg, Johannesburg, South Africa

Gideon Els Department of Accountancy, University of Johannesburg, Johannesburg, South Africa

Botha Ilse Department of Accountancy, University of Johannesburg, Johannesburg, South Africa

Collins Achepsah Leke Department of Accountancy, University of Johannesburg, Johannesburg, South Africa

Benjamin Marx Department of Accountancy, University of Johannesburg, Johannesburg, South Africa

Amanda F. Mhlongo Department of Accountancy, University of Johannesburg, Johannesburg, South Africa

Ahmed Mohammadali-Haji Department of Accountancy, University of Johannesburg, Johannesburg, South Africa

Morepe Ncalo Department of Accountancy, University of Johannesburg, Johannesburg, South Africa

Justine Gomolemo Nkobane Department of Accountancy, University of Johannesburg, Johannesburg, South Africa

Nicolaas Strydom Department of Accountancy, University of Johannesburg, Johannesburg, South Africa

Milan De Wet Department of Accountancy, University of Johannesburg, Johannesburg, South Africa

List of Figures

The Accountancy Profession and the Challenges of Artificial Intelligence

Fig. 1   Number of documents by year (n = 1520)   49
Fig. 2   Top 20 total documents by country or territory (n = 1520)   49
Fig. 3   Frequency of keywords in article titles (n = 880)................   50

The Impact of Artificial Intelligence on the Role of Management Accountants

Fig. 1   Adopted from Kamal (2015)   68
Fig. 2   CIMA Information to impact framework (CIMA 2019)   70
Fig. 3   Different levels of AI—Adopted from AICPA's
Introduction to AI (2019)   72

Integration of Artificial Intelligence into Taxation Processes

Fig. 1   Evolution of Artificial Intelligence: A timeline of key
developments   105

The Benefits and Challenges of Utilising Artificial Intelligence in Enterprise Risk Management

Fig. 1   Documents consulted in the systematic literature review..........   180

Financial Time Series Forecasting in the Artificial Intelligence Domain: Learning Through the Lens of Time

Fig. 1   Objectives of time series forecasting   190
Fig. 2   Time series components   192
Fig. 3   The evolution of time series analysis   192
Fig. 4   Data Science and related terms..............................   196

Fig. 5   The components of machine learning 197
Fig. 6   Annual production over time 200
Fig. 7   Annual citations per year 200
Fig. 8   Impact of journals in the field by H index 201
Fig. 9   Word Cloud 201
Fig. 10   Trending topics 202
Fig. 11   Documents with the highest impact 203

List of Tables

The Accountancy Profession and the Challenges of Artificial Intelligence

Table 1 Inclusion criteria. 50
Table 2 Exclusion criteria 51
Table 3 Data extracted. 51
Table 4 Themes identified from the review. 52

Artificial Intelligence Tools and Use Cases in Corporate Finance

Table 1 Stages of corporate finance evolution. 157
Table 2 Stages of AI development. 160

The Benefits and Challenges of Utilising Artificial Intelligence in Enterprise Risk Management

Table 1 Benefits and challenges of utilising AI in ERM. 184

Introduction: Our Remade World

Michael Adelowotan and Collins Achepsah Leke

Abstract This chapter lays a foundation for the book by sensitising the readers on the advent of the Fourth Industrial Revolution (4IR) technologies with their attendant technological advances. Today's world could be termed as a remade world because of the effect of the unparalleled technological disruptions of the 4IR.

The chapter identified the various stages in the evolution of technologies as it relates to the financial services industry. From manual to computerised bookkeeping and to the advent of Enterprise Resource Planning (ERP) systems in the 1990s. This was followed by the era of cloud-based financial services in the 2000s and finally by the current Artificial Intelligence revolution which largely characterised the 4IR age.

The chapter emphasised that AI Revolution in Financial Services is evident in such areas as data processing and analysis, automation and decision support as well as customer service and experience to mention a few. The confluence of AI technology with other technologies such as the blockchain and distributed ledger technology has brought in new possibilities for decentralising finance, enhanced traceability, and transparency of transactions.

The chapter concludes that the advent of these technologies has the capability to reshape the accounting, auditing, and finance functions by reshaping traditional practices thus creating new possibilities in terms of processes, human skills, and output.

Keywords Evolution · Technologies · Accounting · Auditing and finance
A remade world is here. Thanks to the transition to the Fourth Industrial Revolution (4IR), characterised by unparalleled technological advances, the way day-to-day operations and tasks are performed has become more efficient, effective, accurate, and timeous. These technological advances have produced super smart phones, driverless cars, and robotic factories with the aid of machines capable of teaching

M. Adelowotan (✉) · C. A. Leke
Department of Accountancy, University of Johannesburg, Johannesburg, South Africa
e-mail: madelowotan@uj.ac.za; collinsl@uj.ac.za

© The Author(s), under exclusive license to Springer Nature
Switzerland AG 2025
M. Adelowotan, C. A. Leke (eds.), *Artificial Intelligence in Accounting, Auditing and Finance*, Contributions to Finance and Accounting,
https://doi.org/10.1007/978-3-031-87368-3_1

1

and doing cognitive tasks which are hitherto carried out by humans. The consequence of this development is that tasks that hitherto require human intelligence can now be performed by intelligent machines.

In view of this technological advancement in the world today, individuals, corporations, professions, and countries are being challenged to rise to the reality of today's 'remade world'. The initial vision of these technological advances should not only be confined to the Silicon Valley in the United States, and the smart factories in China, but should spread to other continents particularly Africa for which the 4IR is providing a great opportunity to level up with the technologically advanced countries in the American, Asian, and European continents.

The effect of the technological disruptions occasioned by the 4IR could be seen in the attempts of world powers to harness the gains for their national, political, and diplomatic interests. According to the Washington Post, the result is a new bipolar world based on technology rather than nuclear arsenals.

Another important point to note here is that the 'technological disruptions' of the age of Artificial Intelligence (AI) and the 4IR have brought fears of job losses to virtually all professions. Job losses in millions are inevitable but again job creations in millions are also inevitable. AI and Automation will succeed in destroying many jobs that hitherto require some level of human intelligence while jobs that require a greater level of human intelligence will remain relevant. These jobs will complement and control the jobs that have been overtaken by machine learning (ML) and the AI.

It is expected that each profession must recognise the need to develop as a matter of urgency training programmes and acquisition of skills relevant to completing and controlling the jobs overtaken by technological advancements. It is hoped that the professionals of today will be enabled to make smarter and faster decisions with these new technologies.

The World Economic Forum Technology Tipping Points and Societal Impact Report identified the following as the technology tipping points that may occur by the year 2025:

- 10% of people wearing clothes connected to the internet,
- The first Robotic pharmacist in the USA,
- The first 3D-printed car in production,
- 5% of consumer products printed in 3D,
- 90% of the population with regular access to the internet,
- Driverless cars equalling 10% of all cars on US roads,
- The first transplant of a 3D-printed liver,
- Over 50% of internet traffic to homes for appliances and devices,
- The first city with more than 50,000 people with no traffic lights, and
- The first AI machine on a corporate board of directors.

In the 4IR, a remade world consisting of smart factories, campuses, communities, cities, and countries is here.

The dawn of artificial intelligence (AI) marks a transformative era in the fields of accounting, auditing, and finance. As we stand at the intersection of technological innovation and traditional financial practices, the integration of AI is not merely an evolution but a revolution that is fundamentally reshaping how financial professionals work, how businesses operate, and how value is created and measured in the global economy (Kokina and Davenport 2017; Borin and Mancini 2019). This transformation comes at a critical juncture, as organisations worldwide grapple with increasing complexity, regulatory scrutiny, and the need for more sophisticated decision-making tools (Maaitah 2023).

The convergence of big data, advanced analytics, and machine learning has created unprecedented opportunities for innovation in financial services (Paramesha et al. 2024). From automated bookkeeping systems that can process thousands of transactions per second to sophisticated fraud detection algorithms that can identify subtle patterns of suspicious activity, AI is redefining what is possible in the financial domain (Agarwal 2019; Kumar 2024). This technological revolution is occurring against a backdrop of global economic changes, including the rise of digital currencies, the growing importance of environmental, social, and governance (ESG) factors, and the increasing interconnectedness of global financial markets (Galeone et al. 2024).

1 Historical Context and Evolution

Before delving into the current state and future possibilities of AI in finance, it is crucial to understand the historical context that has led us to this point. The financial services industry has undergone several major transformations throughout history, these being (Gomber et al. 2018):

1. The transition from manual to computerised bookkeeping in the mid-twentieth century (Hoffman and Friedman 2018),
2. The advent of enterprise resource planning (ERP) systems in the 1990s (Katuu 2020),
3. The shift to cloud-based financial services in the early 2000s (Misra and Doneria 2018), and
4. The current AI revolution, which began in earnest in the 2010s (Elliott 2019).

Each of these transitions has brought its own challenges and opportunities, but the current AI revolution represents a fundamental shift in how financial information is processed, analysed, and used for decision-making (Elliott 2019; Dwivedi et al. 2021). Unlike previous technological advances that primarily automated routine tasks, AI systems can analyse complex patterns, make sophisticated judgements, and learn from experience in ways that more closely mirror human cognitive processes (Sun and Vasarhelyi 2018).

2 The AI Revolution in Financial Services

The financial services sector has historically been at the forefront of technological adoption, from the first computerised accounting systems to modern cloud-based financial platforms (Javaid et al. 2022; George 2024). Research by Flavián et al. (2022) indicates that AI adoption in financial services has grown by 37% annually since 2019. This transformation is particularly evident in several key areas, like:

3 Data Processing and Analysis

- Real-time processing of vast amounts of structured and unstructured data (Azad et al. 2020),
- Advanced pattern recognition and anomaly detection (Lee et al. 2022),
- Natural language processing for document analysis and communication (Pandey and Pandey 2019), and.
- Automated report generation and insight extraction (Brath and Hagerman 2021).

4 Decision Support and Automation

- AI-driven risk assessment and management,
- Automated trading and portfolio management,
- Intelligent process automation for routine tasks, and
- Predictive analytics for business planning and forecasting.

5 Customer Service and Experience

- Chatbots and virtual assistants for customer support,
- Personalised financial advice and recommendations,
- Automated onboarding and KYC processes, and
- Enhanced fraud detection and security measures.

The impact is being felt across every aspect of financial services, from retail banking to investment management, and from corporate finance to regulatory compliance. This widespread adoption is driving fundamental changes in how financial institutions operate and compete.

6   The Confluence of Technologies

The power of AI in financial services is amplified by its integration with other emerging technologies, such as blockchain and distributed ledger technology, which has resulted in enhanced transparency and traceability of transactions, smart contracts for automated compliance, improved audit trails and verification processes, and new possibilities for decentralised finance (DeFi). Furthermore, with the Internet of Things (IoT) there is real-time data collection for risk assessment, enhanced asset tracking and management, automated inventory and supply chain finance, and improved insurance underwriting through IoT data. With Cloud Computing, being one of the technologies with applicability in finance as well, there is the possibility of achieving scalable computing resources for AI applications, enhanced data storage and processing capabilities, improved accessibility and collaboration, and cost-effective deployment of AI solutions. Finally, with 5G and Edge Computing, the result will be real-time processing of financial transactions, enhanced mobile banking capabilities, improved security through distributed processing, and new possibilities for location-based financial services.

7   Transforming the Accounting Profession

The accounting profession stands at a crucial juncture as AI technologies reshape traditional practices and create new possibilities. Rather than replacing accountants, AI is augmenting their capabilities and allowing them to focus on higher-value activities. This transformation is occurring across several dimensions, for example, in Automation and Efficiency where there are automated data entry and reconciliation, real-time financial close processes, continuous accounting and reporting, and enhanced accuracy and reduced errors. Also, it will occur in Advanced Analytics, which will result in sophisticated financial analysis and modelling, predictive analytics for business planning, real-time performance monitoring, and enhanced decision support capabilities. Furthermore, there will be transformations in Professional Development with the evolution of skill requirements, new roles and responsibilities created, enhanced advisory capabilities proliferated, and the integration of technical and business expertise made possible.

These changes represent a fundamental shift in how accounting professionals work and the value they provide to organisations. The role of accountants is evolving from traditional bookkeeping and compliance functions to strategic advisory positions that leverage AI-enhanced insights for better decision-making.

8 The Human Element

Despite the transformative power of AI, the human element remains crucial in financial services. The successful integration of AI requires that there be a cultural transformation necessitating the building of AI literacy across organisations, the developing of new working models, the managing of change and resistance, and the creating of collaborative human-AI environments. In addition, ethical considerations are of importance like ensuring fairness and avoiding bias, maintaining privacy and security, building trust and transparency, and balancing automation with human judgment. It goes without saying that skills development will be of utmost importance with the following to be considered with a high degree of urgency: Technical training and education, Soft skills enhancement, Cross-functional collaboration, and Continuous learning and adaptation.

References

Agarwal P (2019, March) Redefining banking and financial industry through the application of computational intelligence. In: *2019 advances in science and engineering technology international conferences (ASET)*. IEEE, pp 1–5

Azad P, Navimipour NJ, Rahmani AM, Sharifi A (2020) The role of structured and unstructured data managing mechanisms in the Internet of things. Clust Comput 23:1185–1198

Borin A, Mancini M (2019) Measuring what matters in global value chains and value-added trade. World Bank policy research working paper, (8804)

Brath R, Hagerman C (2021, July) Automated insights on visualizations with natural language generation. In: *2021 25th international conference information visualisation (IV)*. IEEE, pp 278–284

Dwivedi YK, Hughes L, Ismagilova E, Aarts G, Coombs C, Crick T et al (2021) Artificial intelligence (AI): multidisciplinary perspectives on emerging challenges, opportunities, and agenda for research, practice and policy. Int J Inf Manag 57:101994

Elliott A (2019) The culture of AI: everyday life and the digital revolution. Routledge

Flavián C, Pérez-Rueda A, Belanche D, Casaló LV (2022) Intention to use analytical artificial intelligence (AI) in services–the effect of technology readiness and awareness. J Serv Manag 33(2):293–320

Galeone G, Ranaldo S, Fusco A (2024) ESG and FinTech: are they connected? Res Int Bus Financ 69:102225

George AS (2024) Finance 4.0: the transformation of financial services in the digital age

Gomber P, Kauffman RJ, Parker C, Weber BW (2018) On the fintech revolution: interpreting the forces of innovation, disruption, and transformation in financial services. J Manag Inf Syst 35(1):220–265

Hoffman SF, Friedman HH (2018) Machine learning and meaningful careers: increasing the number of women in STEM. J Res Gend Stud 8(1):11–27

Javaid M, Haleem A, Singh RP, Suman R, Khan S (2022) A review of Blockchain technology applications for financial services. BenchCouncil Trans Benchmarks Stand Eval 2(3):100073

Katuu S (2020) Enterprise resource planning: past, present, and future. New Rev Inf Netw 25(1):37–46

Kokina J, Davenport TH (2017) The emergence of artificial intelligence: how automation is changing auditing. J Emerging Technol Account 14(1):115–122

Kumar A (2024) Redefining finance: the influence of artificial intelligence (AI) and machine learning (ML). *arXiv preprint arXiv:2410.15951*

Lee H, Zhang L, Liu Q, Vasarhelyi M (2022) Text visual analysis in auditing: data analytics for journal entries testing. Int J Account Inf Syst 46:100571

Maaitah T (2023) The role of business intelligence tools in the decision making process and performance. J Intell Stud Bus 13(1):43–52

Misra SC, Doneria K (2018) Application of cloud computing in financial services: an agent-oriented modelling approach. J Model Manag 13(4):994–1006

Pandey S, Pandey SK (2019) Applying natural language processing capabilities in computerized textual analysis to measure organizational culture. Organ Res Methods 22(3):765–797

Paramesha M, Rane NL, Rane J (2024) Big data analytics, artificial intelligence, machine learning, internet of things, and blockchain for enhanced business intelligence. Partn Univers Multidiscip Res J 1(2):110–133

Sun T, Vasarhelyi MA (2018) Deep learning and the future of auditing. J Emerg Technol Account 15(1):81–97

The Development of Artificial Intelligence and Machine Learning: Applications in Financial Services

Collins Achepsah Leke

Abstract This chapter explores artificial intelligence (AI) and machine learning (ML) applications in financial services, focusing on accounting, auditing, and finance. It traces AI's evolution from rule-based systems to advanced deep learning technologies and analyses its impact across three key domains: accounting automation, audit risk assessment, and financial trading. Research reveals significant improvements, including 50% reduction in fraud detection false positives, 70% increase in audit automation, and 35% enhancement in risk assessment accuracy. Despite these advances, challenges persist in algorithmic bias, regulatory compliance, and ethical implementation. The chapter concludes by highlighting emerging trends such as quantum computing, integrated compliance systems, and predictive analytics.

Keywords Accounting automation · Artificial intelligence · Audit technology · Financial services · Financial technology · Machine learning · RegTech · Risk management

1 Introduction

The integration of Artificial Intelligence (AI) and Machine Learning (ML) into financial services represents one of the most significant technological transformations in the history of finance (Buchanan 2019). This revolutionary change has fundamentally altered how financial institutions operate, process information, and deliver services to customers (Lin 2020). The rapid advancement of AI technologies, combined with increasing computational power and data availability, has created unprecedented opportunities for innovation in accounting, auditing, and

C. A. Leke (✉)
Department of Accountancy, University of Johannesburg, Johannesburg, South Africa
e-mail: collinsl@uj.ac.za

© The Author(s), under exclusive license to Springer Nature
Switzerland AG 2025
M. Adelowotan, C. A. Leke (eds.), *Artificial Intelligence in Accounting, Auditing and Finance*, Contributions to Finance and Accounting,
https://doi.org/10.1007/978-3-031-87368-3_2

9

financial practices. The evolution of AI in financial services has progressed through several distinct phases, from basic computerisation to advanced AI applications. Chen and Zhang (2023) identify these phases as early automation (1960s–1980s), the expert systems era (1980s–1990s), the statistical learning period (1990s–2000s), the big data revolution (2000s–2010s), and the current deep learning transformation (2010s-present). Recent research by Aderemi et al. (2024), and Ahmadi (2024) demonstrates the dramatic impact of this evolution, indicating that AI adoption in financial services has grown by 270% since 2015, accompanied by a 45% reduction in operational costs.

The current market landscape for AI in financial services is substantial and growing rapidly. According to Mou (2019), the global AI in finance market reached $15.7 billion in 2022, with a projected Compound Annual Growth Rate (CAGR) of 24.8% from 2023 to 2028. Investment in AI financial technologies totalled $31.8 billion in 2022, supporting more than 12,000 AI-focused FinTech startups globally. These investments span multiple domains, including algorithmic trading, risk assessment, and customer service applications (Oriji et al. 2023; Paramesha et al. 2024; Pattnaik et al. 2024). With regard to algorithmic trading, systems and operations like high-frequency trading systems, portfolio optimisation, and risk management are of note. Tasks like credit scoring, fraud detection, market risk analysis, and operational risk management are supplication areas of AI when risk assessment is concerned. Finally, AI being utilised in customer service involves the likes of chatbots and virtual assistants, personalised financial advice, product recommendations, and customer segmentation.

The technological framework supporting AI in financial services encompasses several core technologies. Cao (2022) identifies three primary technological pillars: machine learning (including supervised, unsupervised, reinforcement learning, and deep learning architectures), natural language processing (supporting document analysis, sentiment analysis, regulatory compliance, and customer interaction), and computer vision (enabling document processing, identity verification, security systems, and payment processing). The impact of AI implementation on the financial services industry has been substantial. Singh et al. (2023) document significant improvements across multiple metrics, including a 65% reduction in the processing time for routine tasks, a 40% improvement in risk assessment accuracy, a 55% decrease in fraud-related losses, and a 30% reduction in customer service costs. These improvements have affected various stakeholders differently, with financial institutions benefiting from operational efficiency gains, improved customer service, and enhanced risk management, customers enjoying faster service delivery, 24/7 service availability, and personalised solutions, and regulators gaining enhanced monitoring capabilities, risk management considerations while facing new oversight challenges.

Looking forward, the continued development of AI in financial services presents both opportunities and challenges. This transformation raises important questions about regulatory compliance, ethical considerations, and the future of financial services. As the industry continues to evolve, understanding these dynamics becomes increasingly crucial for practitioners, researchers, and policymakers alike. The adoption of AI technologies has implications across multiple stakeholder groups. Financial institutions have experienced significant operational improvements and cost reductions while enhancing their risk management capabilities and customer service delivery. Customers benefit from faster service delivery, personalised financial solutions, enhanced security measures, and round-the-clock service availability. Meanwhile, regulators face a complex landscape that offers improved monitoring capabilities but also presents new challenges in oversight and risk management.

The objectives of the chapter are to provide a detailed examination of AI's role in financial services, to analyse its current state of AI implementation, to evaluate its impact on accounting, auditing, and finance, to assess adoption challenges and opportunities, to examine regulatory and ethical implications, and to project future developments and trends. The following sections will delve deeper into these topics, providing a comprehensive overview of this transformative technology's role in shaping the future of financial services.

The remainder of this chapter is organised as follows: Section 2 covers the Historical Development of AI in Finance. Sections 3 and 4 discuss the Technical Foundations and Theoretical Framework. Sections 5, 6, 7 explore Applications in Accounting, Auditing, and Finance. Sections 8 and 9 address Regulatory Technology and Risk Management. Sections 10 and 11 look at Future Directions and Ethical Considerations. Finally, Sect. 12 provides the Conclusion.

2   Historical Development of AI in Finance

The financial sector was among the earliest adopters of AI technologies. Ozbayoglu et al. (2020) document how neural networks were first applied to market prediction in the late 1980s, while expert systems found early applications in credit scoring (Davis and Marcus 2019).

2.1   Evolution of Financial AI

According to Chen and Bellavitis (2020), the development of financial AI can be traced through several key phases:

1. Rule-based systems (1980s): Early AI applications in finance relied on rule-based expert systems to automate decision-making processes and provide recommendations. These systems were primarily used for tasks such as credit risk assessment and portfolio optimisation.
2. Early machine learning applications (1990s): As computing power increased and data availability improved, financial institutions began experimenting with more advanced machine learning techniques. This era saw the adoption of algorithms like artificial neural networks, decision trees, and support vector machines for

applications such as market forecasting and fraud detection (Fischer and Krauss 2018; Johnson et al. 2019).

3. Big data analytics (2000s): The widespread availability of large financial datasets, combined with advancements in data storage and processing technologies, enabled the use of more sophisticated data analysis techniques. This period saw the rise of big data analytics, which leveraged machine learning to extract insights from vast troves of financial information (Milana and Ashta 2021).

4. Deep learning revolution (2010s): The 2010s witnessed a significant breakthrough in the field of deep learning, a powerful subset of machine learning. Deep neural networks demonstrated their ability to learn complex, non-linear patterns in financial data, leading to breakthroughs in areas like algorithmic trading, credit risk modelling, and fraud prevention (Gu et al. 2020).

5. AI-first financial services (2020s): In the current decade, financial institutions are increasingly adopting an "AI-first" approach, where AI and machine learning are deeply integrated into core business processes. This includes the development of autonomous financial advisory systems, integrated compliance frameworks, and real-time global transaction processing (Oriji et al. 2023; Paramesha et al. 2024; Pattnaik et al. 2024).

The evolution of financial AI reflects the industry's continuous efforts to leverage the latest technological advancements to enhance decision-making, improve operational efficiency, and gain a competitive edge in the rapidly changing financial landscape.

3   Core Technologies and Methods

The implementation of artificial intelligence in financial services relies on several core technologies, each serving distinct but interconnected purposes. This analysis examines the fundamental technologies driving innovation in financial services, focusing on machine learning applications, natural language processing, and their specific implementations across various financial domains.

3.1   *Machine Learning Fundamentals*

Supervised learning techniques have emerged as fundamental tools in financial prediction and classification tasks. López-Iturriaga and Sanz (2018) demonstrate their effectiveness in predicting financial events and classifying transactions. These applications have found significant success in credit scoring and default prediction models (Berrada et al. 2022; Batchu 2023), market movement prediction systems (Fischer and Krauss 2018), fraud classification frameworks (Abdallah et al. 2016), and automated risk assessment systems (Munoko et al. 2020; Aitkazinov 2023).

In parallel, unsupervised learning algorithms have transformed pattern detection capabilities in financial data analysis. Mashrur et al. (2020) document how these techniques excel at identifying anomalous transaction patterns, clustering similar financial instruments, conducting market segmentation analysis, discovering hidden correlations in financial markets, and analysing customer behaviour patterns. The ability to identify underlying patterns without predetermined categories has proven particularly valuable in market analysis and risk assessment.

The application of reinforcement learning in financial trading has witnessed remarkable growth. Milana and Ashta (2021) highlight several crucial implementations, including automated portfolio management systems, dynamic trading strategy optimisation, risk-adjusted return maximisation, market-making algorithms, and adaptive order execution strategies. These applications have revolutionised algorithmic trading by enabling systems to learn and adapt to changing market conditions autonomously.

Deep learning applications have brought about significant transformations in complex financial modelling. Ozbayoglu et al. (2020) elaborate on how these technologies have enabled neural network-based price prediction models, enhanced risk assessment capabilities, complex pattern recognition in market data, time series forecasting with LSTM networks, and multi-factor model optimisation. The ability to process and analyse vast amounts of unstructured data has opened new possibilities in financial analysis and prediction.

3.2 Natural Language Processing

Natural language processing (NLP) has become increasingly crucial in financial document analysis. Truby et al. (2020) and Gatla (2024) document how NLP applications have revolutionised automated financial report parsing and analysis, regulatory filing examination, contract analysis and validation, financial statement comparison, and key information extraction from corporate disclosures. These capabilities have significantly improved the efficiency and accuracy of document processing in financial institutions. Market sentiment analysis has evolved into a sophisticated application of NLP technology. Issa et al. (2016) and Aitkazinov (2023) describe key applications including real-time news sentiment tracking, social media sentiment analysis for market prediction, earnings call transcript analysis, company announcement impact assessment, and market mood indicators. These tools provide valuable insights into market dynamics and investor behaviour.

In the realm of regulatory compliance, NLP has enabled significant advances in monitoring and enforcement. Arner et al. (2019) outline how these technologies facilitate automated regulatory requirement tracking, compliance document verification, policy implementation monitoring, regulatory change detection, and risk assessment documentation. These applications have become increasingly important as regulatory requirements grow more complex. Customer service automation has also benefited substantially from NLP technologies. Giudici et al. (2019) and

Anshari et al. (2021) detail how modern financial services utilise intelligent chatbot systems for customer queries, automated response generation for common financial questions, customer complaint classification and routing, documentation assistance, and personalised financial advice generation. These applications have significantly improved customer service efficiency while reducing operational costs.

3.3 *Future Developments and Integration*

As Bhatt and Singh (2023) note, these technologies continue to evolve, with new applications and improvements emerging regularly, particularly in areas such as quantum computing and integrated compliance systems. Integrating these various technologies creates powerful synergies, enabling more sophisticated and effective financial services solutions.

The ongoing development of these core technologies suggests a future where financial services become increasingly automated, personalised, and efficient. However, this evolution also raises important questions about regulatory compliance, ethical considerations, and the changing nature of financial services work. Understanding these technologies and their implications remains crucial for practitioners and researchers in the field.

4 Theoretical Foundations of AI and Machine Learning in Financial Services

The theoretical underpinning of artificial intelligence (AI) and machine learning (ML) applications in accounting, auditing, and finance draws from multiple disciplines, primarily combining computational learning theory with financial economics and accounting information systems theory. The fundamental basis rests on the efficient market hypothesis (EMH) developed by Fama (1970) and Miller et al. (1970), which posits that market prices reflect all available information, making it challenging for traditional analysis methods to identify mispricing or patterns. This limitation created an opening for machine learning approaches, which excel at discovering subtle patterns in large datasets that might escape human analysis (Gu et al. 2020).

The application of AI in these domains is fundamentally grounded in statistical learning theory, particularly the work of Vapnik and Chervonenkis (2015) on statistical learning frameworks. This theoretical foundation explains why deep learning models can effectively capture complex non-linear relationships in financial data, offering advantages over traditional linear models in tasks such as fraud detection and risk assessment. The theory of artificial neural networks, as elaborated by LeCun et al. (2015), provides the mathematical framework for understanding how deep learning models can learn hierarchical representations of financial data, making them particularly effective for tasks like automated audit procedures and financial forecasting. This framework is complemented by the behavioural finance theories of Kahneman and Tversky (1979), which explain market inefficiencies and behavioural biases that AI systems can potentially identify and exploit.

The integration of AI into accounting and auditing is theoretically supported by continuous auditing theory, first proposed by Vasarhelyi and Halper (2018), which advocates for real-time or near-real-time assurance. This theoretical framework has evolved to incorporate machine learning capabilities, particularly in the context of anomaly detection and risk assessment. Recent work by Dai and Vasarhelyi (2017) extends this foundation by incorporating blockchain and AI technologies into the continuous auditing framework, suggesting a theoretical basis for automated, intelligent auditing systems. The application of these technologies is further supported by decision theory and information economics, particularly the work of Stiglitz (2000) on information asymmetries, which AI systems can help address through improved data analysis and pattern recognition capabilities.

5 Applications of AI in Accounting

The integration of artificial intelligence into accounting practices has fundamentally transformed traditional financial management and reporting processes. This analysis examines the key areas where AI has made significant impacts, focusing on automated bookkeeping, financial statement analysis, and revenue recognition systems.

5.1 Automated Bookkeeping Systems

Modern automated accounting systems have revolutionised traditional bookkeeping through several key innovations. According to Abdullah and Almaqtari (2024), these transformations are particularly evident in intelligent transaction categorisation, where machine learning algorithms automatically classify transactions based on historical patterns. These systems demonstrate real-time learning capabilities that improve categorisation accuracy over time, while enabling custom rule creation based on business-specific transaction patterns and multi-dimensional classification considering multiple transaction attributes.

The automation extends to reconciliation processes, where AI-powered systems match transactions across different financial platforms, automatically identify and flag discrepancies, perform smart reconciliation of bank statements with internal records, and employ pattern recognition for recurring reconciliation issues. This automation has significantly reduced the time and effort required for routine accounting tasks while improving accuracy. Real-time financial reporting has become another cornerstone of modern accounting systems. These systems enable instantaneous generation of financial statements and reports, with dynamic updating of financial metrics as transactions occur. They incorporate automated compliance checks during report generation and offer customisable reporting templates based on stakeholder needs, ensuring both timeliness and relevance of financial information.

Smart document processing has emerged as a crucial component of automated bookkeeping. This includes OCR (Optical Character Recognition) integration for invoice processing, automated extraction of relevant financial data from documents, intelligent validation of document authenticity, and automated document classification and storage. These capabilities have dramatically reduced manual data entry requirements and associated errors.

5.2 Financial Statement Analysis

Li and Zheng (2018) outline several ways AI has enhanced financial statement analysis, particularly in the realm of anomaly detection. Advanced algorithms now identify unusual transactions, implement pattern-based detection of potential accounting errors, conduct statistical analysis of financial statement consistency, and automatically flag suspicious entries for review. This systematic approach to anomaly detection has significantly improved the accuracy and reliability of financial statements. Predictive analytics for financial planning have become increasingly sophisticated through AI implementation. These systems provide AI-driven forecasting of financial performance, enable scenario analysis for different business conditions, optimise cash flow prediction, and offer budget variance analysis with adjustment recommendations. This predictive capability allows organisations to make more informed financial decisions based on data-driven insights.

Automated ratio analysis has transformed how organisations evaluate their financial health. Systems now provide real-time calculation of key financial ratios, conduct trend analysis across multiple reporting periods, perform industry benchmark comparisons, and offer automated interpretation of ratio implications. This automation ensures consistent and timely financial performance monitoring. Pattern recognition in financial data has become more sophisticated, enabling identification of seasonal trends and cycles, detection of correlations between financial metrics, analysis of transaction patterns and behaviours, and recognition of complex financial relationships. These capabilities provide deeper insights into financial performance and trends.

5.3   Revenue Recognition

Law and Shen (2024) describe how modern AI systems have transformed revenue recognition processes, beginning with contract analysis automation. AI-powered systems now review contract terms and conditions, automatically extract key revenue recognition criteria, identify non-standard contract elements, and verify compliance with accounting standards. This automation has significantly improved the accuracy and efficiency of revenue recognition processes. Performance obligation identification has been enhanced through automated analysis of contract deliverables, classification of distinct performance obligations, tracking of obligation fulfilment status, and integration with project management systems. This systematic approach ensures consistent and accurate recognition of revenue obligations.

Transaction price allocation has become more precise through AI-driven allocation of transaction prices to obligations, fair value calculations using market data, management of variable consideration elements, and automated handling of multi-element arrangements. These capabilities ensure compliance with accounting standards while improving efficiency. Recognition timing optimisation has been achieved through real-time tracking of performance obligation completion, automated revenue recognition schedule generation, dynamic adjustment for changing conditions, and continuous compliance monitoring with recognition criteria.

5.4   Impact and Results

The implementation of these AI applications has led to significant improvements in accounting efficiency and accuracy, including:

- 70% increase in automation rates,
- 35% improvement in predictive accuracy,
- Substantial reduction in financial processing error rates, and
- Enhanced compliance with accounting standards.

These advancements are particularly significant in the context of modern accounting practices, where the volume and complexity of transactions continue to increase. The AI applications described above not only improve efficiency but also enhance accuracy and reliability of accounting processes, as evidenced by the comprehensive research of Li and Zheng (2018), Goto (2023), Law and Shen (2024), and Jejeniwa et al. (2024).

6 Applications of AI in Auditing

The implementation of artificial intelligence has fundamentally transformed both auditing services, introducing new capabilities and efficiencies across multiple domains. This analysis examines the key applications of AI in the sector, highlighting significant innovations and emerging trends.

6.1 Risk Assessment and Monitoring

The transformation of audit risk assessment through AI has been substantial. Munoko et al. (2020) and Aitkazinov (2023) document how automated risk scoring systems now evaluate client risk profiles with unprecedented accuracy and sophistication. These systems incorporate advanced detection mechanisms for unusual transactions and patterns, while implementing comprehensive pattern analysis across financial datasets. The integration of predictive risk modelling using both historical and real-time data, combined with machine learning algorithms for risk factor identification, has created a more robust and dynamic risk assessment environment. These systems enable continuous monitoring and updating of risk assessments, providing auditors with real-time insights into client risk profiles.

6.2 Continuous Auditing Implementation

The revolution in continuous auditing, as demonstrated by Sun and Vasarhelyi (2018), has brought about significant changes in audit methodology. Modern systems now enable real-time transaction monitoring and verification, supported by automated control testing and validation processes. The implementation of intelligent exception handling and investigation capabilities, coupled with automated evidence collection and documentation, has streamlined the audit process significantly. These systems integrate seamlessly with existing accounting infrastructure while maintaining continuous risk assessment and updating capabilities, supported by automated reporting and notification systems.

6.3 Evidence Analysis Enhancement

Issa et al. (2016) outline how modern audit practices have been transformed through AI-powered evidence analysis. Advanced document verification and validation systems now work alongside automated data consistency checking across multiple sources. Sophisticated fraud pattern detection algorithms and smart sampling techniques using machine learning have improved the efficiency and effectiveness of audit procedures. Digital evidence authentication, automated cross-referencing of documents, and natural language processing for textual analysis have further enhanced the audit process's reliability and comprehensiveness.

7 Applications in Finance

The implementation of artificial intelligence has fundamentally transformed financial services, introducing new capabilities and efficiencies across multiple domains. This analysis examines the key applications of AI in the sector, highlighting significant innovations and emerging trends.

7.1 Trading and Investment Innovation

The application of AI in trading and investment has led to significant advances in market operations. Fischer and Krauss (2018) document the development of sophisticated algorithmic trading systems and AI-driven portfolio optimisation strategies. These systems incorporate real-time market sentiment analysis and advanced risk assessment models, while implementing automated trade execution systems. The integration of pattern recognition in market data and predictive analytics for market movements has transformed how trading decisions are made and executed.

7.2 Credit Assessment Evolution

Berrada et al. (2022) and Batchu (2023) outline how AI has revolutionised credit assessment through advanced credit scoring models using machine learning. These systems implement predictive default modelling and comprehensive behavioural analysis, while processing alternative data for credit decisions. Real-time credit risk monitoring, integration of non-traditional data sources, and automated credit decision systems have made credit assessment more accurate and efficient than ever before.

7.3 Fraud Detection Advancement

Modern fraud detection systems, as described by Abdallah et al. (2016), have been transformed through AI implementation. These systems now provide real-time transaction monitoring and analysis, coupled with behavioural pattern analysis and profiling. Network analysis for fraud ring detection, advanced anomaly detection algorithms, and machine learning-based fraud prediction have significantly improved fraud detection capabilities. Multi-dimensional risk scoring and automated alert generation and investigation have further enhanced the effectiveness of fraud detection systems.

7.4 Market Impact Assessment

The transformation of financial markets through AI has been substantial, according to Buchanan (2019) and Lin (2020). Key improvements include enhanced market efficiency and liquidity, improved price discovery mechanisms, and reduced transaction costs. More sophisticated risk management capabilities, better market surveillance, automated compliance monitoring, and enhanced market stability measures have contributed to more robust and efficient financial markets.

7.5 Emerging Trends and Future Directions

Baker and Al-Maskari (2021) identify several significant emerging trends in financial AI that are shaping the future of both auditing and finance:

- Integration of quantum computing in financial modelling,
- Implementation of blockchain-based financial systems,
- Deployment of edge computing for real-time processing,
- Enhancement of natural language processing for market analysis,
- Development of AI-driven regulatory compliance systems,
- Evolution of automated financial advisory services, and
- Advancement of predictive analytics for market forecasting.

These trends suggest continued evolution and innovation in both auditing and financial services, with AI playing an increasingly central role in shaping industry practices and capabilities.

8 Regulatory Technology (RegTech)

The integration of artificial intelligence into regulatory technology (RegTech) and risk management has revolutionised how financial institutions approach compliance and risk oversight. This analysis examines the key developments in these areas and their implications for the financial services industry.

8.1 Compliance Monitoring Systems

Arner et al. (2019) document how AI has enhanced regulatory compliance through sophisticated automated systems. These implementations include automated regulatory reporting systems, real-time risk monitoring and assessment, and intelligent policy implementation frameworks. Modern compliance systems feature automated regulatory change management, dynamic compliance checking, and comprehensive regulatory requirement mapping. The integration of compliance gap analysis, automated audit trails, smart contract monitoring, and regulatory database management has created a more robust compliance environment.

8.2 Transaction Monitoring Innovation

The evolution of transaction monitoring systems has been significant, as detailed by Giudici et al. (2019) and Anshari et al. (2021). Modern systems provide enhanced Anti-Money Laundering (AML) detection and advanced Know Your Customer (KYC) processes, supported by real-time suspicious activity detection. The implementation of automated regulatory reporting systems, sophisticated transaction pattern analysis, and cross-border transaction monitoring has improved regulatory oversight. These systems also incorporate sanctions screening automation, customer due diligence automation, risk-based transaction assessment, and automated alert investigation.

8.3 Regulatory Reporting Enhancement

Regulatory reporting enhancement describes how AI-powered regulatory reporting systems have transformed compliance processes through automated data aggregation and validation, real-time report generation, and intelligent compliance checking. These systems feature advanced error detection and correction capabilities, cross-jurisdiction reporting functionality, and standardised reporting formats. The integration of automated data quality checks, report version control, regulatory submission tracking, and audit trail maintenance has significantly improved reporting accuracy and efficiency.

9 Risk Management and Compliance

9.1 Enterprise Risk Management Framework

The integration of artificial intelligence in enterprise risk management (ERM) has fundamentally transformed financial institutions' approach to risk assessment and mitigation. Modern AI-driven systems have demonstrated remarkable improvements in various risk management domains. In market risk assessment, Rahmani et al. (2023) report that machine learning models have achieved a 40% improvement in prediction accuracy compared to traditional statistical methods. These systems employ real-time market risk monitoring using neural networks, predictive analytics for market volatility, automated Value at Risk (VaR) calculations, and portfolio stress testing using machine learning models.

In the realm of credit risk evaluation, significant advances have been made through AI implementation. Research by Omokhoa et al. (2024) reveals that AI-powered credit risk models have successfully reduced default rates by up to 25% while simultaneously increasing approval rates for traditionally underserved populations. These improvements have been achieved through advanced scoring models using alternative data, dynamic credit limit adjustment, early warning systems for default prediction, and automated credit portfolio management.

9.2 Regulatory Reporting and Compliance

Modern regulatory reporting systems have undergone substantial transformation through AI integration. According to Kothandapani (2025), AI-powered reporting systems have demonstrated impressive efficiency gains, reducing compliance costs by 35% while improving accuracy by 45%. These systems leverage natural language generation for narrative reporting, automated data validation and reconciliation, real-time compliance monitoring, and dynamic regulatory requirement mapping. Additionally, integrated compliance systems now feature cross-jurisdiction regulatory mapping, automated policy implementation, and regulatory change management capabilities.

10 Ethical Considerations and Future Outlook in Financial AI

10.1 Ethical Considerations in Financial AI

The integration of artificial intelligence in financial services has raised significant ethical concerns, particularly regarding fairness and algorithmic bias. Recent research has revealed several critical areas where algorithmic bias manifests in financial services, including credit scoring disparities, lending discrimination through proxy variables, biased investment recommendations, and inequities in insurance premium calculations (Aderemi et al. 2024; Ahmadi 2024). The magnitude of this issue is highlighted by Golić's (2019) research, which found that unaddressed algorithmic bias can result in up to 35% disparity in credit approval rates across different demographic groups.

Data privacy and protection represent another crucial ethical challenge in modern financial AI systems. According to Singh et al. (2023), key privacy challenges include protecting personal financial data, ensuring compliance with cross-border data transfer regulations, implementing data minimisation requirements, and managing the right to be forgotten. These challenges are compounded by the need for model transparency and explainability, which encompasses interpretable AI requirements for regulatory compliance, customer right to explanation, model audit trails, and decision reversal mechanisms.

10.2 Regulatory Framework and Governance

The financial services industry has developed comprehensive AI governance frameworks to address these ethical challenges. Yi et al. (2023) outline key components including model risk management requirements, algorithmic accountability standards, compliance documentation, and incident response protocols. Financial institutions are increasingly adopting ethical AI guidelines that incorporate fairness metrics and monitoring, bias detection and mitigation, transparency requirements, and accountability structures. The effectiveness of these frameworks is evident in research by Mou (2019), which shows that institutions implementing comprehensive ethical AI frameworks experience a 40% reduction in customer complaints related to automated decisions.

10.3 Current State and Quantifiable Improvements

The integration of AI and machine learning into financial services has led to significant transformations. Recent industry analyses by Anderson et al. (2023) demonstrate impressive improvements, including a 60% reduction in processing time for routine financial tasks, 45% improvement in fraud detection accuracy, 30% cost reduction in regulatory compliance, and 50% increase in customer satisfaction with automated services. These improvements have been accompanied by fundamental operational changes, including automated decision-making processes, real-time risk assessment capabilities, enhanced customer service through AI, and improved regulatory compliance mechanisms.

10.4 Future Outlook and Developments

Looking ahead, Oriji et al. (2023), Paramesha et al. (2024), and Pattnaik et al. (2024) project several significant developments in the short term (1–3 years), including widespread adoption of explainable AI systems, integration of quantum-resistant security measures, enhanced privacy-preserving computation methods, and standardisation of AI governance frameworks. Long-term implications (3–10 years) suggest even more dramatic changes, with expectations of fully autonomous financial systems, quantum-enhanced AI applications, decentralised AI governance, and advanced ethical AI frameworks.

10.5 Recommendations for Stakeholders

For financial institutions, key recommendations include investing in ethical AI development, enhancing data governance frameworks, developing AI talent and expertise, and strengthening cybersecurity measures. Regulators should focus on developing adaptive regulatory frameworks, enhancing cross-border cooperation, implementing AI audit standards, and establishing ethical AI guidelines. Technology providers are advised to concentrate on explainable AI solutions, develop privacy-preserving technologies, create standardised AI frameworks, and enhance model transparency.

11   The Future Directions

11.1   Emerging Technologies and Future Applications

The future of financial services is being shaped by groundbreaking technological advances, particularly in quantum computing. Baker and Al-Maskari (2021) highlight promising applications including portfolio optimisation using quantum algorithms, risk calculations with quantum speedup, and quantum-resistant cryptography for financial security. Further research by Wang et al. (2024) suggests that quantum computing could provide a remarkable 100–1000x speedup in complex financial calculations within the next decade. Advanced AI integration is also reshaping the industry through hybrid AI systems combining multiple learning approaches, explainable AI for regulatory compliance, edge computing for real-time processing, and federated learning for privacy-preserved analysis. These developments are driving the evolution towards more sophisticated financial systems.

11.2   Industry Transformation and Autonomous Systems

The financial services industry is moving towards increased autonomy, as documented by Gill et al. (2015), Kashyap and Weber (2016), and Gleasure and Feller (2016). This transformation encompasses self-optimising trading systems, autonomous risk management, smart contract-based financial products, and AI-driven market making. Next-generation compliance systems are expected to feature real-time regulatory compliance, automated policy implementation, cross-border regulatory harmonisation, and dynamic risk assessment capabilities.

11.3   Emerging Challenges and Considerations

The advancement of AI in financial services faces several technical challenges that need to be addressed. These include model interpretability requirements, data quality and standardisation issues, system interoperability concerns, and computational resource optimisation. Additionally, regulatory considerations present ongoing challenges in areas such as AI governance frameworks, cross-border data sharing, model risk management, and privacy preservation.

11.4   Operational Risk Management

Financial institutions are expanding their operational risk monitoring capabilities through process automation risk assessment, cyber risk detection and prevention, employee behaviour analysis, and infrastructure resilience evaluation. These developments represent a comprehensive approach to managing operational risks in an increasingly digital financial environment.

In summary, the evolution of risk management and compliance in financial services continues to be driven by technological innovation and regulatory requirements. As the industry moves towards more autonomous and integrated systems, the balance between technological advancement and risk management becomes increasingly critical. Success in this evolving landscape will require continued innovation in both technical capabilities and regulatory frameworks while addressing emerging challenges and opportunities.

12   Conclusion

The integration of artificial intelligence into financial services represents a pivotal moment of technological transformation that extends far beyond mere technological innovation. This evolution demands a holistic approach that synthesises technological capabilities, ethical considerations, and regulatory frameworks. AI technologies are revolutionising financial services by introducing unprecedented levels of efficiency, accuracy, and predictive capabilities. From algorithmic trading and risk assessment to personalised financial advice and fraud detection, AI is fundamentally reshaping how financial institutions operate and deliver value to customers.

As AI becomes increasingly sophisticated, the ethical dimensions of its implementation become critically important. Financial institutions must prioritise transparency in AI decision-making processes, fairness and non-discriminatory algorithmic design, protection of individual privacy and data rights, and maintain human oversight and accountability. Furthermore, the rapid evolution of AI necessitates a dynamic and responsive regulatory environment. Policymakers and financial regulators must develop comprehensive frameworks that balance innovation with consumer protection, create adaptive guidelines that can keep pace with technological advancements, and ensure that AI implementations align with broader societal values and economic goals.

Beyond technological and financial metrics, AI in financial services must be evaluated through the lens of broader social and environmental impact. This includes promoting financial inclusion, supporting sustainable economic development, addressing environmental challenges through intelligent financial strategies, and ensuring that technological benefits are equitably distributed across different socio-economic groups. Success in this complex landscape will require a multidisciplinary approach that integrates technological expertise, ethical reasoning, regulatory compliance, and a forward-looking vision. Financial institutions must view AI not just as a technological tool, but as a transformative force with the potential to create more intelligent, responsive, and equitable financial ecosystems.

The future of AI in financial services is not predetermined but will be shaped by our collective choices. By maintaining a balanced, thoughtful, and proactive approach, we can harness the immense potential of AI to create financial systems that are not only more efficient and intelligent but also more just, sustainable, and aligned with broader human and environmental needs. The road ahead demands continuous learning, adaptation, and a commitment to responsible innovation.

References

Abdallah A, Maarof MA, Zainal A (2016) Fraud detection system: a survey. J Netw Comput Appl 68:90–113

Abdullah AAH, Almaqtari FA (2024) The impact of artificial intelligence and industry 4.0 on transforming accounting and auditing practices. J Open Innov: Technol Mark Complex 10(1):100218

Aderemi S, Olutimehin DO, Nnaomah UI, Orieno OH, Edunjobi TE, Babatunde SO (2024) Big data analytics in the financial services industry: trends, challenges, and future prospects: a review. Int J Sci Technol Res Arch 6(1):147–166

Ahmadi S (2024) A comprehensive study on integration of big data and AI in financial industry and its effect on present and future opportunities. Int J Curr Sci Res Rev 7(01):66–74

Aitkazinov A (2023) The role of artificial intelligence in auditing: opportunities and challenges. Int J Res Eng Sci Manag 6(6):117–119

Anderson P, Wilson M, Brown K (2023) Early expert systems in finance: a historical analysis. J Financ Hist 25(3):178–195

Anshari M, Almunawar MN, Masri M, Hrdy M (2021) Financial technology with AI-enabled and ethical challenges. Society 58(3):189–195

Arner DW, Barberis J, Buckley RP (2019) The evolution of FinTech: a new post-crisis paradigm? Georget J Int Law 47:1271–1319

Baker HK, Al-Maskari M (2021) Fintech and artificial intelligence in finance: current applications and future prospects. Eur J Financ 27(4–5):367–390

Batchu RK (2023) Artificial intelligence in credit risk assessment: enhancing accuracy and efficiency. Int Trans Artif Intell 7(7):1–24

Berrada IR, Barramou FZ, Alami OB (2022, February) A review of artificial intelligence approach for credit risk assessment. In: 2022 2nd international conference on artificial intelligence and signal processing (AISP). IEEE, pp 1–5

Bhatt S, Singh P (2023, September) A comprehensive review of AI-enabled financial domain: past, present & future aspects. In: 2023 3rd international conference on innovative sustainable computational technologies (CISCT). IEEE, pp 1–5

Buchanan BG (2019) Artificial intelligence in finance. J Financ 74(4):1665–1699

Cao L (2022) Ai in finance: challenges, techniques, and opportunities. ACM Comput Surv (CSUR) 55(3):1–38

Chen MA, Bellavitis C (2020) Blockchain disruption and decentralized finance: the rise of decentralized business models. J Bus Ventur Insights 13:e00151

Chen Y, Zhang X (2023) Evolution of AI in financial services: a historical perspective. J Financ Technol 17(2):89–112

Dai J, Vasarhelyi MA (2017) Toward Blockchain-based accounting and assurance. J Inf Syst 31(3):5–21

Davis E, Marcus G (2019) Rebooting AI: building artificial intelligence we can trust. Pantheon, New York

Fama EF (1970) Efficient capital markets: a review of theory and empirical work. J Financ 25(2):383–417

Fischer T, Krauss C (2018) Deep learning with long short-term memory networks for financial market predictions. Eur J Oper Res 270(2):654–669

Gatla TR (2024) AI-driven regulatory compliance for financial institutions: examining how AI can assist in monitoring and complying with ever-changing financial regulations

Gill A, Bunker D, Seltsikas P (2015) Moving forward: emerging themes in financial services technologies' adoption. Commun Assoc Inf Syst 36(1):12

Giudici P, Hochreiter R, Osterrieder J, Papenbrock J, Schwendner P (2019) AI and financial technology. Front Artif Intell 2:25

Gleasure R, Feller J (2016) Emerging technologies and the democratisation of financial services: a metatriangulation of crowdfunding research. Inf Organ 26(4):101–115

Golić Z (2019) Finance and artificial intelligence: the fifth industrial revolution and its impact on the financial sector. Zbornik radova Ekonomskog fakulteta u Istočnom Sarajevu 19:67–81

Goto M (2023) Anticipatory innovation of professional services: the case of auditing and artificial intelligence. Res Policy 52(8):104828

Gu S, Kelly B, Xiu D (2020) Empirical asset pricing via machine learning. Rev Financ Stud 33(5):2223–2273

Issa H, Sun T, Vasarhelyi MA (2016) Research ideas for artificial intelligence in auditing: the formalization of audit and workforce supplementation. J Emerg Technol Account 13(2):1–20

Jejeniwa TO, Mhlongo NZ, Jejeniwa TO (2024) A comprehensive review of the impact of artificial intelligence on modern accounting practices and financial reporting. Comput Sci IT Res J 5(4):1031–1047

Johnson K, Pasquale F, Chapman J (2019) Artificial intelligence, machine learning, and bias in finance: toward responsible innovation. Fordham L Rev 88:499

Kahneman D, Tversky A (1979) Prospect theory: an analysis of decision under risk. Econometrica 47(2):263–291

Kashyap KM, Weber G (2016) How emerging technologies will change financial services. In: The FinTech book: the financial technology handbook for investors, entrepreneurs and visionaries, pp 226–228

Kothandapani HP (2025) AI-Driven Regulatory Compliance: Transforming Financial Oversight through Large Language Models and Automation. Emerging Science Research 12–24

Law KK, Shen M (2024) How does artificial intelligence shape audit firms? Manag Sci

LeCun Y, Bengio Y, Hinton G (2015) Deep learning. Nature 521(7553):436–444

Li Z, Zheng L (2018, September) The impact of artificial intelligence on accounting. In: *2018 4th international conference on social science and higher education (ICSSHE 2018)*. Atlantis Press

Lin TCW (2020) Artificial intelligence, finance, and the law. Fordham Law Rev 88(2):531–598

López-Iturriaga FJ, Sanz IP (2018) Predicting public corruption with neural networks: an analysis of Spanish provinces. Soc Indic Res 140(3):975–994

Mashrur A, Luo W, Zaidi NA, Robles-Kelly A (2020) Machine learning for financial risk management: a survey. IEEE Access 8:203203–203223

Milana C, Ashta A (2021) Artificial intelligence techniques in finance and financial markets: a survey of the literature. Strateg Chang 30(3):189–209

Miller CN, Roll R, Taylor W (1970) Efficient capital markets: a review of theory and empirical work. J Financ 25(2):383–417

Mou X (2019) Artificial intelligence: investment trends and selected industry uses. Int Financ Corp 8(2):311–320

Munoko I, Brown-Liburd HL, Vasarhelyi M (2020) The ethical implications of using artificial intelligence in auditing. J Bus Ethics 167(2):209–234

Omokhoa HE, Odionu CS, Azubuike CHIMA, & Sule AK (2024) Innovative credit management and risk reduction strategies: AI and fintech approaches for microfinance and SMEs. IRE Journals 8(6):686

Oriji O, Shonibare MA, Daraojimba RE, Abitoye O, Daraojimba C (2023) Financial technology evolution in Africa: a comprehensive review of legal frameworks and implications for AI-driven financial services. Int J Manag Entrep Res 5(12):929–951

Ozbayoglu AM, Gudelek MU, Sezer OB (2020) Deep learning for financial applications: a survey. Appl Soft Comput 93:106384

Paramesha M, Rane NL, Rane J (2024) Artificial intelligence, machine learning, deep learning, and Blockchain in financial and banking services: a comprehensive review. Partn Univers Multidiscip Res J 1(2):51–67

Pattnaik D, Ray S, Raman R (2024) Applications of artificial intelligence and machine learning in the financial services industry: a bibliometric review. Heliyon 10(1):e23492

Rahmani AM, Rezazadeh B, Haghparast M, Chang WC, Ting SG (2023) Applications of artificial intelligence in the economy, including applications in stock trading, market analysis, and risk management. IEEE Access 11:80769–80793

Singh S, Bhagat R, Preeti SH, Girish GP (2023, April) Transforming the financial industry through machine and deep learning innovations. In: International conference on Intelligent Computing & Optimization. Springer Nature Switzerland, Cham, pp 167–176

Stiglitz JE (2000) The contributions of the economics of information to twentieth century economics. Q J Econ 115(4):1441–1478

Sun T, Vasarhelyi MA (2018) Embracing textual data analytics in auditing with deep learning. Int J Digit Account Res 18:49–67

Truby J, Brown R, Dahdal A (2020) Banking on AI: mandating a proactive approach to AI regulation in the financial sector. Law Financ Mark Rev 14(2):110–120

Vapnik VN, Chervonenkis AY (2015) On the uniform convergence of relative frequencies of events to their probabilities. In: Measures of complexity: festschrift for alexey chervonenkis. Springer International Publishing, Cham, pp 11–30

Vasarhelyi MA, Halper FB (2018) The continuous audit of online Systems1. In: Continuous auditing. Emerald Publishing Limited, pp 87–104

Wang J, Xu J, Cheng Q, Kumar R (2024) Research on finance credit risk quantification model based on machine learning algorithm. Acad J Sci Technol 10(1):290–298

Yi Z, Cao X, Chen Z, Li S (2023) Artificial intelligence in accounting and finance: challenges and opportunities. IEEE Access 11:129100–129123

The Development of Accounting as a Service Activity

Michael Adelowotan

Abstract This chapter reviews the development of accounting as a service activity to various organisations and industries. In theory, Accounting is described as a system of recording, classifying, and summarising financial information in such a way that users of the information can make economic decisions based on such information. Accounting as a science has its own history, which could be traced from 6000 BC until 1900s before the advent of computers and accounting software packages. However, accounting from 2000s has been greatly influenced by the advent of the Fourth Industrial Revolution Technologies notably artificial intelligence, machine learning, Internet of Things, Big Data Analysis and Blockchain Technology among others. Therefore, this chapter explores the roots of accounting from the earliest history of civilisation through to the double-entry bookkeeping to the modern professional and specialised accounting. The chapter also touched briefly on the influence of industrial revolutions on accounting as a service activity and accounting as a profession.

Keywords Accounting · History · Development · Service activity · Profession · Fourth Industrial Revolution

1 Introduction

The history and development of accounting is a "specialist research area in itself" (Carnegie 2014, p. 1241). In order to support the development of accounting, researchers need to continuously evaluate its history (Previts et al. 1990) to inform its development. Since ancient civilisations, accounting has evolved as a social practice, shaping organisations, industries, and nations (Soll 2014). It has been, and remains, a pivotal

M. Adelowotan (✉)
Department of Accountancy, University of Johannesburg, Johannesburg, South Africa
e-mail: madelowotan@uj.ac.za

© The Author(s), under exclusive license to Springer Nature
Switzerland AG 2025
M. Adelowotan, C. A. Leke (eds.), *Artificial Intelligence in Accounting, Auditing and Finance*, Contributions to Finance and Accounting,
https://doi.org/10.1007/978-3-031-87368-3_3

31

aspect of capitalism, enabling businesses to manoeuvre intricate financial landscapes. Along the way, economic interests, institutional forces, technology, and socio-economic dynamics have significantly influenced accounting practice. Bearing in mind the ever-changing business environment, it is critical to continuously understand and document the historical background of accounting. History allows a better understanding of the past and provides insights into present practices, enabling forecasting or controlling its future (Kulikova 2015; Sokolov 2004).

In order to keep history up to date, accounting researchers are called upon to identify and evaluate contemporary issues and how they continue to shape the practice. If historical perspectives are ignored, current accounting practices and ideas could be rootless (Carnegie 2014). Because of the fast-paced business environment and the significant changes in various factors such as technology, several underexplored issues remain in the historical accounting literature. While previous studies have documented accounting history, the narrative history could be insufficient because of these changes.

The chapter maintains that with the changes in technology, the methods and the means of information processing are also changing in the process, influencing how accounting is perceived and understood. For this reason, the chapter aims to review the development of accounting as a service activity for organisations and industries and how the Fourth Industrial Revolution has shaped the accounting practice. The chapter also explores the history of accounting from the earliest civilisation to the double-entry bookkeeping to modern professional and specialised accounting. The final section of the chapter discusses the influence of industrial revolutions on accounting as a service activity and accounting as a profession.

The development of accounting in the earlier period was related to occurrences in the counting and writing of transactions involving exchange of goods and services. The step taken in Mesopotamia with regard to accounting and money was pivotal to the development of counting with its accompanying transition from concrete counting to abstract counting. Thus the history of Accounting could be seen as having emanated from thousands of years ago before the advent of the cradle of civilisation in Mesopotamia which relates to the inventions of the counting and writing of money. It was observed that the Babylonians and the Egyptians in the earlier times invented a system of audit while the idea of the collation of financial information was first practised by the Romans.

The Italian Luca Pacioli has been referred to as the father of accounting and bookkeeping because he first described the system of double-entry bookkeeping used by Venetian merchants in his Summa de Arithmetica, Geometria, Proportioni et Proportionalita (Summary of Arithmetic and Geometry) in 1494. While he was not the inventor of accounting, Pacioli was the first to describe the system of debits and credits in journals and ledgers that is still the basis of today's accounting systems. Thus, Luca Pacioli was the first person to publish a work on double-entry bookkeeping and introduced the field in Italy (Berisha and Asllanaj 2017).

However, the advent of the nineteenth century marks the beginning of transition of accounting into an organised profession culminating into the formation of the Institute of Chartered Accountants of England and Wales in the year 1880 as a result of the merger between some local professional organisations in England.

The practice of accounting existed from the beginning of humanity because the writings of the Assyrians, Babylonians, Chaldeans, and the Sumerians formed the basis of the earliest sample of accounting records.

The literature on accounting history presents various versions of the history and development of Accounting as a profession. However, this chapter will glean literatures to come up with stages in the development of Accounting from earliest period to date.

2   Methodology

The author adopted a systematic literature review which involves the identification of relevant works; assessing the quality of studies; summarising the evidence obtained; and finally interpreting the findings. Thus, the author analysed various sources of information where the origin and the development of accounting were discussed. The author's main sources of information include journal articles, blogs, and websites of professional organisations (Mukhametzyanov et al. 2017).

A systematic literature review aims to identify and evaluate relevant literature on a topic so as to arrive at conclusions about the subject that is being considered. Feak and Swales (2009) stated that *"Systematic reviews are undertaken to clarify the state of existing research and the implications that should be drawn from this"*. It can be stated that a systematic literature review has the capability to demonstrate the present state of research on a subject so as to identify gaps necessitating further research on the subject matter.

M. H. Abrams identified four theories that could be used in systematic literature reviews. These are objective theories, mimetic theories, pragmatic theories and the expressive theories. According to Abrams, *"the objective view treats each poem as its own self-contained world or object. The mimetic view sees poetry as imitating or reflecting the real world. The pragmatic view focuses on how poetry achieves effects in its audience. The expressive view emphasises the poet's feelings and experience"*. However, the author leaned towards expressive theories because they lay emphasis on the authors' account which is considered relevant for a work on history and development of accounting.

3   Discussion and Results

3.1   History of Accounting

"It is impossible to imagine modern business and economy without accounting" (Mukhametzyanov et al. 2017, p. 1227). These words demonstrate the significance of accounting in fostering sustainable business practices and illustrate how accounting has evolved to become a science on its own. The history of accounting as a service activity spans thousands of years, evolving in response to various factors such as changing societal needs, economic systems, and technological changes. Some scholars contend that accounting emerged as far back as 7000 years ago (Kulikova 2015; Napier 2006). Accounting historians have documented the development of accounting at every turn. Understanding the history of accounting is critical because it informs development (Sokolov 2004). Development builds on history; new accounting practices and theories emerge from existing foundations.

Accounting historians suggest that accounting history could be divided into six main phases. These include ancient civilisation (3000 BC-500 CE), the mediaeval period (500–1500 CE), the Renaissance and Enlightenment period (1500–1800 CE), the Industrial Revolution (1800–1900 CE), the twentieth Century (1900–2000 CE), and the present (2000 to date). Accounting in the ancient civilisation was dominated by the Mesopotamians, Egyptians, and Babylonians, who used accounting for trade and taxation (Phatshwane and Mbekomize 2017). Because of the increase in trade during this time, record-keeping became essential. Clay tablets were used to record accounting transactions. Ancient successful farmers kept commercial records in the Mesopotamian valley, using silver and gold as standard value measures to external credit for certain transactions (Soll 2014). These practices provided a solid foundation for what we know today as professional accounting. Building on these developments, Egyptians later kept accounting records that a system of internal controls could verify. However, some literature (Phatshwane and Mbekomize 2017) suggests that although Egyptians kept accounting records, they never progressed beyond simple lists of warehouse items. Nevertheless, Egyptian practices significantly shaped the accounting practice.

The mediaeval period was characterised by increased barter trade. It saw the emergence of merchant capitalism and guilds in Europe (Hoopwood and Miller 1994). During this time, the so-called accountants began to develop ethics and professional standards to ensure that the profession maintained a high standing, professionalism, and responsibility in their work (Phatshwane and Mbekomize 2017).

Meanwhile, the establishment of joint-stock companies characterised the Renaissance and Enlightenment periods. Luca Pacioli's "Summa de Arithmetica" of 1494 introduced the double-entry bookkeeping system and, consequently, accounting as it is known today (Napier 2006; Sokolov 2004). It is generally believed that 1494 saw the beginning of modern accounting. These civilisations provided the first evidence of surviving scripted records that indicate the establishment of formal business structures (Soll 2014). The double-entry system was characterised by a separate balance sheet consisting of debits and credits in order to assist the business in efficiently tracking their transactions. It is essential to mention that accounting information was unavailable for the general stakeholders during this time. It was only for the company. The history highlights the transformation of accounting from simple record-keeping to an established social practice shaping economies, organisations, and societies (Mukhametzyanov et al. 2017).

Accounting adapted to new manufacturing technologies during the Industrial Revolution because of increased business activities. Since 2000, accounting has undergone significant changes because of the Fourth Industrial Revolution. More professional accounting bodies emerged during this period. The contemporary period, characterised by globalisation, saw the adoption of accounting standards worldwide, including technological advances such as blockchain, cloud computing, and machine learning.

The developments in counting, writing and money could be linked to the development of accounting in the earlier times. For instance, the change from concrete to abstract counting resulted in the development of accounting in monetary terms in Mesopotamia (Blog-Erasmus Rekenmeesters). As far back as over 7000 years ago, other early accounting records were discovered from the remains of ancient Babylonian and Assyrian empires. It was further discovered that the people used a form of accounting method in recording the growth in the level of production relying on the seasons of animal rearing and cultivation of crops (Blog-Erasmus Rekenmeesters).

The second century BC witnessed the need for the recording of payments for tax purposes. Again, during the second century BC, the ancient Babylonians and Egyptians empires, developed systems for checking in and out movements of stock items thus establishing a form of audit systems. This is the origin of the term "audire" a Latin word meaning "to hear" (Blog-Erasmus Rekenmeesters). Evidence of early form of accounting were found in the Bible where Moses the leader of the Israelites engaged a man called Ithamar to account for materials that were contributed for the building of tabernacle for worship. *"This is the sum of the tabernacle, even of the tabernacle of testimony, as it was counted, according to the commandment of Moses, for the service of the Levites, by the hand of Ithamar, son to Aaron the priest"* (Exodus 38:21;Holy Bible, King James Version).

According to TheStreet, the roles played by the practice of accounting from the earliest time to the present times includes observing the growth in animal and crop rearing, taking record of transactions, measurement of organisational performance, establishing risk management processes through adequate regulatory compliance and ensuring reduction in fraud, errors, and irregularities through auditing and investigations. The figure below summarises the historical development of accounting practice.

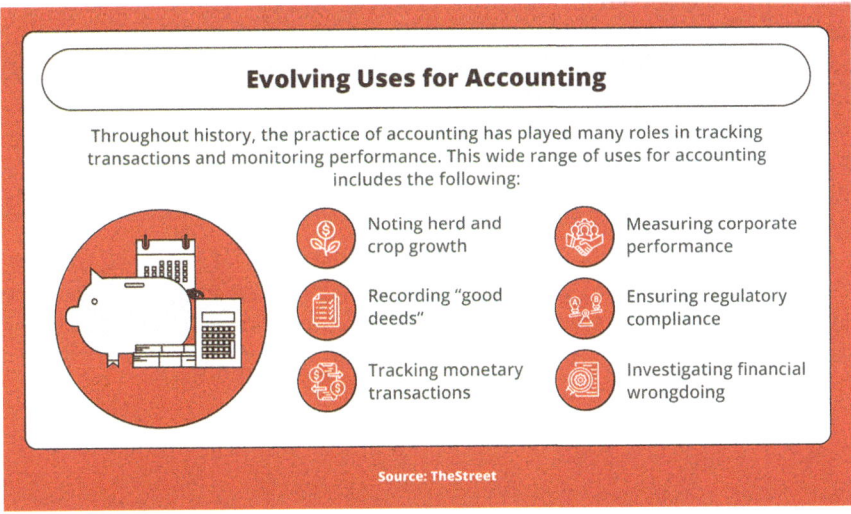

3.2   History of Accounting Timelines

As mentioned, early accounting systems are believed to have been developed by the Mesopotamians in ancient civilisations. The Egyptians, Greeks, and Romans later developed what was known as basic accounting principles. In 1494, a period known as the Middle Ages, Luca Pacioli published the famous "Summa de Arithmetica", which introduced the double-entry bookkeeping system (Phatshwane and Mbekomize 2017). In the later years (Renaissance and Enlightenment), a German merchant, Simon Stevin, published "Tafelen van Interest" on compound interest in 1543. The twentieth century saw the establishment of organisations such as the American Institute of Certified Public Accountants (AICPA) in 1900, the Securities and Exchange Commission (SEC) in 1934, and the American Accounting Association in 1953. In 2001, the International Accounting Standards Board (IFRS) was established.

4   Development of Accounting

History and development are intertwined. There is no development without history because history informs development. "The development of any science is studied in order to ensure the continuity in its development" (Mukhametzyanov et al. 2017, p. 1228). Accounting development has been influenced by factors such as history, technology, globalisation, regulatory requirements, and the continued changes in business needs. The late nineteenth and early twentieth centuries saw the establishment of professional accounting bodies, such as the Institute of Chartered Accountants in England and Wales (1890). These organisations were tasked with developing ethics, standards, and certification programmes. The introduction of Generally Accepted Accounting Principles (GAAP) and International Financial Reporting Standards (IFRS) improved the consistency and comparability of accounting information. As mentioned, while history looks backwards, development looks forward and focuses on improving current and future practices. Thus, development is the ongoing process of improving and expanding practices, theories, and accounting standards. In recent years, technology has transformed accounting practices by introducing software solutions. The emergence of cloud computing, artificial intelligence, and blockchain technology continues to reshape the accounting development landscape.

The development of accounting spreads over thousands of years and has witnessed series of transformation from mere recording of transactions to the present day's comprehensive recording, investigations, and prediction of results of financial transactions.

4.1 Accounting from Clay Tablets to Computers

Clay tablets were used in ancient civilisations, particularly in Mesopotamia, for record-keeping and taxation. In the later years, papyrus scrolls were used in ancient Egypt for royal treasuries and wax tablets were used in Rome and Greece for merchants' records and financial transactions. Manuscript ledgers were later developed in the mediaeval period. These consisted of records that were handwritten for trade and commerce. As mentioned, Luca Pacioli's "Summa de Arithmetica" introduced the double-entry bookkeeping system and modern accounting principles (Previts et al. 1990). The industrial revolution culminated in printing ledgers where arithmetic calculations were automated. In the modern era, typewriters (1874), electronic calculators (1960s), and mainframe computers were introduced for faster data entry, electronic calculations, computerised accounting, and spreadsheet and accounting software. Personal computers were developed in the 1980s. The Fourth Industrial Revolution increased the importance of accounting, and technological innovations produced more business transactions. Computer software has made accounting easier and more efficient.

4.2 Accounting from Computers to Software

After the development of computers, the 1980s to the 1990s saw the emergence of accounting software such as QuickBooks—an accounting software for small businesses, which was later developed into QuickBooks online—a cloud-based version of QuickBooks. These led the automation of accounting transactions and real-time reporting, accessible on the desktops.

According to BSB and Medius, the following timelines could be identified in relation to the historical development of accounting:

- *"Circa 3300 B.C.: Earliest documented use of accounting. Artefacts show tax records on clay tablets.*
- *1458: Invention of double-entry accounting method. Benedetto Cotrugli invented the double-entry accounting system, establishing the foundation for modern accounting.*
- *1494: Publication of the first book describing the double-entry accounting method. Luca Bartolomeo de Pacioli, known as the father of accounting, published Summa de Arithmetica, Geometria, Proportioni et Proportionalita.*
- *1854: Establishment of the first accounting professional organisations. The members of the Institute of Accountants and Actuaries in Glasgow and the Edinburgh Society of Accountants called themselves chartered accountants.*
- *1880s: Invention of the adding machine. William Burroughs invented the adding machine, improving accounting's speed and accuracy.*
- *1930s: First high-profile use of forensic accounting. IRS accountant Frank Wilson uncovered financial irregularities that led to the arrest of Al Capone.*

- *1955: First purchase of a computer for accounting use. General Electric made the first purchase of a computer to perform accounting functions such as payroll processing.*
- *1978: Introduction of spreadsheet software. VisiCalc was the first spreadsheet software to allow financial modelling on the computer".*

In summary, it was noted that major developments in Accounting include the recording of tax on clay tablets around 3300 BC; the introduction of double-entry accounting system in 1458; the introduction of first book with accounting concepts in 1494; the establishment of first organisation of professional accountants in 1854; the introduction of adding machines (calculators) in 1880s; the introduction of computers for accounting purposes in 1955; the introduction of first spreadsheet software in 1978 and the automation of some accounting processes in the year 2000.

These developments have also been summarised in the figure below:

Thus, the earliest records of financial and business transactions started with clay tablets, the first examples of these records were found in Egypt and Mesopotamia. Since then, accounting has evolved to complex processes enabled by automated technology used for debtors and creditors control processes. Today, automation has led to the emergence and the application of Fourth Industrial Revolution technologies. The thirteenth century was noted for the advancement of money economy in mediaeval Europe. This necessitated reliance of merchants on bookkeeping as a step forward from record-keeping.

The year 1458 witnessed the invention of the double-entry system of accounting by Benedetto Contrugli. This bookkeeping system involves a debit to the receiver and a credit to the giver for all transactions. Later in 1494, Luca Pacioli—a Franciscan monk and Italian Mathematician—wrote a book which included a 27-page treatise on bookkeeping emphasising the use of memorandum, journal, and ledger. In the year 1854, the Glasgow Institute of Accountants and the Edinburgh Society of Accountants were formed in Scotland as the first set of professional organisations for Accountants. Later in 1887, the Accountants in America came together to form the American Institute of Certified Public Accountants.

4.3   The Early Systems and Electronic Data Interchange

One great invention occurred in the 1880s when an American-born William Burroughs invented the adding machine (calculator) which made it possible to do arithmetical calculations with greater efficiency and higher accuracy. By the end of eighteenth century, technological advancement led to the development of punch-card machine by American Herman Hollerith with the aim of speeding up data handling and analysis processes for the United States Census. Hollerith eventually used the punch-card machine concept to develop the IBM tabulator which could process up to 100 cards per minute.

At the end of the Second World War, the company known as General Electric purchase a special computer known as UNIVAC (the UNIVersal Automatic Computer) for running its payroll processes. The special computer developed by J. Mauchly and J. P. Eckert was able to process General Electric payroll within a short time interval of 40 h.

4.4   The Ongoing Evolution of Accounting Automation Tools

The first spreadsheet software named VisiCalc was developed in 1978. This software made it possible for financial modelling to be done on the computer. Again, the Peachtree accounting software was also developed around the same time in which VisiCalc was developed. These software enabled the computerisation of accounting functions at a much lower cost. Another notable software referred to as Quickbooks was introduced in 1998. It was designed for day-to-day bookkeeping and became the most popular accounting software in the late 1990s and early 2000s.

4.5 Optical Character Recognition (OCR) and Intelligent Data Capture (IDC)

Also in the early 2000s, another notable advancement in the history of accounting is the development of Advanced Data Capture in the forms of Optical Character Recognition (OCR) and Intelligent Data Capture (IDC). These technologies enabled the account payable process to be automated from the beginning to the end. This has resulted in increasing the efficiency of accounts payable processes.

5 Accounting from Software to Technological Revolutions

5.1 Artificial Intelligence (AI)

AI has influenced accounting in recent years, enabling companies to make, for example, financial forecasting and improved risk management. It has improved the efficiency and effectiveness of accounting by reducing the possibility of fraud, improving the quality of accounting information and promoting the reform of traditional accounting. The focus areas of application of AI in accounting include expert systems, decision support systems, and natural language processing, among other areas (Hasan 2022). Processing time has been reduced, enabling real-time analysis and improved compliance.

5.2 Machine Learning

Machine learning broadly involves the science of computers without being explicitly programmed (Yu et al. 2019). This includes applying several statistical techniques, including data visualisation and mathematical modelling for pattern and trend prediction (Yu et al. 2016). Using machine learning, companies can forecast revenues and make decisions on investments. In addition, companies can also predict customer purchase intentions (Zhang et al. 2020).

5.3 Big Data Analysis

Big data involves large volumes of data analysed using algorithms (data analytic technique). Variety, speed, and volume characterise big data. Analysis of big data has transformed accounting, enabling accountants to extract valuable insights from large data sets, such as identifying trends and anomalies and optimising tax strategies. Companies are able to extract some value for the business in order to understand their customers, competitors, and the business environment (Zhang et al. 2020). Big data supports decision-making and improves prediction accuracy and in addition to data visualisation, big data analysis can transform large volumes of data into information, enhancing decision-making processes (Hoelscher and Mortimer 2018).

5.4 Blockchain Technology

Blockchain is a technology for storing and verifying transactional records that work by adding data blocks to a ledger maintained across a network of peer-to-peer computers (Coyne and McMickle 2017). Fanning and Centers (2016, p. 53) define blockchain as "a database that maintains a continuously growing list of data records that are hardened against tampering and revision, even by operators of the data stores modes". Blockchain could be a secure accounting information system (Garanina et al. 2022). In a blockchain, the process of verification of transactions is not centrally managed. Instead, all the computers in the network are involved, and individuals cannot collude to override controls or illicitly alter official accounting records. Transactions cannot be deleted. Blockchain technically allows for the secure and cost-effective transmission of any value in real-time (Zhang et al. 2020). Although the use of blockchain can potentially change the nature of accounting can potentially change the nature of accounting, cyber-security, and privacy concerns will demand reconciliation before business commits their data to blockchain-based systems and solutions. The non-tamperable features of blockchain enhance the reliability and authenticity of data (Zhang et al. 2020). Blockchain technology can simplify the transfer of any value in real time. Besides, it can also make it easier to detect errors and fraud by providing transparent information about transactions.

With advancements in technology, the majority of accounting processes can now be done more efficiently because they facilitate the generation of numerical figures, thus enabling accountants today to focus on analysis and advice that will facilitate the formulation and execution of corporate strategies for improved performance.

In the modern days, accounting methods make use of specialised tools and processes such as cloud storage, blockchain, digital payment systems, artificial intelligence, and machine learning.

According to Software Suggest, the emerging technologies with reference to accounting include robotic process automation, cloud-based operations, blockchain, data analytics, and others.

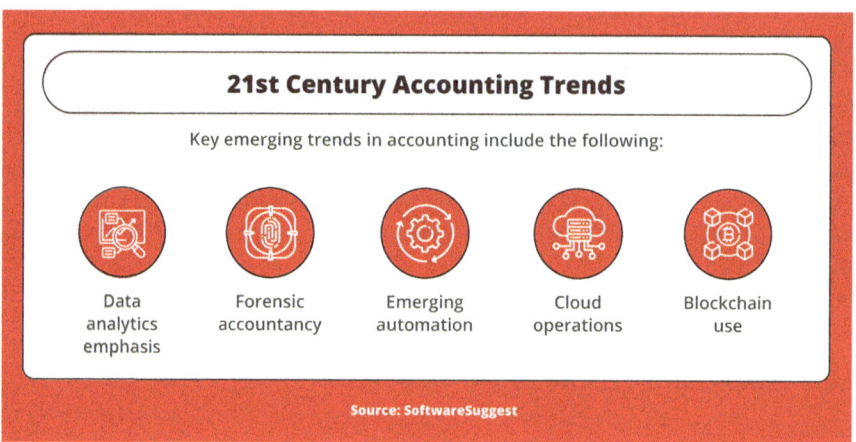

6   Conclusion

In the study by Atherton Research in 2018, it was predicted that accounting processes, internal and external audits, payroll operations, taxation will be fully automated through AI-based technologies by the year 2020. Four years now, AI has phenomenal transformation to accounting processes although this has come with various challenges and opportunities.

It is obvious that studying the history of accounting will enable accounting professionals and practitioners to understand and recognise the past and the present developments and leverage on the present to advance accounting processes and practice particularly in the Fourth Industrial Revolution Era. However, the history of accounting is evolving and its continuous study will enable accounting professionals to improve accuracy and achieve greater efficiency with a view to facilitate optimal growth of businesses all over the world.

This chapter discussed the evolution of accounting and how the current development of technology is influencing accounting as a service activity. Development has been shaped by historical, social, economic, and technological factors. While significant progress has been made, accounting only maintains relevance and effectiveness in an ever-changing business environment by embracing innovation and standardisation. This includes embracing sustainability-focused accounting. The advent of the Fourth Industrial Revolution is expected to continue transforming accounting practice. Accounting efficiency is set to improve tremendously.

References

Atherton Research (2018). https://www.linkedin.com/company/atherton-research/

Berisha V, Asllanaj R (2017) Literature review on historical development of accounting. *Acta Univ Danubius* 13(6)

Carnegie GD (2014) The present and future of accounting history. Account Audit Account J 27(8):1241–1249. https://doi.org/10.1108/AAAJ-05-2014-1715

Coyne J, McMickle P (2017) Can Blockchains serve an accounting purpose. J Emerging Technol Account 14(2):101–111. https://doi.org/10.2308/jeta-51910

Fanning K, Centers DP (2016) Blockchain and its coming impact on financial services. J Corp Account Finance 27(5):53–57. https://doi.org/10.1002/jcaf.22179

Feak CB, Swales JM (2009) Telling a research story: writing a literature review. In: English in today's research world 2. University of Michigan Press, Ann Arbor. https://doi.org/10.3998/mpub.309338

Garanina T, Ranta M, Dumay J (2022) Blockchain in accounting research: current trends and emerging topics. Account Audit Account J 35(7):1507–1533). Emerald Group Holdings Ltd. https://doi.org/10.1108/AAAJ-10-2020-4991

Hasan AR (2022) Artificial intelligence (AI) in Accounting & Auditing: a literature review. Open J Bus Manag 10(01):440–465. https://doi.org/10.4236/ojbm.2022.101026

Hoelscher J, Mortimer A (2018) Using tableau to visualise data and drive decision-making. J Account Educ 44:49–59. https://doi.org/10.1016/j.jaccedu.2018.05.002

Hoopwood AG, Miller P (1994) Accounting as a social and institutional practice. Cambridge University Press

Kulikova LI (2015) The historical aspect of bookkeeping science origin and development. Bull Adygei State Univ 3(165):97–105

Mukhametzyanov R, Nugaev F, Muhametzyanova L (2017) History of accounting development. J Hist Cult Art Res 6(4):1227. https://doi.org/10.7596/taksad.v6i4.1163

Napier CJ (2006) Accounts of change: 30 years of historical accounting research. Account Org Soc 31(1):445–507

Phatshwane PMD, Mbekomize CJ (2017) Special issue: 50th anniversary special issue. Botswana J Bus 10(1):1–2

Previts GJ, Parker LD, Coffman EN (1990) Accounting history: definition and relevance. Abacus 26(1):1–16. https://doi.org/10.1111/j.1467-6281.1990.tb00229.x

Sokolov LI (2004) History of accounting: a textbook. Finance and Statistics

Soll J (2014) The reckoning: financial accountability and the rise and fall of nations. Basic Books

Yu Y, Yin G, Wang T, Yang C, Wang H (2016) Determinants of pull-based development in the context of continuous integration. Sci China Inf Sci 59(8):080104. https://doi.org/10.1007/s11432-016-5595-8

Yu H, Yang X, Zheng S, Sun C (2019) Active learning from imbalanced data: a solution of online weighted extreme learning machine. IEEE Trans Neural Netw Learn Syst 30(4):1088–1103. https://doi.org/10.1109/TNNLS.2018.2855446

Zhang Y, Xiong F, Xie Y, Fan X, Gu H (2020) The impact of artificial intelligence and block-chain on the accounting profession. IEEE Access 8:110461–110477. https://doi.org/10.1109/ACCESS.2020.3000505

The Accountancy Profession and the Challenges of Artificial Intelligence

Nicolaas Strydom and Ahmed Mohammadali-Haji

Abstract The accountancy profession is undergoing a transformative shift driven by the integration of artificial intelligence (AI) and other technologies of the Fourth Industrial Revolution (4IR). With the rapid pace of technological advancement, the profession must quickly adapt to new technologies and their impact on the accountant's role to remain relevant and continue adding value. Given the availability of systematic literature reviews on the potential impact of 4IR on the accountancy profession, this chapter provides a review of reviews to highlight the challenges and opportunities that AI and 4IR technologies present to the accountancy profession. Thirty-two reviews are included in the study.

The analysis highlights a shift in accountants' role from routine financial tasks to strategic advisory positions that require technological proficiency, critical thinking, and data-driven decision-making. While automation enhances efficiency and fraud detection, concerns about job displacement, ethical risks, and the widening skills gap persist. The study emphasises the need for lifelong learning and industry-academia collaboration to equip future accountants with digital acumen. Despite the challenges faced by the profession, 4IR technologies present significant opportunities for accountants to drive innovation, enhance financial transparency, and improve efficiency. The findings call for proactive adaptation by stakeholders - including educators, professional bodies, and policymakers - to ensure that the profession remains relevant in an increasingly digital economy.

Keywords Accountancy profession · Fourth Industrial Revolution · Digital transformation · Emerging technologies · Digital acumen · Review of reviews

N. Strydom (✉) · A. Mohammadali-Haji
Department of Accountancy, University of Johannesburg, Johannesburg, South Africa
e-mail: nicost@uj.ac.za; ahmedh@uj.ac.za

© The Author(s), under exclusive license to Springer Nature Switzerland AG 2025
M. Adelowotan, C. A. Leke (eds.), *Artificial Intelligence in Accounting, Auditing and Finance*, Contributions to Finance and Accounting,
https://doi.org/10.1007/978-3-031-87368-3_4

45

1   Introduction

The Fourth Industrial Revolution (4IR) is reshaping professions and industries globally, and accountancy is no exception. The emergence of digital technologies such as generative artificial intelligence (AI), blockchain, and advanced data analytics has set the accounting profession on a new course towards the "digitised world of work" (Tsiligiris and Bowyer 2021:621; Barac et al. 2021). Given the rapid technological development of the 4IR era, the accountant's skillset is shifting from "manual and basic cognitive skills" towards "technological, social, and emotional skills" (Tsiligiris and Bowyer 2021:630; cf. Landsberg and Van den Berg 2023; Richins et al. 2017). This is supported by recent developments in the competency frameworks of several professional bodies (CGMA 2019; SAICA 2021), which have argued for technological and other pervasive skills to move from the periphery to the core of accounting education. Similarly, Jackson et al. (2022) argue that the role of accountants has shifted beyond the traditional focus on transactions towards technology-driven decision-making and strategic support. Kroon et al. (2021) summarise the shift as (1) a change in *how tasks are performed*, and (2) a change in *which tasks are performed* by accountants (cf. Damasiotis et al. 2015).

The rise of AI and 4IR technologies presents both opportunities and challenges for the profession. On the one hand, automation enhances efficiency by minimising human errors, reducing operational costs, and freeing accountants from repetitive tasks. This shift allows professionals to assume more strategic and advisory roles, supporting business decision-making and offering value-added services. On the other hand, the transformation brings concerns about job displacement, ethical risks, and the need for new skills to remain relevant in a technology-driven environment. Accountants must now develop expertise in data analytics, technology governance, and cybersecurity to adapt to these emerging roles. Accountants need to adopt a digital mindset that embraces lifelong learning and technological fluency while maintaining the core values of the profession, such as integrity and public trust.

The purpose of this study is to explore how artificial intelligence (AI) and Fourth Industrial Revolution (4IR) technologies are transforming the role of accountants. As technology reshapes industries worldwide, the accountancy profession is witnessing a shift from performing routine tasks such as data entry and financial reporting towards strategic advisory roles that require a deeper understanding of technology and business. This transformation demands not only an evaluation of how these technologies impact the profession but also an understanding of the challenges and opportunities that accompany them.

This study aims to provide a structured literature review of existing research on the impact of AI and 4IR technologies on the accounting profession. Through a critical analysis of relevant studies, the chapter identifies the key areas where automation, machine learning, data analytics, and other emerging technologies are driving change. The focus is on understanding how the adoption of these technologies is reshaping core accounting processes, redefining required skill sets, and introducing new ethical and professional challenges.

The study also seeks to highlight strategies that accountants, educators, and professional bodies can adopt to effectively respond to these changes. By examining how accountants can move towards more advisory and analytical roles, the study offers practical insights into maintaining the relevance and value of the profession in a technology-driven world. Additionally, it discusses the importance of balancing technological fluency with the core professional values that define the accounting field, such as integrity, trust, and responsibility.

This chapter explores how AI and 4IR technologies are transforming the accountancy profession. It begins by outlining the shift from routine tasks, such as bookkeeping, towards more strategic, advisory roles as automation and data analytics reshape traditional accounting processes. The introduction highlights both the opportunities, such as increased efficiency and new advisory services, and the challenges, including job displacement, ethical concerns, and the need for advanced digital skills.

The methodology section details the structured literature review approach, including the search strategy, inclusion and exclusion criteria, and the process for analysing relevant studies. The review identifies key themes: the evolving role of accountants, the challenges and opportunities posed by AI and 4IR, and strategies for adapting to these technologies. These themes form the basis for exploring how the profession can embrace change while maintaining core values like integrity and trust.

The discussion synthesises insights from the literature, addressing practical implications for accountants, educators, and professional bodies and identifying gaps for future research. The chapter concludes by emphasising the importance of continuous learning and proactive adaptation to remain relevant in the 4IR era. A call to action encourages stakeholders to engage with these changes and shape the future of the profession.

2   Methodology

2.1   Review of Reviews

Given the general growth in publications, Faulkner et al. (2022) note that the number of systematic reviews has also grown as a result. Thus, when a field is well-researched to the point where several systematic reviews have been conducted, a review of reviews may become necessary to further synthesise findings and identify gaps in the literature.

A review of reviews, also known as an umbrella review or meta review, is a structured and systematic approach used to locate and analyse multiple systematic reviews and meta-analyses. This method allows for a comparison of findings across different reviews, offering a comprehensive summary of the existing research on a specific topic (Faulkner et al. 2022; cf. Pollock et al. 2024). As such, a review of reviews represents the pinnacle of evidence synthesis (Faulkner et al. 2022; Fusar-Poli and Radua, 2018).

Systematic review of reviews are commonly conducted in *medical research* (Mokhatri-Hesari and Montazeri 2020; Kafadar et al. 2023), *psychological research* (Eklund and Meranius 2021; Lange-Smith et al. 2024), *technological research* (Raman et al. 2024; Khosravi et al. 2024), *management research* (Marsilio and Pisarra 2021; Risso et al. 2023), *social research* (Fakoya et al. 2020; Bezgrebelna et al. 2021), and *education research* (Gessler and Siemer 2020; Hassan et al. 2022).

2.2 Search Strategy and Databases

The review follows a systematic search strategy to ensure the identification of relevant and high-quality sources. The search was conducted using academic databases such as Google Scholar, Scopus, and Web of Science. A comprehensive search term was developed to capture the relevant literature. The search string combined multiple terms related to the accountancy profession and emerging technologies, as follows:

> ("accountancy" OR "accounting profession" OR "accountants" OR "chartered accountants" OR "financial accountants" OR "professional accountants" OR "certified accountants" OR "public accountants") AND ("artificial intelligence" OR "AI" OR "machine learning" OR "automation" OR "robotic process automation" OR "RPA") AND ("Fourth Industrial Revolution" OR "4IR" OR "Industry 4.0" OR "digital transformation" OR "emerging technologies") AND ("challenges" OR "barriers" OR "obstacles" OR "risks" OR "opportunities" OR "benefits" OR "advantages" OR "impact" OR "influence" OR "effect" OR "transformation")

This search strategy ensured a broad coverage of studies that address both the challenges and opportunities AI and 4IR technologies present to the accountancy profession. Applying the search strategy to the Google Scholar database yielded 13,800 articles published between 2017 and 2024, while Scopus yielded 1520 articles for the same period. Web of Science yielded only 18 articles for the same period. Therefore, to aid the feasibility of the study and ensure that high-quality sources are included, the study was limited to the results from Scopus. The number of articles per year is depicted in Fig. 1, which shows that a sharp increase in articles occurs from 2021 onwards. The search strategy also yielded a wide range of perspectives from various countries or territories, as shown in Fig. 2.

Despite the reduction in time period to only include articles published in 2023 and 2024, the articles remained somewhat fragmented in terms of focus, as illustrated in Fig. 3. Perspectives ranged from healthcare and mining to ethical considerations and implications for sustainability. This motivated the review of reviews, given the disparate nature of the existing literature for this period.

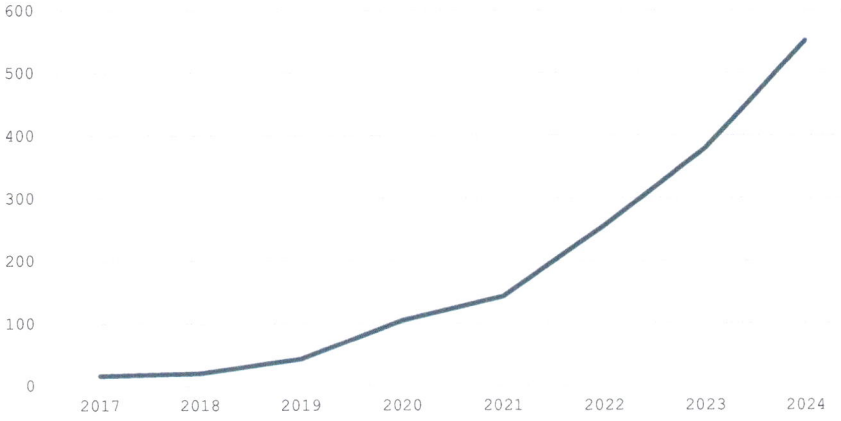

Fig. 1 Number of documents by year (n = 1520). Source: Authors' construction using Scopus data

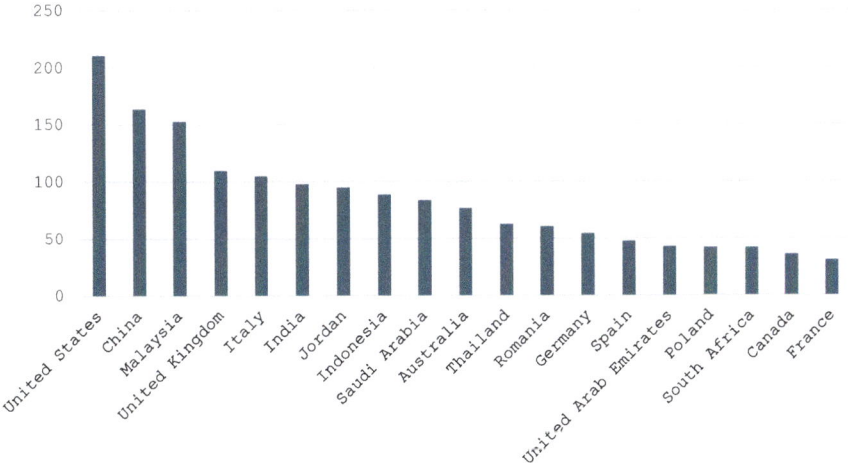

Fig. 2 Top 20 total documents by country or territory (n = 1520). Source: Authors' construction using Scopus data

With search terms, 880 relevant papers were identified. This was categorised to get further insight into the structure of extant literature. From the 880 papers, 87 (or 10% of the original set of papers) papers were identified as being either systematic reviews or bibliometric studies of literature. Based on the final list of systematic reviews, 55 papers were excluded for not being substantially about accountancy and related fields or lacking a strong technological element or focus. Therefore, ulti-mately, 32 papers were included in the study. While the reviews have diverse focus areas, each review highlights important implications of technological development for the accountancy profession. The thirty-two reviews included in the study col-lectively analysed a total of 1 185 articles.

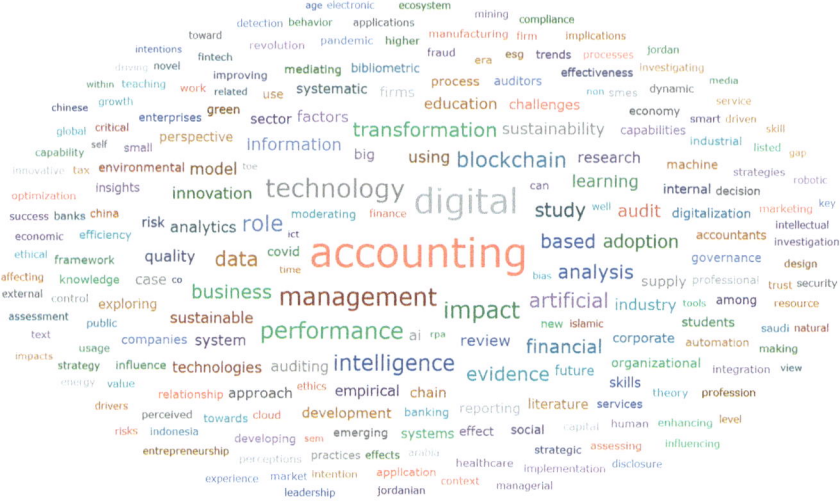

Fig. 3 Frequency of keywords in article titles (n = 880). Source: Authors' construction using Scopus data and ATLAS.ti 24

Table 1 Inclusion criteria

Inclusion criteria	Explanation
Focus on the accounting profession	Studies substantially addressing the impact of AI and 4IR technologies on the accounting profession or practice.
Recent research	Given the recency of the technological developments, studies published in 2023 and 2024 were included to ensure relevance to current technological advancements.
Peer-reviewed and reputable sources	Articles from peer-reviewed Scopus-indexed journals were included.
English-language publications	Only sources published in English were included to ensure comprehension and consistency.
Must be a meta-analysis	Articles following a systematic or structured literature review, or bibliometric approach were included

Source: Authors' construction

2.3   Inclusion and Exclusion Criteria

The inclusion and exclusion criteria were applied to refine the search results and ensure the relevance and quality of the selected studies (Tables 1 and 2).

2.4   Data Extraction and Analysis Process

The data extraction and analysis process were designed to ensure a systematic and comprehensive synthesis of relevant literature. After identifying studies through the defined search strategy, each article, report, or paper was carefully screened to

Table 2 Exclusion criteria

Exclusion criteria	Explanation
Non-relevant disciplines	Studies focusing on industries or professions unrelated to accounting or not substantially about accounting were excluded.
Preliminary findings	Early-stage conference papers or working papers that were later published in peer-reviewed journals were excluded to avoid duplication.

Source: Authors' construction

Table 3 Data extracted

Data extracted	Explanation
Author(s) and year of publication	To track the timeline and source of contributions.
Study objective and scope	To understand the specific focus of each study.
Technologies discussed	To identify the relevant technologies impacting the accountancy profession.
Challenges identified	To understand specific accountancy-related challenges identified in the literature.
Opportunities highlighted	To explore specific accountancy-related opportunities identified in the literature.
Recommendations or strategies	Approaches suggested for adapting to technological change, including education reforms and skill development.

Source: Authors' construction

extract key information related to the research question: What is the impact of AI and 4IR technologies on the accounting profession? This process involved organising the extracted data into predefined categories aligned with the chapter's themes.

Table 3 summarises the key information extracted from each study.

Once the relevant data were extracted, the next step involved a thematic analysis. The studies were grouped based on recurring themes, including the evolving role of accountants, challenges facing the profession, opportunities for accountants, and strategies for adaptation. Each theme was analysed to identify patterns, contradictions, and gaps in the literature. The analysis also involved comparing insights from academic sources with industry reports to ensure a balanced perspective. This approach allowed for the synthesis of key findings, providing a clearer understanding of how accountants can proactively embrace AI and 4IR technologies while maintaining core professional values. The themes are summarised in Table 4. Subsequently, each theme is discussed in more detail.

2.5 The Evolving Role of the Accountant

The role of accountants is undergoing significant transformation, driven by advances in technology, changing business landscapes, and the increasing complexity of stakeholder demands (Afsay et al., 2023; Agustí & Orta-Pérez, 2023). Traditionally

Table 4 Themes identified from the review

Theme	Summary	References
Evolving role of the accountant	Accountants are transitioning from routine tasks to strategic decision-making roles. Professionals must develop critical thinking, problem-solving, and leadership skills to adapt to changing job demands.	Afsay et al. (2023); Agustí & Orta-Perez (2023); Murphy et al. (2024); Suta et al. (2023); Salleh et al. (2023); Nikolova (2023); Lyeonov et al. (2024); Han et al. (2023); Shahana et al. (2023)
Technological proficiency as a core skill	Accountants must develop proficiency in emerging technologies like AI, blockchain, data analytics, and automation to remain competitive. The integration of such technologies can enhance efficiency, fraud prevention, and transparency.	Afsay et al. (2023); Agustí & Orta-Perez (2023); Murphy et al. (2024); Gupta et al. (2024); Landsberg and Van den Berg (2023); Nikolova (2023); Han et al. (2023); Suta et al. (2023); Lyeonov et al. (2024); Shahana et al. (2023)
Bridging the industry-academia gap	Stronger collaboration between academia and industry is essential to align accounting education with industry requirements. Accounting education must reflect industry needs, emphasising interdisciplinary approaches and tools to prepare students for tech-driven roles.	Thottoli et al. (2024); Agustí & Orta-Pérez (2023); Landsberg and Van den Berg (2023); Rego et al. (2024); Uyar et al. (2023); Afsay et al. (2023; Handoyo (2024); Ballantine et al. (2024); Indrayani et al. (2024); Desai (2023); Murphy et al. (2024); Nikolova (2023); Salleh et al. (2023); O'Hara et al. (2024)
Ethical and governance challenges	Ethical considerations must guide the implementation of AI and blockchain to ensure fairness, transparency, and compliance. Accountants must address data privacy, security concerns, and ethical issues related to automation and digital transformation.	Murikah et al. (2024); Afsay et al. (2023); Han et al. (2023); Chávez-Díaz et al. (2024); Dong et al. (2024); Anica-Popa et al. (2024); Barr-Pulliam et al. (2024); Brabete et al. (2024)
Lifelong learning and continuous professional development	Accountants need to engage in lifelong learning to keep pace with rapidly evolving technologies and industry changes. Learning should focus on emerging skills in technology, analytics, and strategy.	Salleh et al. (2023); Murphy et al. (2024); Afsay et al. (2023); Brabete et al. (2024); Anica-Popa et al. (2024); Shahana et al. (2023); Suta et al. (2023)
Fraud detection and risk management	Under the guidance of accountants, AI and machine learning can enhance fraud detection by identifying anomalies and patterns in financial data. Blockchain provides a secure and transparent platform for reducing fraud risks in transactions and reporting.	Shahana et al. (2023); Han et al. (2023); Lyeonov et al. (2024); Suta et al. (2023); Kumar et al. (2023); Murphy et al. (2024); Brabete et al. (2024)

Source: Authors' construction

focused on bookkeeping and financial reporting, accountants are now transitioning into strategic advisory roles, leveraging data to provide actionable insights for decision-making. This shift is facilitated by technologies like artificial intelligence (AI), blockchain, and big data analytics, which automate routine tasks and enable real-time financial analysis (Murphy et al. 2024; Suta et al. 2023; Salleh et al., 2023). Strategic decision-making, critical thinking, and problem-solving are emerging as key competencies, requiring accountants to develop interdisciplinary knowledge and advanced analytical skills (Nikolova 2023; Salleh et al. 2023; Lyeonov et al., 2024; Murphy et al., 2024). Moreover, accountants are increasingly involved in areas such as sustainability reporting, fraud detection, and risk management, highlighting their evolving importance in governance and compliance frameworks (Han et al. 2023; Shahana et al. 2023).

2.6   Integration of Technology and Digital Tools

The integration of technology and digital tools is revolutionising the accounting profession, fundamentally altering how financial data is processed, analysed, and reported (Afsay et al., 2023; Agustí & Orta-Pérez, 2023). Technologies such as artificial intelligence (AI), blockchain, data analytics, and robotic process automation (RPA) are automating routine tasks, improving accuracy, and enabling real-time decision-making (Murphy et al. 2024; Gupta et al. 2024; Afsay et al., 2023). This shift allows accountants to transition from transactional roles to strategic advisory positions, focusing on insights and value creation (Landsberg and Van den Berg, 2023; Nikolova, 2023). Blockchain, for instance, enhances transparency and security in financial reporting by creating immutable ledgers, reducing fraud risks, and improving audit efficiency (Suta et al. 2023; Han et al. 2023). Similarly, AI-powered tools enable advanced fraud detection, anomaly identification, and predictive analytics, supporting compliance and risk management efforts (Shahana et al. 2023; Lyeonov et al. 2024).

2.7   Bridging the Industry-Academia Gap

Bridging the gap between industry and academia in accounting is essential to prepare newly qualified accountants for the demands of a rapidly evolving profession (Thottoli et al., 2024; Agustí & Orta-Pérez, 2023; Landsberg and Van den Berg, 2023). The disconnection often stems from mismatches between academic curricula and industry needs, particularly in areas such as technology integration, practical application of knowledge, and critical skills like problem-solving and decision-making (Uyar et al. 2023; Rego et al. 2024; Thottoli et al., 2024). Collaboration between academic institutions and the industry is pivotal for addressing this gap (Afsay et al., 2023; Thottoli et al., 2024). Initiatives such as incorporating real-world case studies, vacation work, and experiential learning opportunities can better equip students with the skills required in professional environments (Handoyo, 2024; Ballantine et al., 2024; Indrayani et al., 2024; Desai, 2023). Furthermore, integrating advanced technologies, such as AI and data analytics, into accounting programs ensures that graduates are proficient in tools increasingly used in the field (Murphy et al. 2024; Agustí & Orta-Pérez, 2023). To harness the full potential of these technologies, accounting education and professional training programs must incorporate digital competencies into their curricula (Agustí & Orta-Pérez, 2023; Nikolova, 2023). Courses in programming languages like Python and tools such as Tableau are becoming crucial in preparing accountants for data-driven roles (Salleh et al., 2023; O'Hara et al., 2024). This integration not only enhances efficiency but also ensures that accountants remain pivotal in driving innovation and organisational strategy in an increasingly digital economy. Aligning educational objectives with industry expectations requires continuous engagement and partnership. Bridging this gap not only enhances the employability of accounting graduates but also ensures that they contribute effectively to the strategic goals of organisations, fostering innovation and excellence in the profession.

2.8   Ethical and Governance Challenges

The rapid integration of technology into accounting practices presents significant ethical and governance challenges, necessitating a balanced approach to innovation and accountability (Murikah et al., 2024; Afsay et al., 2023). Artificial intelligence (AI), blockchain, and automation are transforming traditional roles, but their use raises critical concerns about transparency, data privacy, and ethical decision-making (Murikah et al. 2024; cf. Han et al. 2023). For example, AI systems can inadvertently perpetuate biases if trained on flawed data, leading to unfair outcomes in financial reporting or auditing (Chávez-Díaz et al. (2024); Murikah et al., 2024; Dong et al., 2024; Anica-Popa et al., 2024). Governance frameworks are essential to manage these risks, ensuring that technological tools align with professional standards and societal expectations (Afsay et al., 2023; Murikah et al., 2024). Similarly, reliance on automation and machine learning necessitates robust oversight mechanisms to prevent over-dependence and ensure accountability in decision-making (Barr-Pulliam et al., 2024; Murikah et al., 2024; Dong et al., 2024). Educational institutions and professional bodies play a pivotal role in addressing these challenges by integrating ethical training into accounting programs and establishing clear guidelines for technology use (Afsay et al., 2023; Brabete et al., 2024). By fostering ethical awareness and reinforcing governance standards, the accounting profession can leverage technological advancements responsibly while maintaining stakeholder trust and public confidence.

2.9 Lifelong Learning and Continuous Professional Development

Lifelong learning and continuous professional development (CPD) have become imperative for accountants to remain competitive in an era of rapid technological and regulatory changes. Emerging technologies such as artificial intelligence (AI), blockchain, and data analytics are redefining accounting roles, requiring professionals to constantly update their skills to adapt to evolving industry demands (Salleh et al. 2023; Murphy et al. 2024; Afsay et al., 2023). Lifelong learning ensures that accountants are equipped with both technical and strategic competencies, enabling them to transition from routine tasks to higher-value advisory roles. Professional bodies and institutions are playing a key role by providing training programs and certifications tailored to new skill sets, such as programming, data visualisation, and digital acumen (Afsay et al., 2023; Brabete et al., 2024; Anica-Popa et al., 2024). These initiatives not only improve individual employability but also enhance organisational resilience in a dynamic business environment. Moreover, continuous learning fosters innovation and critical thinking, which are essential for addressing complex challenges, such as sustainability reporting and fraud detection (Shahana et al. 2023; Suta et al. 2023). By embracing lifelong learning, accountants can maintain professional relevance, contribute to organisational growth, and uphold the credibility of the profession in a rapidly changing global landscape.

2.10 Fraud Detection and Risk Management

Fraud detection and risk management have become critical areas of focus in the accounting profession, especially with the increasing complexity of financial systems and the emergence of sophisticated fraud schemes. The integration of advanced technologies, such as artificial intelligence (AI), machine learning, and blockchain, has significantly enhanced the ability to identify and mitigate fraudulent activities (Shahana et al. 2023; Han et al. 2023; Lyeonov et al., 2024). AI-powered tools, for instance, can analyse vast datasets in real time, detecting anomalies and patterns indicative of fraud, thereby enabling more proactive risk management. Blockchain technology further strengthens fraud prevention by creating tamper-proof ledgers that ensure transparency and traceability in financial transactions. This innovation minimises the opportunities for data manipulation and facilitates secure, verifiable records (Suta et al. 2023; Lyeonov et al. 2024; Kumar et al., 2023). However, these advancements also bring challenges, such as addressing biases in AI algorithms and ensuring the security of blockchain systems. Accountants must possess the technical skills to implement and oversee these tools effectively while maintaining ethical and regulatory compliance (Murphy et al. 2024; Brabete et al., 2024). Through continuous professional development and collaboration across disciplines, the profession can leverage these technologies to enhance fraud detection, safeguard organisational assets, and uphold public trust in financial reporting.

3 Conclusion

The integration of artificial intelligence (AI) and Fourth Industrial Revolution (4IR) technologies is reshaping the accountancy profession, offering both challenges and opportunities. This review of reviews underscores the significant transformation in the roles and skillsets required for accountants. Routine tasks are increasingly automated, enabling accountants to transition into strategic advisory positions that require advanced technological proficiency and critical thinking. Key themes identified in the literature include the evolving role of accountants, the necessity for technological fluency, and the importance of bridging the gap between academia and industry. Ethical considerations and governance challenges also emerge as critical aspects that must be addressed to harness these technologies responsibly. Lifelong learning and continuous professional development are paramount, ensuring that accountants remain agile and competent in a rapidly evolving digital landscape. The findings highlight the need for accounting education to incorporate interdisciplinary approaches, digital competencies, and ethical awareness into curricula. By aligning academic training with industry requirements, the profession can better prepare its members for the demands of a technology-driven future. Professional bodies also have a pivotal role in facilitating this transition through certification programs and advocacy for technological standards. Ultimately, the accountancy profession stands at a crossroads, where proactive adaptation to technological advancements is not only necessary but also an opportunity to redefine its value in the modern economy. This chapter calls for stakeholders—academics, practitioners, and policymakers— to collaborate in shaping a sustainable, ethical, and forward-looking profession.

4 Suggestions for future research

Despite a growing body of literature, research on AI and 4IR in the accounting profession remains fragmented. Studies cover diverse themes (including automation, fraud detection, ethics, and sustainability), but there is a lack of integration and synthesis across these topics. More interdisciplinary research is needed to bridge these themes and provide a holistic view of AI's impact on the profession. Furthermore, a significant gap exists between the skills emphasised in the academic curricula and the competencies required by the profession. Universities still focus heavily on traditional accounting skills, while employers increasingly demand digital literacy, data analytics, and AI proficiency. Future research may focus on ways to foster greater collaboration between academia, industry, and professional bodies, to align education with industry needs. AI and blockchain introduce new ethical dilemmas, such as bias in algorithms, data privacy concerns, and the need for transparent decision-making. Existing research does not provide clear governance frameworks for accountants to navigate these ethical challenges effectively. More studies are needed on regulatory adaptations, ethical AI use, and accountability structures in AI-driven financial decision-making. Finally, most research is dominated by studies from the global north, with limited contributions from developing countries and the global south. Given the unique economic and regulatory environments in these regions, more context-specific research is needed to understand AI's impact on accounting in different global contexts.

Appendix 1: List of Included Reviews

Title	Reference
Artificial intelligence in accounting and auditing: bibliometric analysis in Scopus 2020–2023	Chávez-Díaz et al. (2024)
Bias and ethics of AI systems applied in auditing—A systematic review	Murikah et al. (2024)
Artificial intelligence and machine learning in combating illegal financial operations: Bibliometric analysis	Lyeonov et al. (2024)
Exploring accounting and AI using topic modelling	Murphy et al. (2024)
A scoping review of ChatGPT research in accounting and finance	Dong et al. (2024)
Digital transformation, skills, and education: A systematic literature review	Rêgo et al. (2024)
Blockchain in the age of industrial revolution: A systematic literature review using bibliometric analysis	Gupta et al. (2024)
Evolution of blockchain accounting literature from the perspective of CiteSpace (2013–2023)	Liu et al. (2024)
Exploring journal of emerging Technologies in Accounting: A content and citation analysis of JETA	Göktürk et al. (2024)
Exploring publication trends in accounting information systems and identifying research positions in Indonesia: A bibliometric analysis	Anriva and Hamidah (2024)
Mapping research landscape of emerging technology in the accounting field: A bibliometric analysis	Indrayani et al. (2024)
Audit evidence, technology, and judgement: A review of the literature in response to ED-500	Barr-Pulliam et al. (2024)
Towards the intelligent automation of accounting research: Systemised literature reviews	Łada et al. (2023)
Systematic review on blockchain research for sustainability accounting applying methodology coding and text mining	Suta and Tóth (2023)
A review of scholarly discourses on accounting technical skills for IR 4.0	Salleh et al. (2023)
State of the art in financial statement fraud detection: A systematic review	Shahana et al. (2023)
A meta-analysis of factors affecting acceptance of information technology in auditing	Afsay et al. (2023)

Title	Reference
Accounting and auditing with blockchain technology and artificial intelligence: A literature review	Han et al. (2023)
Artificial intelligence and Blockchain integration in business: Trends from a bibliometric-content analysis	Kumar et al. (2023)
4th industrial revolution skills in the current south African accountancy curricula: A systematic literature review	Landsberg and Van den Berg (2023)
Big data and artificial intelligence in the fields of accounting and auditing: A bibliometric analysis	Agustí and Orta-Pérez (2023)
The big data crossroads: Accounting education and the challenge of the twenty-first century technology	Fogarty and Campbell (2024)
Evolving paradigms in accounting education: A bibliometric study on the impact of information technology	Handoyo (2024)
Developing a STEM-designated accounting curriculum	O'Hara et al. (2024)
Framework for integrating generative AI in developing competencies for accounting and audit professionals	Anica-Popa et al. (2024)
A critical review of AI in accounting education: Threat and opportunity	Ballantine et al. (2024)
Enricher learning: Bridging the gap between academics and practising accounting professionals	Thottoli et al. (2024)
Redesign of accounting education to meet the challenges of artificial intelligence—A literature review	Brabete et al. (2024)
Infusing Blockchain in accounting curricula and practice: Expectations, challenges, and strategies	Desai (2023)
Education quality, internet access in schools, and research performance in management and accounting domains: A cross-country investigation	Uyar et al. (2023)
The extent to which textbooks fulfil the requirements of digital transformation in accounting and auditing	Oleiwi (2023)
The accounting education: Is a paradigm shift needed?	Nikolova (2023)

References

Afsay A, Tahriri A, Rezaee Z (2023) A meta-analysis of factors affecting acceptance of information technology in auditing. Int J Account Inf Syst 49:100608

Agustí MA, Orta-Pérez M (2023) Big data and artificial intelligence in the fields of accounting and auditing: a bibliometric analysis. Span J Financ Acc/Revista Española de Financiación y Contabilidad 52(3):412–438

Anica-Popa IF, Vrîncianu M, Anica-Popa LE, Cişmaşu ID, Tudor CG (2024) Framework for integrating generative AI in developing competencies for accounting and audit professionals. Electronics 13(13):2621

Anriva DH, Hamidah. (2024) Exploring publication trends in accounting information systems and identifying research positions in Indonesia: a bibliometric analysis. Int J Econ Bus Res 27(5):29–44

Ballantine J, Boyce G, Stoner G (2024) A critical review of AI in accounting education: threat and opportunity. Crit Perspect Account 99:102711

Barac K, Plant K, Olivier MM (2021) Preparing Chartered Accountants who are fit for purpose in the Fourth Industrial Revolution (4IR). SAQA Bulletin 20(1):220–233

Barr-Pulliam D, Calvin CG, Eulerich M, Maghakyan A (2024) Audit evidence, technology, and judgement: a review of the literature in response to ED-500. J Int Financ Manag Acc 35(1):36–67

Bezgrebelna M, McKenzie K, Wells S, Ravindran A, Kral M, Christensen J et al (2021) Climate change, weather, housing precarity, and homelessness: a systematic review of reviews. Int J Environ Res Public Health 18(11):5812

Brabete V, Barbu CM, Cîrciumaru D, Goagără D, Berceanu D (2024) Redesign of accounting education to meet the challenges of artificial intelligence: a literature review. Amfiteatru Econ 26(65):275–293

CGMA (2019) CGMA® competency framework: 2019 update. Online: https://www.cgma.org/content/dam/cgma/resources/tools/downloadabledocuments/cgma-competency-framework-2019-edition.pdf?vngagetrans=tM9eZrqBy6wXlq63M6sw

Chávez-Díaz JM, Aquiño-Perales L, De-Velazco-Borda JL, Villagómez-Chinchay JA, Flores-Sotelo WS (2024) Artificial intelligence in accounting and auditing: bibliometric analysis in Scopus 2020–2023. Indones J Electr Eng Comput Sci 36(2):1319–1328

Damasiotis V, Trivellas P, Santouridis I, Nikolopoulos S, Tsifora E (2015) IT competences for professional accountants. A review. Procedia-Soc Behav Sci 175:537–545

Desai H (2023) Infusing blockchain in accounting curricula and practice: expectations, challenges, and strategies. Int J Digit Account Res 23:97–135

Dong MM, Stratopoulos TC, Wang VX (2024) A scoping review of ChatGPT research in accounting and finance. Int J Account Inf Syst 55:100715

Eklund JH, Meranius MS (2021) Toward a consensus on the nature of empathy: a review of reviews. *Patient Educ Couns* 104(2):300–307

Fakoya OA, McCorry NK, Donnelly M (2020) Loneliness and social isolation interventions for older adults: a scoping review of reviews. *BMC Public Health* 20:1–14

Faulkner G, Fagan MJ, Lee J (2022) Umbrella reviews (systematic review of reviews). Int Rev Sport Exerc Psychol 15(1):73–90

Fogarty TJ, Campbell C (2024) The big data crossroads: accounting education and the challenge of 21st-century technology. J Account Educ 68:100914

Fusar-Poli P, Radua J (2018) Ten simple rules for conducting umbrella reviews. Evidence-Based Ment Health 21(3):95–100. https://doi.org/10.1136/ebmental-2018-300014

Gessler M, Siemer C (2020) Umbrella review: methodological review of reviews published in peer-reviewed journals with a substantial focus on vocational education and training research. Int J Res Vocat Educ Train 7(1):91–125

Göktürk IE, Güvemli B, Sarısoy Ö (2024) Exploring journal of emerging technologies in accounting: a content and citation analysis of JETA. J Emerging Technol Account 21(1):1–13

Gupta R, Meena A, Dhir S (2024) Blockchain in the age of industrial revolution: a systematic literature review using bibliometric analysis. Glob Bus Organ Excell 43(5):5–23

Han H, Shiwakoti RK, Jarvis R, Mordi C, Botchie D (2023) Accounting and auditing with blockchain technology and artificial intelligence: a literature review. Int J Account Inf Syst 48:100598

Handoyo S (2024) Evolving paradigms in accounting education: a bibliometric study on the impact of information technology. Int J Manag Educ 22(3):100998

Hassan E, Groot W, Volante L (2022) Education funding and learning outcomes in Sub-Saharan Africa: a review of reviews. *Int J Educ Res Open* 3:100181

Indrayani, Sukoharsono EG, Djamhuri A, Roekhudin (2024) Mapping research landscape of emerging technology in the accounting field: a bibliometric analysis. Cogent Bus Manag 11(1):2407044

Jackson D, Michelson G, Munir R (2022) New technology and desired skills of early career accountants. Pac Account Rev 34(4):548–568

Kafadar AH, Tekeli GG, Jones KA, Stephan B, Dening T (2023) Determinants for COVID-19 vaccine hesitancy in the general population: a systematic review of reviews. J Public Health 31(11):1829–1845

Khosravi M, Zare Z, Mojtabaeian SM, Izadi R (2024) Artificial intelligence and decision-making in healthcare: a thematic analysis of a systematic review of reviews. *Health Serv Res Manag Epidemiol* 11:23333928241234863

Kroon N, do Céu Alves M, Martins I (2021) The impacts of emerging technologies on accountants' role and skills: Connecting to open innovation—a systematic literature review. J Open Innov: Technol Mark Complex 7(3):163

Kumar S, Lim WM, Sivarajah U, Kaur J (2023) Artificial intelligence and blockchain integration in business: trends from a bibliometric-content analysis. Inf Syst Front 25(2):871–896

Łada M, Haslam J (2023) Towards the intelligent automation of accounting research: systemised literature reviews. Theor J Account 47(4):155–171

Landsberg E, van den Berg L (2023) 4th Industrial Revolution skills in the current South African accountancy curricula: a systematic literature review. S Afr J Account Res 37(3):177–201

Lange-Smith S, Cabot J, Coffee P, Gunnell K, Tod D (2024) The efficacy of psychological skills training for enhancing performance in sport: a review of reviews. *Int J Sport Exerc Psychol* 22(4):1012–1029

Liu C, Muravskyi V, Wei W (2024) Evolution of blockchain accounting literature from the perspective of CiteSpace (2013–2023). Heliyon 10(2024):e32097

Lyeonov S, Draskovic V, Kubaščikova Z, Fenyves V (2024) Artificial intelligence and machine learning in combating illegal financial operations: bibliometric analysis. Hum Technol 20(2):325–360

Marsilio M, Pisarra M (2021) Lean management in health care: a review of reviews of socio-technical components for effective impact. *J Health Organ Manag* 35(4):475–491

Mokhatri-Hesari P, Montazeri A (2020) Health-related quality of life in breast cancer patients: review of reviews from 2008 to 2018. *Health Qual Life Outcomes* 18:1–25

Murikah W, Nthenge JK, Musyoka FM (2024) Bias and ethics of AI systems applied in auditing: a systematic review. Scientific African 16:e02281

Murphy B, Feeney O, Rosati P, Lynn T (2024) Exploring accounting and AI using topic modelling. Int J Account Inf Syst 55:100709

Nikolova B (2023) The accounting education: is a paradigm shift needed? J High Edu Theory Prac 23(5):1–12

O'Hara RC, Simmons V, Kogan G, Boyle DM (2024) Developing a STEM-designated accounting curriculum. J Account Educ 69:100918

Oleiwi R (2023) The extent to which textbooks fulfill the requirements of digital transformation in accounting and auditing. Int J Prof Bus Rev 8(5):Article 18

Pollock M, Fernandes RM, Becker LA, Pieper D, Hartling L (2024) Chapter V: overviews of reviews [last updated August 2023]. In: JPT H, Thomas J, Chandler J, Cumpston M, Li T, Page MJ, Welch VA (eds) *Cochrane handbook for systematic reviews of interventions* version 6.5. Cochrane. www.training.cochrane.org/handbook

Raman R, Pattnaik D, Hughes L, Nedungadi P (2024) Unveiling the dynamics of AI applications: A review of reviews using scientometrics and BERTopic modeling. *J Innov Knowl* 9(3):100517

Rêgo BS, Lourenço D, Moreira F, Pereira CS (2024) Digital transformation, skills, and education: a systematic literature review. Ind High Educ 38(4):336–349

Richins G, Stapleton A, Stratopoulos TC, Wong C (2017) Big data analytics: opportunity or threat for the accounting profession? J Inf Syst 31(3):63–79

Risso LA, Ganga GMD, Godinho Filho M, de Santa-Eulalia LA, Chikhi T, Mosconi E (2023) Present and future perspectives of blockchain in supply chain management: a review of reviews and research agenda. *Comput Ind Eng* 179:109195

SAICA (2021) CA(SA) competency framework. Online: https://saicawebprstorage.blob.core.windows.net/uploads/Competency-Framework-2021.pdf

Salleh NMZN, Moorthy K, Jasmon A (2023) A review of scholarly discourses on accounting technical skills for IR 4.0. J High Edu Theory Prac 23(9):1–15

Shahana T, Lavanya V, Bhat AR (2023) State of the art in financial statement fraud detection: a systematic review. Technol Forecast Soc Chang 192:122527

Suta A, Tóth Á (2023) Systematic review on blockchain research for sustainability accounting applying methodology coding and text mining. Cleaner Eng Technol 14:100648

Thottoli MM, Islam MA, Abdullah ABM, Hassan MS, Ibrahim S (2024) Enricher learning: bridging the gap between academics and practicing accounting professionals. J Educ Bus 99(5):300–311

Tsiligiris V, Bowyer D (2021) Exploring the impact of 4IR on skills and personal qualities for future accountants: a proposed conceptual framework for university accounting education. Account Educ 30(6):621–649

Uyar A, Nimer K, Kuzey C (2023) Education quality, internet access in schools, and research performance in management and accounting domains: a cross-country investigation. Scientometrics 128(10):5441–5475

The Impact of Artificial Intelligence on the Role of Management Accountants

Amanda F. Mhlongo

Abstract The field of management accounting has been transforming tremendously because of the rapid advancements in the business world. Naturally, as one of key supporting structures of business, the necessity of agile integration to the new business landscape is essential for the profession. This chapter unpacked how artificial intelligence (AI), as one of the critical 4IR technologies, is redefining the management accounting profession. Historically, the role of management accountants has been to collect and analyse relevant data and provide businesses with information for decision-making purposes. The increasing complexities of business operations, globalisation, and developments in technology have at times made this role challenging and necessitated its evolution for adaptation and relevance. This chapter explored how the need to transform the profession infused with AI integration has resulted in improved operational efficiency (because of automation), improved accuracy (because of reduced human errors) and enabled businesses to pursue more strategic decisions that have resulted in higher profits and sustainable practices. Despite the many benefits of AI to the profession, the debate of whether to perceive it as a threat or an opportunity continues to limit its application. This chapter will also explore both views focusing on how opportunities can be leveraged on while limiting exposure to threats. The chapter will provide an overview of real-world AI applications in the field with the focus of future disruptions including real-time data analysis and predictive analytics that could yield greater benefits. Ethical considerations of AI applications will also be discussed including data privacy concerns, transparency, and biases in AI judgement. Through this examination, the chapter will offer comprehensive insights on how AI is uniquely positioned to influence the role of management accountants.

Keywords Artificial intelligence · Business · Management accounting

A. F. Mhlongo (✉)
Department of Accountancy, University of Johannesburg, Johannesburg, South Africa
e-mail: amandam@uj.ac.za

© The Author(s), under exclusive license to Springer Nature
Switzerland AG 2025
M. Adelowotan, C. A. Leke (eds.), *Artificial Intelligence in Accounting, Auditing and Finance*, Contributions to Finance and Accounting,
https://doi.org/10.1007/978-3-031-87368-3_5

1 Introduction and Background

Artificial intelligence (AI), a friend or a foe to management accounting? This is the question that many professionals in the industry struggle to answer. On the one hand, technology has been instrumental in improving efficiency by automating routine tasks and enhancing accuracy (among other things) therefore freeing up time for management accountants to focus on more strategic tasks in the organisations they support. According to Adelakun et al. (2024), these strategic tasks include advisory services, leading to provide insights that will improve financial outcomes and increase productivity. However, on the other hand, technologies such as AI are radically changing the identity of management accountants, and many professionals find themselves misplaced or incompatible to perform their guardian role to the organisations they support. Despite these mixed feelings within the profession, businesses are transforming at a rapid rate, and they require a new set of hybrid skills and competences that transcend technical expertise (Ala-Heikkilä and Järvenpää 2023). The scope of management accounting has certainly escalated beyond the traditional tasks such as reporting, analysing, risk management, and internal control and has integrated forward-looking aspects of business partnering and forecasting (Ala-Heikkilä and Järvenpää 2023). Artificial intelligence can therefore aid this transition into modern business.

Evolution is also not a new concept to the profession and according to management accounting scholars, this transformation will continue over time as modern businesses become increasingly complex (Dahal 2023). Digitalisation of businesses has also been a catalyst justifying the integration of AI into the management accounting field. According to Korobeynikova et al. (2021), this is a logical continuation of digital innovation. The researchers further assert that AI should be viewed as an applied tool along with other digital innovations that management accountants can utilise to improve efficiency in their function. In addition, AI has the potential to reshape existing business processes and add value to businesses (Abu Afifa et al. 2024). The use of AI can improve the management accounting profession, and the quality of financial support afforded to businesses. This chapter focuses on how AI could improve the profession while acknowledging some of the concerns that have been raised by AI critics, including potential of job losses, transparency in AI-decision making, algorithm bias and violation of privacy, to mention a few. One key observation is that AI is not going anywhere, in fact it is everywhere from virtual assistants to navigation applications and according to a study conducted by AICPA (American Institute of Certified Public Accountants), we are still just scratching the surface of how it will transform how we work and live (CPA, Canada). Management accountants have an opportunity to embrace AI as it has the potential to significantly impact the support they offer to businesses.

1.1   Literature Review

Digitalisation has been a vital catalyst for transforming many industries and professions, at times disrupting but more often enhancing efficiency. The management accounting profession has not been an exception, having been impacted by technologies such as big data analytics, Internet of Things, cloud computing, and artificial intelligence (Arkhipova et al. 2024). Despite the ability to provide more accurate analysis, faster processing times, and increased efficiency sometimes at lower costs in a long run, these technologies also present some challenges (Rakhmawati et al. 2023) that still require human intelligence. As a result, hybrid skills integrating both digital and human intelligence are important for the sustainability of the management accounting profession. Artificial Intelligence, more specifically, has been instrumental in offering automation of repetitive skills (Adeyelu et al. 2024; Bose et al. 2023), improving accuracy in processing financial data, and providing analytical insights from historical data (Alldén and Norén 2023; Dahal 2017).

Several researchers have defined artificial intelligence but according to Bako and Tanko (2022) it means programming robots to act in the same way that people do, meaning they will have capacity for knowledge acquisition, judgement, and ability to recognise relationships between variables. This definition is also supported by Sheikh et al. (2024) who state that AI is the imitation of intelligence intrinsic in humans, by computers. AI is often used interchangeably with machine learning or deep learning despite the subtle differences in all three. According to Du-Harpur et al. (2020) machine learning is a step ahead of AI, referring to algorithms and statical models that are programmed to learn from labelled training data enabling computers to perform tasks without instructions from a human.

Deep learning, on the other hand, is a subset of machine learning that stimulates neurons which are the functionality of our brain leading to the idea of neural networks (Bhatt et al. 2020). Simple put, deep learning-driven algorithms have better outputs than machine learning-driven algorithms and therefore each representing an elevated level of AI application. This chapter is based on the theory foundations described above and that of a study conducted by LeCun et al. (2015) suggesting that deep learning has capabilities of solving problems that AI has not been able to do in many years. In summary, AI is the intelligence exhibited by machines while machine learning and deep learning are AI's advanced application to data—both are parts of the AI, but they represent more complex and deeper levels of AI.

However, when it comes to the management accounting profession, the current state of AI integration is underdeveloped, and its scope and impact are limited (Ranta et al. 2023) but in the past decade it has been growing at an accelerated rate as the relationship between AI and the management accounting profession is evolving (Allden and Noren 2023). Despite AI solutions not yet reaching self-conscious intelligence, Varzaru (2022) asserts that the management accounting profession can benefit from the automation of repetitive tasks and the human support element. In addition, the researcher states that AI will not make management accountants extinct but rather absorb low skill competencies and alleviate professionals to high competency roles such as strategic partnering and high-level decision making.

The role of management accountants has historically been that of a controller (whether financial, business, or more recently, sustainability controller), predominantly responsible for creating reports that interpret and analyse patterns to improve business processes for greater success (Allden and Noren 2023). However, the introduction of AI could enhance how management accountants support businesses by shifting their focus from operational and tactical issues to strategic levels of decision making (Varzaru 2022). As data has become a new way for businesses to create value, the use of AI in the management accounting profession has also become critical (Ranta et al. 2023).

1.2   Research Methodology

This section provides a description of how data was collected, analysed, and interpreted. A systematic literature review (SLR) was the research analysis tool used for this chapter. Several steps were followed as part of the analysis of the articles reviewed. Top academic journal databases were searched to access related articles and the keywords that were included—artificial intelligence, management accounting, AI in MA, deep learning, ethics in AI and machine learning. The time frame that was used is 2018–2024. After a thorough review a total of 50 articles were selected from various sources including journals, book chapters, and conference proceedings.

2   Historic Role of a Management Accountant

Historically, the purpose of management accounting has been to provide information to the management team, and this has largely been labour-intensive (Korobeynikova et al. 2021). Over the years this role has transitioned from basic bookkeeping to the preparation of budgets and expense reports to a strategic business partner that we now observe in this new era (Walker 2008). While most of the historic responsibilities are still a fundamental part of a management accountants' role, most of these functions are now largely automated or performed by an accounting software. The core function that has remained organic to management accounting function throughout its evolution is the production of information to support business decisions. Despite the changing times, technological developments, digital advancements, and globalisation, this core function has remained throughout history. In this section we will explore the origins of management accounting and how instrumental technology has been in reshaping the industry.

2.1 Origins of Management Accounting

Management accounting dates back to the ancient times and according to Ovunda (2015) it is one of the oldest managerial tools that was used by kings to determine the amount of taxes that were taken and later used to determine the prices of the products. Even though the double-entry system of accounting was officially published in the late 1400s, some researchers believe that the formal beginning of cost and management accounting was the nineteenth century as this century was characterised by the emergence of large business enterprises (Ovunda 2015). Since then, management accounting has continued to advance in order to remain relevant to the core function of supporting the ever-changing business environment. Prior to 1950, the focus was on technical activities that were required for organisational objectives, primarily focusing on the determination of product cost (Kamal 2015). It was also referred to as accounting for processes and then later renamed to cost accounting (Kaplan 1984).

It was only after 1950 where the concept of management accounting was established, resulting in a shift from data capturing for record keeping to the provision of financial information for planning and control. Despite this shift, the financial support offered to businesses remained largely reactive (Kamal 2015), only identifying problems when there were deviations from the business plans and budgets (Ashton et al. 1995). Prior to 1980, data capturing and processing were largely performed manually which meant that management accountants had limited capacity for providing insights on, the financial data they reported on as all their time was focused on generating the management reports. As new costing techniques were developed from 1980 onwards, such as target costing and activity-based costing, supported by technological developments, there was another shift to strategic planning. This era brought about cost reductions that ultimately resulted in increased profits. This timeline is demonstrated in Fig. 1 below.

From the 1980s, management accounting started to shape into what we witness today, embracing a more proactive approach propelled by the continued evolution of technological advancements. Techniques such as the balanced scorecard were developed which focused on understanding costs as opposed to merely reporting them. As a result, there was improved resource allocation and a rise to strategic planning. This era is the foundation of what management accounting is today—a central part of a business strategic direction that has been further propelled by today's business landscape which requires a management accountant with hybrid skills, occupying both technical knowledge and strategic partner attributes. While both attributes are essential, ethical considerations especially for the use of technology in the management accounting profession cannot be ignored and professionals must uphold data privacy laws, maintain transparency and accountability in decision making, and reduce the exposure to algorithm bias (Adelakun et al. 2024).

A study by Spraakman et al. (2021) identified several factors that influence the effectiveness of a management accountant in transforming data insights into decisions that add value, and they include:

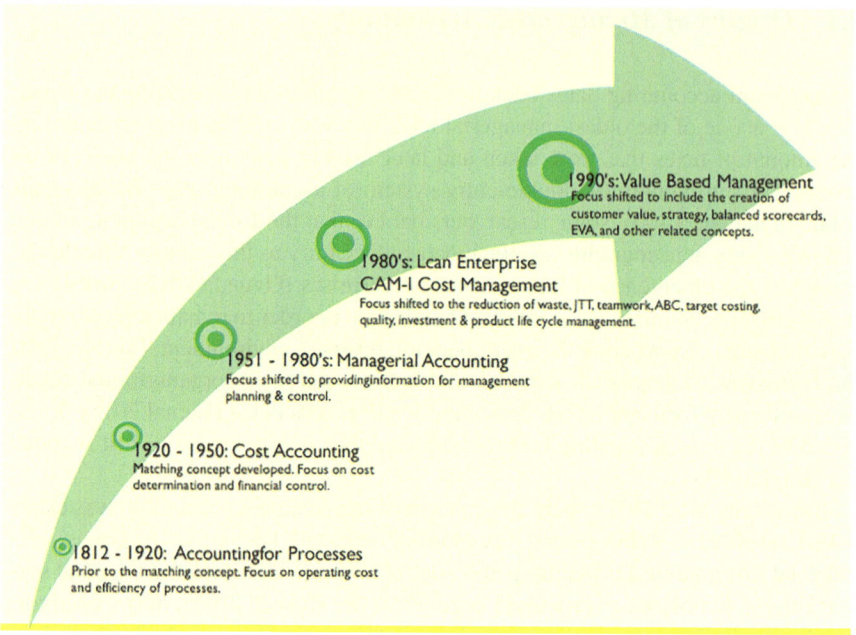

Fig. 1 Adopted from Kamal (2015)

- Management accountants must have a good knowledge of the kind of business their organisations operate in.
- Management accountants must take different perspectives into consideration when doing data analysis.
- Management accountants must be able to communicate results effectively and in a way that is clear and understandable, and lastly
- Management accountants must be able to add value to decision making by providing insights that senior management needs for decision making.

Historically, the role of management accountants has often been performed by chartered accountants, who have continued to be dominant in heading up the finance function and filling managerial positions (Boyns and Edwards 2006). These researchers further state that prior to that, these functions were seconded to engineers but in both instances, there were concerns that businesses were not being provided with the information they required for critical decision making. This resulted in the expansion of a scope of management accounting and clearly differentiated between financial accounting functions and cost accounting (management accounting) functions. However, in the last three decades, there has been an integration of the roles as automation of routine tasks has led to need of a more strategic finance business partner.

2.2   Evolution of Management Accounting (from Cost to Strategic Partner)

It is evident that management accounting is no stranger to transformation, from the fourteenth century till today, it has continued to evolve to ensure that financial information provided to support to businesses remains relevant to decision making. From its infancy when the sole focus was on costing techniques to its current position of strategic business partnering, the changes in management accounting reporting (among other things) were heavily necessitated by the developments within the business landscape. Over time, cost accounting grew to include information that businesses could use for planning and control. This included variance analysis, budgeting, and responsibility accounting. It is evident that in today's business environment a different kind of management accountant is required to ethically deal with rapid changes in a digital world while effecting relevant financial support that will lead to sustainable profits.

According to a study conducted by Dobroszek et al. (2024), management accountants must be SMART, where SMART is defined by the following characteristics:

(S) Strategic—being able to take a long-term view when supporting a business' strategic objectives.

(M) Meaningful—being able to verify the meaning of the current situations with regard to strategy implementation and value creation.

(A) Agile—being able to react quickly to the changing situation of the company and the market and the changing needs of all stakeholders.

(R) Resilient—being able to survive or quickly overcome difficulties in unpredictable situations.

(T) Transparent—being able to provide clarity and transparency of management accounting processes, which can be supported by advanced technology.

The characteristics cited above broadly encompass what it will take for the role of management accountants to remain relevant during the era of disruption and digitalisation, where they are not only expected to be uphold a strategic focus but also be intentional about integrating technology in their processes to provide real-time and sustainable solutions. Organisations will continue to face common challenges that require technical skills, such as cash flow management, insolvency, access to capital, budgeting, and forecasting, but operating in a digital world also brings a new set of complex challenges. These challenges include data security concerns, shifting customer expectations, and the need to integrate complex new technologies to stay ahead of the competition, and the rate at which these technologies are developed and updated requires businesses to be agile.

Despite the numerous benefits that can be leveraged from digitalisation, if not managed effectively, it could destroy organisations and make many professions extinct. The insights gained in real time from customer expectations, for example, could lead to businesses making hurried decisions without sufficient research. As a result, modern management accountants are expected to have the wisdom to make impactful decisions amidst all the data they now have available. To conceptualise this new and evolved role, CIMA (Chartered Institute of Management Accountants—the international professional body of Management Accountants) developed the CGMA (Chartered Global Management Accountant) Competency Framework in 2019 to assist management accountants in developing the skills needed in the digital era, which include technical skills, business skills, leadership skills, and people skills, all of which are bound together by digital skills (CIMA 2019). It is important to note that the foundation of these skills are ethics, integrity, and professionalism. The framework further details the transformed role of management accountants from assembling information to applying their influence to make meaningful impact in the organisations they support—see Fig. 2 below.

Other critical challenges of integrating AI-driven solution to financial systems include lack of transparency and accountability, bias, data privacy issues and poor professional judgement and management accountants must be proactive in addressing these challenges to ensure that the profession's reputation is preserved and continues to add value to businesses (Adelakun 2022). According to Adeyelu (2024) resistance to change and scepticism of AI is another consideration that can lead to slow adoption in the accounting profession as a whole but effective change management strategies coupled with clear communication about AI benefits can overcome resistance. It is also important to monitor for the initial establishment costs for AI-driven solutions because at times, the costs can outweigh the benefits. This can include hardware installations and training resources required to integrate current financial systems with AI that other organisations may lack (Rane 2023). It is also important to note that while other functions of management accounting such as portfolio optimisation, bankruptcy and fraud prediction, and market risk and credit risk management may have effectively integrated AI solutions, other tasks have not, as they require self-conscious levels of human intelligence and these include (but not limited to) corporate finance decision making and financial project management (Yi et al. 2023). Despite this, the authors assert that the accounting professionals have much to gain from leveraging AI technologies especially at advanced levels of deep learning.

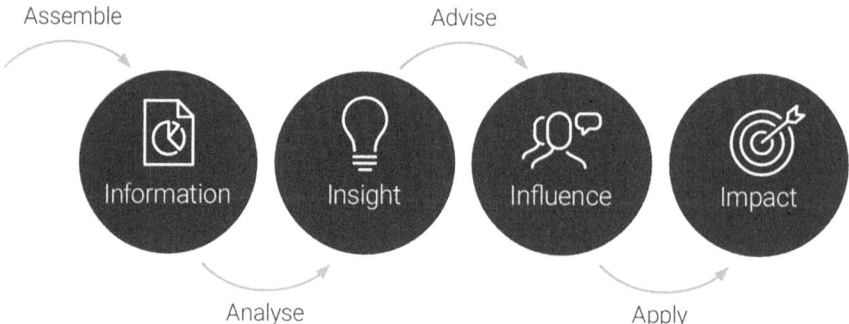

Fig. 2 CIMA Information to impact framework (CIMA 2019)

2.3   Role of Technology in Reshaping Management Accounting

Secondary to professional extinction, technology has been the biggest driver of the demand of highly skilled workers. Over the years, the adoption and adaptation of new technologies have not only improved productivity but also put many accounting functions at risk. This 'good–bad' notion can be infused to describe technological adaptation as bringing change to the way work is performed but not eliminating the work completely (Birnberg and Sisaye 2010). The perception of technology as threat generally limits any industry's growth while embracing change often leads to new norms, only requiring a different kind of human capital. This is also true for the role of a management accountant, where automation of routine and repetitive tasks has led to the need of a more strategic business partner.

The role of a strategic business partner requires a management accountant who perceives technology—such as big data—as a holistic database, AI as a convenient tool for data analysis, and blockchain as a disrupter with error-free data management to enable effective and relevant decision making that will place organisations at the best possible position to gain sustainable competitive advantage (Allen and Jackson 2024). These are some of the key examples of how management accountants can leverage technology to provide improved financial information for strategic planning and management control.

3   AI—Improving the Role of Management Accountants

In the context of management accounting, AI is broadly defined by AICPA as the science of teaching programmes and machines to complete tasks that normally require human intelligence; in simple terms, it is technology that simulates human intelligence. Figure 2 below is a visual representation of the scope of AI technologies that management accountants can integrate into their functions to improve the information they provide to businesses. Starting from no integration, where Robotic Process Automation (RPA) is the key driver, AI is evolving toward deep learning and a future with cognitive technologies. Each level represents a different level of AI application to the management accounting profession.

An important piece missing from Fig. 3 is data, which serves as the foundation of management accounting. Data and data management has always played a critical role in decision making but it cannot be used by businesses without a systematic analysis being undertaken (Bose and Bhattacharjee 2023). As internal structures depend on effective data analysis, it is a core function of management accountants to transform data into accurate and timely information that support the sustainability of businesses. Over the years, this role has been extended to include the support of strategic initiatives that drive value creation, because of informed decision making. Additionally, the insights gained by management accountants when they analyse financial data facilitate forward-thinking solutions to some of business's

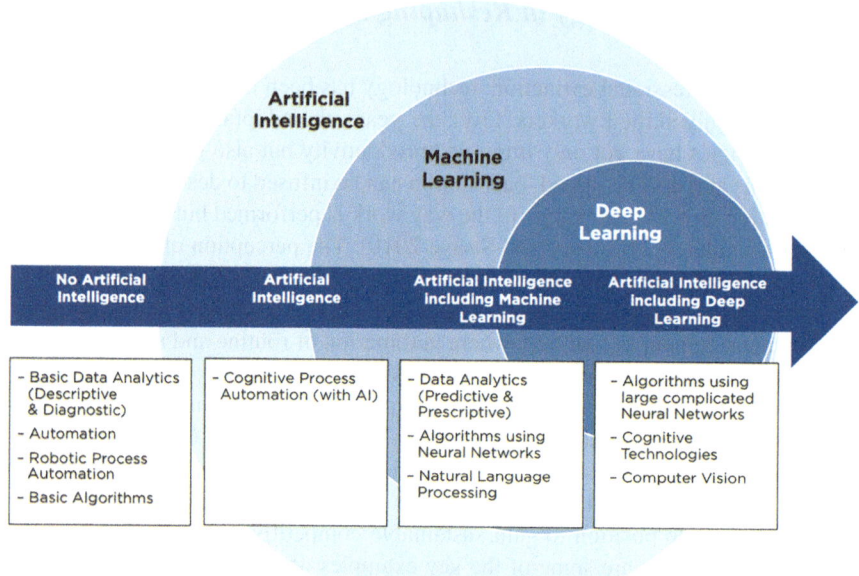

Fig. 3 Different levels of AI—Adopted from AICPA's Introduction to AI (2019)

complex problems. According to Appelbaum et al. (2017) management accountants are now able to fulfil these challenging tasks that help organisations stay competitive with the use of analytical tools such as prescriptive analysis to support decision makers against the uncertainties by recommending possible solutions and showing the likely outcome of each.

Over the years, data has become a source of competitive advantage shaping almost every attribute of decision making and effective data analysis can allow businesses to have real-time responses to market changes and market trends that could result in increased productivity and profitability. Data management and data analysis of financial information are key responsibilities of management accountants and integrating data analytics into managerial accounting practices could result in recommendations that drastically improve profitability.

3.1 Automation of Routine Tasks

One of the key benefits of integrating AI with management accounting functions is the automation of routine tasks which can improve accuracy and efficiency of the information produced for decision making. Automating repetitive tasks such as data entry, processing transactions, and bookkeeping entries can increase operational efficiency. According to a study by Eziefule et al. (2022) automating routine tasks that are performed by accountants can result in the following benefits:

- **Reduction of human errors:** AI systems are not affected by fatigue and distraction which are the common causes of human error. Instead, AI can perform data entry and analysis simultaneously with high precision and because of its ability to learn, it can adapt from past errors which can further enhance accuracy.
- **Consistency of information:** As a result of error-free data entry, processing the output cannot be influenced by human judgement. The results that are produced by AI will uniform across all tasks to ensure that high standards are maintained in line with regulations and compliance.
- **Data Integrity:** Data verification and validation can be augmented by AI systems as it helps in identifying inconsistencies with data entry to ensure that only accurate and consistent information is entered into databases. Because AI has the potential to detect glitches, data integrity can be achieved.
- **Operational efficiency:** The ability of AI to streamline and simplify workflows through automation can result in cost and time-saving efficiencies. Freeing time of key personnel can allow them to focus on more strategic activities rather than mundane tasks.
- **Real-time monitoring:** One of the biggest benefits of AI is enabling management accountants real-time monitoring. Historically reporting would have to be completed before any insights could be gained but integrating AI into business processes can enable analysis of data streams to quickly determine patterns as they occur.

Despite the numerous benefits that can be leveraged from automating routine tasks, it is no secret that these routine tasks previously required large numbers of human capital that will be exposed to job redundancy and displacement. The transforming role of the management accountant will also require upskilling, which will result in new opportunities and advisory roles with the ability to interpret insights and make strategic decisions that will have a shaping effect in industries (Reference).

3.2   Transforming Data Analysis

'Data for decision making' is an organic and integral part of the management accounting role. In fact, businesses rely on this data to improve performance, gain competitive advantage, and attain shareholder wealth. In our previous discussion, we have noted the supreme data collection and processing capabilities of AI, and we will now consider data analysis through AI. In order to consider the transformation of data analysis we must consider the infusion of big data and AI. Over the past decade, there has been a lot of attention on how businesses can derive value from the use of big data and AI has played a significant role in analysing data to provide insights (Munir et al. 2021; Knauer et al. 2020).

For management accountants, the integration of big data and AI can revolutionise how financial information is utilised in decision making going beyond the capabilities of conventional accounting software tools that are unable to keep up with capturing, curating, handling, and processing data within a tolerable amount of time (Tiron-Tudor and Deliu 2021). It is evident that AI can enable efficient data management, encompassing data capturing and processing while also serving as a technology that analyses data to produce useful information for management. Data analysis includes techniques such as:

- **Data Mining**—which involves discovering patterns and relationship, helping businesses identify trends, customer preferences, and potential business opportunities.
- **Natural Language Processing**—which enables machines to interpret text or voice commands, helping businesses gain insights from social media.
- **Statistical analysis**—using techniques such as regression analysis and hypothesis testing to summarise or establish patterns from data.
- **Descriptive analysis**—involves analysing historic data in order to understand past actions, allowing businesses to learn from past mistakes when planning for the future.
- **Diagnostic analysis**—aims to gain insights on historical causes to potentially unveil factors that influence financial performance.
- **Predictive analysis**—involves the use of past data with statistical analysis and machine learning to predict the future and is used in business for resource allocation, planning, and budgeting.
- **Prescriptive Analytics**—goes beyond predictive analysis by recommending actions and is the ultimate tool that businesses can use to aid informed and strategic decision making.

3.3 Improving Insights for Decision Making

As AI transforms the role of management accountants from a technical specialist, it frees up their time to focus on more strategic activities. Additionally, it creates opportunities for new roles that require advanced skills in AI and data analytics (Eziefule et al. 2022). These researchers further state that, in this new role, management accountants must be able to understand how AI tools function and how to interpret the data they produce, as this is crucial for value-adding. They will acquire skills that will provide insights into cost management, revenue optimisation, and investment opportunities based on data-driven analysis (Eziefule et al. 2022). In addition, management accountants will drive and reshape the financial direction of a business through strategic decision making that will be gained from AI.

Moreover, this new era might bring about the merger of the financial accounting roles with the managerial accounting roles in businesses. This is also evidenced by the agreements negotiated and signed between accounting professional bodies in

South Africa, namely South African Institute of Chartered Accountants (SAICA) and The Chartered Institute of Management Accountants (CIMA). The two bodies believe that dual membership will enhance members' skillsets and enable them to pursue new career paths (CIMA 2019). Another notable marriage is that of CIMA and American Institute of Certified Public Accountants (AICPA) who joined forces to create a new association following a joint venture that existed since 2011 (CFO—SA 2016).

3.4 Empowering Management Accountants to Navigate the New Business Environment

To effectively support the business and fulfil their strategic role, management accountants must be adequately equipped with the skills needed for the new business landscape. The new business environment is not only complex but also multi-layered and is transforming at a rapid pace. In addition, digitalisation has given rise to new industries such as streaming services, e-hailing services, e-commerce, and cybersecurity. These industries have not only transformed how accountants do their work but also require new skills, as traditional accounting practises may be mis-aligned with their financial needs. Management accountants can empower themselves through continuous professional development and training. Many professional bodies offer short-learning programmes specifically designed to upskill their members.

One of the critical areas for development for management accountants that might not have been acquired in their formal tertiary education is data management and proficiency to utilise analytical tools to interpret large volume of data and draw meaningful insights. Cybersecurity is another critical skill that can elevate the competency of a management accountant. The AI-powered databases and data management technologies are vulnerable to external breaches, which could compromise businesses. This is a result of the new way of managing information (Wamba-Taguimdje et al. 2020) that is backed by AI technologies. In addition, businesses should promote an environment that does not only promote innovation but also a culture of life-long learning to promote change and allow exploration with new approaches. This will enable their accounting teams to be competent to manage change in an evolving business landscape.

4 Real-Life Applications

Integrating AI into accounting practices is no longer a futuristic possibility but it is at our doorstep, and not only have we witnessed its integration in our everyday lives with innovations backed by AI such as virtual assistants (which are now a multi-million-dollar industry) but AI is also revolutionising the finance industry. Transforming business processes because of AI includes the use of AI for repetitive tasks, AI-powered robots taking over concierge tasks, and AI-driven automation such as chatbots to increase customer service. These changes require a different kind of financial support.

As such, leading accounting firms globally have begun to leverage AI tools to improve the support they offer to businesses and in this section, we will explore various real applications on AI in the accounting profession and how management accountants can take advantage of the new paradigm that has emerged because of AI.

4.1 Deloitte—Omnia AI

Omnia AI is an end-to-end AI solution that Deloitte offers to its clients providing services, such as development of a business AI's strategy, management and transformation of data, integrating efficient processes, and ensuring that organisation can gain insights from its data through AI-powered technologies. Among other things, Deloitte's AI solution promises to advanced analytics, data engineering, cloud infrastructure, and operational excellence. The three pillars on Omnia AI are strategy, data, and insights (Deloitte 2024).

4.2 KPMG—Ignite

Harvesting new data, interpreting signals to uncover complex patterns is what KPMG Ignite promises to its clients. It is a platform that is designed to accelerate its clients AI initiatives. Like other platforms it promised data solutions backed up by natural language processing, machine learning, and deep learning. Their clients can gain meaningful insights from various types of data including structured, unstructured, and semi-structured data; images and videos and voice data (i.e. call transcripts). In addition, the KPMG Ignite platform guarantees to solve complex business challenges and deploy AI-enabled solutions (KPMG 2024).

4.3 BDO—BDOLexi and BDODrive

Recognising the ever-changing business environment their clients operate in, BDO has prioritised innovation and the transformation of their audit practises. They have been actively involved in developing several AI-backed technologies such as the BDO*Lexi* Translation App which is designed to help manage information in multiple languages to support their global audits. Another notable innovation was the launch of BDO*Drive* which they describe as an integrated cloud technology solution powered by Microsoft and Intuit to support their advisory services for outsourced accounting and finances services (BDO 2024).

4.4 PwC—Audit.AI/GL.AI

PWC has partnered with H2O.ai which is a Silicon Valley-based AI company to develop its first bot which promises to do what humans can't. GL.ai is the first module of Audit.ai, which has capabilities to analyse billions of data in seconds. It also promises to offer judgement that can detect anomalies in general ledger transactions without bias and variability. Some of the benefits that PwC promises its clients with the integration of GL.ai include faster audits and the generation of additional insights that can help improve efficiency. Other AI products that are offered by PwC include H2O AI cloud, H2O Document AI, and H2O Driverless offering services from fully hosted and hybrid cloud solutions to predictive data processing and automated machine learning capable of extracting patterns and predicting outcomes (PwC 2024).

4.5 EY—EY Helix

EY Helix is analytical tool and integral element of EY audits. EY describes this analytics platform as the edge that gives their teams the ability to analyse large volume of audit-relevant data to derive insights of their client's business operation. This being at the core of a management accountant's function demonstrates how AI can enable accountants to provide client-orientated financial support. EY further describe their platform to have data capturing features that can handle data of any size and analytical tools that increase value of insights derived from the inputted data and can support all areas of audit from risk assessment to execution (EY 2024).

It is evident that AI has disrupted the accounting firms, challenging them to re-imagine how they offer support to their clients. Accountants in general have an opportunity to utilise AI-powered technologies to not only streamline their work but also offer a holistic and end-to-end solutions to their clients. It is clear though that we are in the era of data as data management has become source of competitive advantage, with each firm offering an AI-based solution with data management capabilities.

5 Ethical Considerations for AI

Throughout this chapter, we have discussed various benefits of integrating AI into management accounting functions. However, neglecting the ethical issues in AI solutions could lead to organisational problems (Vărzaru 2022). According to Zhang et al. (2023), examples of the ethical risks include those related to data security and privacy, expectation gap, accountability, bias, auditor competency, and audit quality standards—in addition to those previously discussed earlier. Management accountants are trusted with highly confidential financial information and securing it against infiltration, breach, and hacking is a substantial problem (Ahmad and Ahmada 2024). They can play an important role within the organisations they support by advocating for ethical practices that safeguard sensitive financial and personal data because in many countries it is a legal requirement (i.e. data protection regulations such as the General Data Protection Regulation—GDPR) (Schweitzer 2024).

Another primary ethical concern for management accountants in using AI-technologies is algorithm bias, which could lead to discriminatory outcomes that perpetuate inequalities. This is one key example why AI technologies should not operate fully autonomously, requiring some level of human interaction (Schweitzer 2024). Management accountants must take extra care when capturing data and developing algorithms to ensure that outcomes promote fairness and equality. Another often forgotten ethical issue with the use of AI-powered technology is accountability allocation (Schweitzer 2024). With each dataset inputted, AI tools become better experts in making decisions, but problems often arise when errors are made that are detrimental to the organisation. Often, the biggest question is who will be held accountable and without clear ethical guidelines, accountability cannot be assigned (Adelakun 2022).

It is important for management accountants to follow a clear framework for ethical considerations in the use of AI because unlike financial accounting, which is grounded in widely accepted standards, management accounting processes are more flexible (Zhang et al. 2023). There are two notable ethical frameworks that Management accountants can refer to namely, Artificial Intelligence Governance Principles in the New Generation: Developing Responsible Artificial Intelligence and the Statement on Artificial Intelligence, Robotics, and 'Autonomous' Systems, which will be discussed below.

In 2019, the European Group on Ethics (EGE) in Science and New Technologies published the 'Statement on Artificial Intelligence, Robotics, and Autonomous Systems' providing a proposed ethical and legal framework for the design, production, use and governance of artificial intelligence, robotics, and 'autonomous' systems. The framework has seven ethical principles which include:

- **Human Dignity**—promoting the inherent human state of being, worthy of being respected and not exposed to violation by autonomous technologies.

- **Autonomy**—promoting the freedom of human beings, where autonomous systems technologies must honour the human ability to choose whether, when, and how to delegate decisions and actions to them.
- **Responsibility**—implying that autonomous systems must be designed in a way that their effects align with a plurality of fundamental human values and rights.
- **Justice, equity, and solidarity**—promoting AI's contribution to global justice and equal access while preventing or detecting, reporting and nuetralising discriminatory biases in data sets used to train and run AI systems.
- **Democracy**—promoting democratic debate and public engagement on key decisions on the regulation of AI development and application.
- **Rule of law and accountability**—promoting clear allocation of responsibility in all AI legal challenges.
- **Security, safety, bodily and mental integrity**—promoting strict testing by AI developers before release of all dimensions of safety.
- **Data protection and privacy**—promoting the right to protection of personal information and the right to respect for privacy from AI robots and AI softbots.

Lastly, it is important to note that management accountants are responsible for their own empowerment in pursuit of making ethically sound decisions and continuously maintaining integrity to uphold professional due care in their engagements (Enslin 2019). The researcher further states that continuous education on ethical considerations surrounding AI is one way management accountants can fulfil their ethical responsibility as this is critical in preserving trust and confidence in their accounting processes.

6 Conclusion: The Future of Management Accountants

The functions of management accountants have existed since the concept of business emerged. Like businesses themselves, these functions have transformed over time to remain relevant to their core purpose, which is to provide financial support to businesses. As a result of the recent and expedited technological advancements, it has seen its most significant transformation in the past three decades. This change has been so immense that it has threatened the extinction of some roles that historically fell under its function. While this can be cause for concern, it is not unique to the profession as the Fourth Industrial Revolution (4IR) has had this effect on many industries and professions. What is exciting for management accountants though are the new opportunities and roles that have become available for management accountants to support businesses in the digital age. Enabling organic adaption to technologies like AI can ensure seamless transition into this new era. As businesses gear up to navigate these complex and unique challenges brought about by digitalisation, if management accountants evolve with them, it could only deepen the support they offer to business.

One important transition is the shifting focus on financial reporting and cost control to strategic business partnering, where management accountants are becoming instrumental in shaping and driving value creation. Data management has always been the 'super-power' of management accountants, but AI has enabled them to elevate it to the next level, not only by processing magnitudes of datasets in minutes but by also providing insights in real time, enhancing decision making that supports the success of businesses. AI has also taken management accountants out of the shadow to the forefront, enabling them to utilise technologies such as data visualisation techniques to present complex concepts in a way that is understandable to all stakeholders.

References

Abu Afifa MM, Nguyen TH, Le MTT, Nguyen L, Tran TTH (2024) Accounting going digital: a Vietnamese experimental study on artificial intelligence in accounting. VINE J Inf Knowl Manag Syst

Adelakun BO (2022) Ethical considerations in the use of AI for auditing: balancing innovation and integrity. Eur J Account Audit Finance Res 10(12):91–108

Adelakun BO, Majekodunmi TG, Akintoye OS (2024) AI and ethical accounting: navigating challenges and opportunities. Int J Adv Econ 6(6):224–241

Adeyelu OO, Ugochukwu CE, Shonibare MA (2024) The impact of artificial intelligence on accounting practices: advancements, challenges, and opportunities. Int J Manag Entrep Res 6(4):1200–1210

Ahmad A, Ahmada YAB (2024) Ethical implications of artificial intelligence in accounting: a framework for responsible ai adoption in multinational corporations in Jordan. Int J Data Netw Sci 8(1):401–414

AICPA (2019) A CPA's introduction to AI: from algorithms to deep learning, what you need to know

Ala-Heikkilä V, Järvenpää M (2023) Management accountants' image, role and identity: employer branding and identity conflict. Qual Res Account Manag 20(3):337–371

Alldén S, Norén G (2023) What is the influence of artificial intelligence (AI) on management accounting and control?

Allen C, Jackson D (2024) Enablers, barriers and strategies for adopting new technology in accounting. International Journal of Accounting Information Systems, 52, 100666

Appelbaum D, Kogan A, Vasarhelyi M, Yan Z (2017) Impact of business analytics and enterprise systems on managerial accounting. Int J Account Inf Syst 25:29–44

Arkhipova D, Montemari M, Mio C, Marasca S (2024) Digital technologies and the evolution of the management accounting profession: a grounded theory literature review. Meditari Account Res 32(7):56–85

Ashton D, Hopper T, Scapens R (1995) The changing nature of issues in management accounting. In: Issues in management accounting. Prentice Hall

Bako PM, Tanko UM (2022) The place of artificial intelligence in accounting field and the future of accounting profession. J Artif Intell Machine Learning Neural Netw 25:15–21

BDO (2024) Artificial Intelligence Retrieved August, 2024 from https://www.bdo.co.za/en-za/microsites/bdo-drive

Bhatt DL, Gersh BJ, Oren O (2020) Artificial intelligence in medical imaging: switching from radiographic pathological data to clinically meaningful endpoints. The Lancet Digital Health, 2(9), e486–e488

Birnberg JG, Sisaye S (2010) Organizational development and transformational learning approaches in process innovations: a review of the implications to the management accounting literature. Rev Acc Financ 9(4):337–362

Bose S, Dey SK, Bhattacharjee S (2023) Big data, data analytics and artificial intelligence in accounting: an overview. In: Handbook of big data research methods, pp 32–51

Boyns T, Edwards JR (2006) The development of cost and management accounting in Britain. In: Handbooks of management accounting research, vol 2, pp 969–1034

CFO-SA (2016) SAICA and CIMA work together to advance accountancy in SA. https://cfo.co.za/articles/saica-and-cima-work-together-to-advance-accountancy-in-sa/. Accessed 10 Oct 2024

CIMA (2019) CIMA's CGMA competency framework: a framework for success

Dahal, RK (2017) The changing role of management accountants in the modern business environment

Dahal SB (2023) Utilizing generative AI for real-time financial market analysis opportunities and challenges. Adv Intell Inf Syst 8(4):1–11

Deloitte (2024) Omnia AI. Retrieved August, 2024 from https://www2.deloitte.com/ca/en/pages/deloitteanalytics/articles/omnia-artificial-intelligence.html

Dobroszek J, Paientko T, Walińska E (2024) Management accounting professionals in the SMART economy. Cent Eur Econ J 11(58):320–338

Du-Harpur X, Watt FM, Luscombe NM, Lynch MD (2020) What is AI? Applications of artificial intelligence to dermatology. Br J Dermatol 183(3):423–430

Enslin Z (2019) Behavioural aspects that influence business decision-making by management accounting professionals. University of Pretoria (South Africa)

EY (2024) EY Helix. Retrieved August, 2024 from https://www.ey.com/en_gl/services/audit/technology/helix

Eziefule AO, Adelakun BO, Okoye IN, Attieku JS (2022) The role of AI in automating routine accounting tasks: efficiency gains and workforce implications. Eur J Account Audit Finance Res 10(12):109–134

Kamal S (2015) Historical evolution of management accounting. Cost Manag 43(4):12–19

Kaplan RS (1984) The evolution of management accounting. In: Readings in accounting for management control, pp 586–621

Knauer T, Nikiforow N, Wagener S (2020) Determinants of information system quality and data quality in management accounting. J Manag Control 31(1):97–121

Korobeynikova OM, Korobeynikov DA, Popova LV, Chekrygina TA, Shemet ES (2021, March) Artificial intelligence for digitalization of management accounting of agricultural organizations. In: IOP conference series: earth and environmental science, vol 699, No. 1. IOP Publishing, p 012049

KPMG (2024) KPMG Ignite. Retrieved August, 2024 from https://kpmg.com/us/en/capabilities-services/advisoryservices/data-analytics-ai/artificial-intelligence-ignite.html

LeCun Y, Bengio Y, Hinton G (2015) Deep learning. Nature 521(7553):436–444

Munir S, Rasid SZA, Aamir M, Jamil F, Ahmed I (2021) Big data analytics and innovation performance with the transformational role of management accountant. J Acad Res Bus Soc Sci 11(11):1180–1197

Ovunda AS (2015) The development of cost and management accounting: a historical perspective. Eur J Humanit Soc Sci 34(1)

PwC (2024) Harnessing the power of AI to transform the detection of fraud and error. Retrieved August, 2024 from https://www.pwc.com/gx/en/about/stories-from-across-the-world/harnessing-the-power-of-ai-to-transform-thedetection-of-fraud-and-error.html

Rakhmawati H, Kurniawan U, Prasetyo A (2023) Implications of the use of artificial intelligence in management accounting: a literature review. Int J Econ Lit 2(10)

Rane N (2023) Role and challenges of ChatGPT and similar generative artificial intelligence in finance and accounting. Available at SSRN 4603206

Ranta M, Ylinen M, Järvenpää M (2023) Machine learning in management accounting research: literature review and pathways for the future. Eur Account Rev 32(3):607–636

Schweitzer B (2024) Artificial intelligence (AI) ethics in accounting. J Account Ethics Public Policy, JAEPP 25(1):67–67

Sheikh M, Iqra F, Ambreen H, Pravin KA, Ikra M, Chung YS (2024) Integrating artificial intelligence and high-throughput phenotyping for crop improvement. J Integr Agric 23(6):1787–1802

Spraakman G, Sanchez-Rodriguez C, Tuck-Riggs CA (2021) Data analytics by management accountants. Qual Res Account Manag 18(1):127–147

Tiron-Tudor A, Deliu D (2021) Big data's disruptive effect on job profiles: management accountants' case study. J Risk Financ Manag 14(8):376

Vărzaru AA (2022) Assessing the impact of AI solutions' ethical issues on performance in managerial accounting. Electronics 11(14):2221

Walker SP (2008) Innovation, convergence and argument without end in accounting history. Account Audit Account J 21(2):296–322

Wamba-Taguimdje SL, Wamba SF, Kamdjoug JRK, Wanko CET (2020) Influence of artificial intelligence (AI) on firm performance: the business value of AI-based transformation projects. Bus Process Manag J 26(7):1893–1924

Yi Z, Cao X, Chen Z, Li S (2023) Artificial intelligence in accounting and finance: challenges and opportunities. IEEE Access 11:129100–129123

Zhang C, Zhu W, Dai J, Wu Y, Chen X (2023) Ethical impact of artificial intelligence in managerial accounting. Int J Account Inf Syst 49:100619

The Impact of Artificial Intelligence on Auditing and Assurance Services

Morepe Ncalo and Benjamin Marx

Abstract In the era of digital transformation and the evolving landscape of Artificial Intelligence (AI), external auditors have an indispensable need to modernize their skill sets and be adaptable to the ever-evolving environment they are auditing in. As AI technologies advance, change to traditional approaches of audit methodology and processes followed by external auditors in executing audits is required. AI could revolutionalize various audit phases, such as the risk assessment, planning, gathering of audit evidence and reporting stages. This chapter will focus on the use of AI in the gathering of audit evidence stage, which has been proven to reduce testing time, allow for the testing of larger populations, and improve overall audit quality compared to traditional approaches of handling data. This chapter further explores how AI has shaped and influenced traditional external audit processes through a critical literature review with two main objectives. Firstly, to evaluate the existing literature on the impact of AI on external audit processes. Secondly, to link the impact explored in the literature review to the framework on gathering audit evidence as proposed by the International Standard on Auditing 500 (ISA 500) revised. The qualitative research approach, employing critical literature review, reflects and consolidates research on the impact of AI on external auditing, using International Standards on Auditing, specifically ISA 500 revised framework as its broad theoretical lens. The role of AI in gathering audit evidence promises to enhance the efficiency of auditors by cultivating modern audit skills and allowing for increased focus of their role toward unpacking more complex and unstructured data. The use of AI in gathering audit evidence comes with its challenges. As this chapter highlights the possible use and adoption of AI in gathering audit evidence, limitations such as ethical concerns on handling of data and insufficient documentation on the use of these technologies together with the lack of uniform regulations across the audit profession need to be considered. These challenges provide for

M. Ncalo (✉) · B. Marx
Department of Accountancy, University of Johannesburg, Johannesburg, South Africa
e-mail: morepen@uj.ac.za; benm@uj.ac.za

© The Author(s), under exclusive license to Springer Nature
Switzerland AG 2025
M. Adelowotan, C. A. Leke (eds.), *Artificial Intelligence in Accounting, Auditing and Finance*, Contributions to Finance and Accounting,
https://doi.org/10.1007/978-3-031-87368-3_6

83

areas of further research, especially on proposed measures that can be adopted to mitigate the concerns.

Keywords Artificial Intelligence · Digital transformation · Audit standards · Automated tools and techniques · Fraud detection · Audit quality

1 Introduction

The rapid advancement of Artificial Intelligence (AI) in recent years has compelled organizations and businesses to adopt new processes in order to meet overarching organizational objectives set by management (Schneider and Leyer 2019). This further impacted management's processes and resource allocations to achieve long-term sustainability and growth for their organizations (Kuo and Smith 2018, Wirtz and Müller 2019). AI can have a significant impact on organizations' financial reporting objectives, as it can improve accounting practices toward providing high-quality and timely financial information to various stakeholders (Jejeniwa et al. 2024). Similarly, AI has a substantial effect on auditing and assurance service providers, helping them achieve their objectives and enhance the trustworthiness of financial and non-financial information.

The prominence and focus of audit and assurance services increased in the late 1980s when users noted a need for access to timely and reliable information that aligns to the evolving markets and technological advancements (Coksun Arslan and Dermirkan 2017). As far as accounting and audit functions are concerned, technology remains a key focus in the analysis of an entity's performance within economies that are constantly developing (Sobel and Reding 2004).

Various corporate failures that are often linked to audit failures pose a significant threat and challenge for audit practitioners. It reduces the public trust in the value of auditors' and the work they provide. This has not only affected the auditor's values, professional and ethical attitudes but further impacted on the need for adapting audit and assurance methodologies and tools in the audit of integrated financial report (Maroun 2018). In external auditing, processes are followed whereby the registered auditor uses the audit report as the primary tool to communicate to various stakeholders their opinion on whether the financial and non-financial information in integrated reports of an entity is reliable, timely, and of quality (Coksun Arslan and Dermirkan 2017). An external audit report thus has the potential to increase the confidence of various stakeholders in decision making—namely, shareholders, potential investors, lenders, government, stock exchange regulators, and the industry at large.

The paradigm shift of accounting practices in the era of digital transformation and the evolving landscape of AI consequently requires external auditors to reevaluate, adapt, and modernize their skill sets to be adaptable to the ever-evolving landscape they are auditing in (Elliott 1998). This is evident in the view of the International Auditing and Assurance Standards Board (IAASB), which notes that the audit profession, as we know it today, will need to be reevaluated and transformed to align with changes in the global economy, and accordingly it is imperative to reflect on the factors that influence the efficiency of modern-day auditors (IAASB 2024).

This chapter delves into the impact of AI on the external audit of financial reporting following the technological advancements and eminence of AI. The use of cutting-edge AI technologies and the value they can bring to audit processes are explored. A qualitative research approach is used, employing a critical literature review that reflects and consolidates research on the impact of AI on external auditing, using International Standard on Auditing (ISA) frameworks as its broad theoretical lens. The study aims to bring awareness of the impact of AI on external audit processes following a structured approach to the various stages of an audit as contained in the widely accepted ISAs proposed by the IAASB. The study further aims to offer considerations and insights aligned to the ISA standards recommendations to serve the foundation of how audit practitioners and academics can consider the practical impact of AI on the audit processes.

Audit assurance consists of two categories: reasonable and limited assurance audits. The overall objective of the registered auditor in the audit of financial statements is to obtain reasonable assurance about whether or not the financial statements are free from material misstatements. To achieve this goal, a series of procedures and activities are performed to obtain evidence to support the auditor's opinion. The procedures and activities are referred to as an audit process. AI could revolutionalize various phases of audit processes, such as the risk assessment, planning, gathering of audit evidence and reporting stages (Seethamraju and Hecimovic 2020). In general, artificial intelligence for auditing is expected to affect various elements and audit functions at each stage of the audit process.

2 Pre-Engagement Stage (ISA 220)

2.1 Impact of AI on Client Acceptance

The independence of an auditor when providing assurance services is crucial for ensuring the objectivity and reliability of the audit report issued and accordingly it is critical that the auditor should consider aspects that have or can be seen as threats to the auditor's independence and objectivity. The use of AI-enabled technologies such as data analytics and visualization can aid in the identification of possible independence issues, conflict of interest and matters affecting the firm's independence (Seethamraju and Hecimovic 2020). The use of data analytics and machine learning can further assist the auditor in the evaluation of auditor independence, including assessing the completeness of related party relationship and disclosures in the integrated report. Through visualization, the auditor can map the organization's structure to a live database to make sure that all entities within a group structure are accounted for. If done manually, such mapping can take a substantial amount of time, with the risk that as the client continues to invest in new entities, manually keeping track could result in omissions and errors. Consider the audit of a multinational group company with operations and investments in over 17 countries. To ensure independence the auditor needs to investigate if the audit team members have direct or indirect business dealings, family ties, or recent employment history with the management personnel of the various entities in subsidiaries across all 17 countries. Data analytics and visualization are useful tools that the auditor can use to investigate relationships that could compromise their objectivity and ultimately reduce stakeholder confidence in the assurance reports issued.

3   Risk Assessment and Planning Stage (ISA 300 and 315)

Risk assessment and planning procedures, as well as activities, are outlined in ISA 315 and 300. The ISAs are written linearly, while in practice, planning and risk assessment considerations are often performed iteratively as discussed below.

3.1   Impact of AI on Planning of Audit Engagements

The objective of planning an audit involves establishing the overall audit strategy that represents the foundation of the external auditor's general approach to achieving the audit objectives through outlining the nature, timing, and extent of audit procedures required. An audit strategy represents a high-level overview of how the audit will be conducted, which could include testing an entity's controls, performing substantive procedures, or a combination of both. An audit strategy also outlines the timing and scope of audit procedures. One of the important considerations for an audit strategy is the team's skills, expertise, and firm technologies needed to effectively respond to engagement risks and conduct the audit efficiently. The audit strategy is influenced by observations from risk assessments at the financial statement level, the client's control environment, and its information systems. The impact of AI on audit strategy can be related to an audit firm's investment in AI technologies to support their teams, while others are purposely composing their audit teams to include members with broadened technological skill sets (Kend and Nguyen 2022; Seethamraju and Hecimovic 2020).

3.2 Audit Firm Technologies

The modern business environment calls for advanced analytical tools to interpret vast and complex financial data and identify meaningful patterns. The Independent Regulatory Board of Auditors (IRBA), who regulate the audit profession in South Africa, highlights that some of the good practices noted in the 2022/2023 audit quality reviews relate to the use of AI enhanced audit software specializing in analytics, research, and risk monitoring (IRBA 2022). Notably, the firms will require significant investments in the development and maintenance of such software to keep up with the constantly evolving AI technologies, which also will impact the composition of teams on client engagements.

3.3 Engagement Team Specifics

Audit teams should comprise a balanced mix of knowledge and experience related to the technologies adopted by the client, such as data analytics, machine learning, and other cognitive technologies. It is becoming increasingly evident that AI impacts the recruitment and hiring practices of audit firms. It has been observed that audit firms are now prioritizing employing candidates with a strong foundation in accounting and auditing, coupled with sound awareness of programming skills (Cooper et al. 2019). This shift underscores the growing importance of technological proficiency in the accounting industry. As early as 2003, the Education Committee of the American Accounting Association noted that audit education would need to be transformed to incorporate information technology into the syllabus to develop prospective auditors fit for the twenty-first century (2003), while the 2023 future of jobs report highlights that businesses consider the third fastest growing skill to be technology literacy (World Economic Forum 2023). The lack of skilled staff on audit engagements is identified as one of the root causes of audit quality deficiencies, as identified in the IRBA inspection reports (IRBA 2022), which can then accordingly be correlated further to the technology skills of staff members on the audit engagements, especially in highly complex and computerized environments. This then follows that in response to the rapidly changing business environments driven by AI, the composition of engagement teams should evolve to include staff with the right knowledge, understanding, and experience related to these technologies. For example, if an organization uses robotics and blockchain, the audit engagement team should include members with sufficient expertise in these technologies. In addition, staff support and training is essential to ensure continuous modernizing of auditor skill sets to promote the execution of high-quality audits.

In its infancy, it was widely promulgated that AI would be disruptive resulting in employees being redundant or laid-off. Although retrenchments were noted due to the fourth industrial revolution, it became evident that as AI progresses the auditor and AI tools can co-exist (Issa et al. 2016). While it is argued that auditors working side to side with AI, focusing on higher-order thinking to interpret the output of these AI tools becomes imperative for effective audits (Hasan 2022). It is also evident that AI is taking significantly longer than expected to replace tasks requiring judgmental skills, with the argument being made that in fact it would not be the case at all, experts are of the opinion that AI can supplement auditors capabilities (Agrawal et al. 2017). This view is strongly supported by the International Auditing and Assurance Standards Board, which emphasizes that these tools cannot replace the auditor's knowledge and professional judgment, no matter how powerful the tool is (IAASB 2024). Further, although the auditor may have access to a wide array of data, including from varying sources, the application of professional skepticism is critical to evaluate the reliability of the data and outputs from using automated tools and techniques. PWC notes "automation is how technology can harness points in the audit process to achieve synergy between our people and the machines that they use, so that the sum is greater than those individual parts" (PWC 2024). Auditing firms across the globe could consider making use of in-house AI powered tools to streamline day-to-day work performed at various clients. For example, PwC has developed assets within its lab tool that primarily focus on workflow automation and bots designed to eliminate manual processes in the auditing of tangible assets (PWC 2024).

3.4 Timing of Engagements

The timing of audit engagements depends on multiple factors such as the size of the client's operations, listing on stock exchanges and other regulatory considerations relating to the presentation and release of annual financial statements. The Johannesburg Stock Exchange (JSE) requires listed entities to issue audited financial statements within 3 months after the reporting period, which can be considered a tight deadline depending on the readiness of the client post year-end. Accordingly, the opportunity exists for auditors to leverage the use of AI enhanced tools and techniques to conclude audits within the required timeframe without compromising quality and reliability. Audit firms have made notable investments to incorporate AI into their in-house audit software which is aimed at increasing audit process efficiencies through the elimination of time-consuming data-related audit tasks (IRBA 2022). PWC and Deloitte leverage Aura and Omnia, respectively, as their in-house cloud-based technology platform powering the audit of financial statements (PWC 2024; Deloitte 2024).

Continuous monitoring of audit engagements involves using automated tools and techniques to track data and audit progress throughout the client's financial period until year-end, with AI positively impacting audit deadlines. Continuous monitoring using various AI tools enables upfront risk assessment and planning, ultimately reducing pressure on the team and allowing more time for obtaining audit evidence. Through the use of neural networks and visualization techniques, the auditor can continuously monitor client data to understand in-depth who passed the transactions, the timing thereof, and how the system processed the transactions (Zemánková 2019). In a population of hundreds of entries, detecting anomalies that could indicate areas of fraud traditionally required more experienced auditors to use their judgment to sense any potential risks. EY Helix GL Anomaly Detector is an AI-empowered tool that can assist auditors to detect anomalies in data entries in the reporting of financial statements (EY 2024a, 2024b). The outcome of AI-empowered tools such as Helix GL has the impact of indicating significant areas of focus for overridden controls or possible fraudulent activities upfront and continuously throughout the audit. However, it is important to understand that the insights and output generated through neural networks and other AI tools cannot blindly be relied upon as sufficient audit procedure and evidence. Auditors must exercise professional skepticism and further probe the outcome to determine whether the output from these tools highlights other significant areas of focus.

3.5   Audit Materiality

An independent audit aims to provide an opinion on the fairness and conformity of financial statements with a specific financial reporting framework. This is done on the basis of reasonable assurance deploying the concept of materiality. An auditor's understanding of the entity and risk assessment procedures informs the setting of planning materiality. The calculated planning materiality is then used to identify classes of transactions and account balances that will be significant for the auditor. Materiality consists of both qualitative and quantitative considerations and while auditors normally confirm to the prescribed standards on setting materiality, a contested issue is around the disclosure of the set materiality for transparency to stakeholders (Quick et al. 2023). Setting materiality requires judgment in identifying relevant benchmarks, using budgeted or actual financial information, assessing data stability and weighing qualitative factors. The use of AI can assist auditors in making this binary decision and promote auditor confidence toward transparency in their disclosures of materiality used during the audit.

The use of AI-enabled tools assists the auditor to predict a materiality range acceptable for an engagement at hand, enhancing the auditors use of reasonability and sensitivity checks of audit evidence and findings, while fuzzy logic expert system allows auditors to assess materiality on a continuous basis both quantitatively and qualitatively by allocating on a scale of 0–1, a degree of value to each misstatements and omissions (Rosner et al. 2006). The results from the fuzzy logic expert system can be utilized by an external auditor to conduct a sensitivity analysis of their own calculated materiality figure in both developed and developing economies.

3.6 Understanding Entity and Its Operations Including Information Systems

As part of audit processes, an auditor performs risk assessment procedures. The auditor identifies risks by obtaining an understanding of the organization and the environment, including the relevant controls.

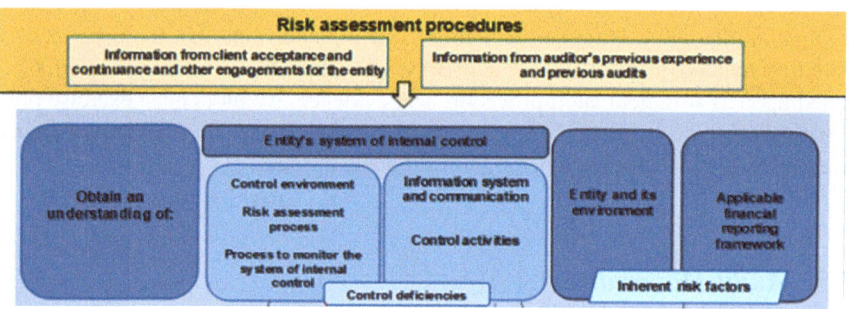

Extract—ISA 315 (Revised 2019)

With the increasing use of computers and automation in entity environments, new business risks emerge relating to IT, including inadequate or inappropriate design and implementation of controls, thus, requiring external auditors to be vigilant about how these risks can lead to increased audit risks. New-age accounting is enormously data-driven and automated, while such data and digitalization within businesses can lead to non-compliance with various rules and regulations such as International Financial Reporting Standards (IFRS), Cybercrimes Act, and the Protection of Personal Information Act (POPIA) among others (Agrawal et al. 2017, Hasan 2022; IAASB 2024).

3.7 Identifying Risks of Material Misstatements Including Considerations for Fraud

Auditors are leveraging the use of automated tools and techniques to assist in assessing the risk of material misstatements (IRBA 2022). By applying automated tools or techniques to a client's database information, the auditor may enhance their understanding of the flow of transactions through the entity's IT systems by continually monitoring the processing of transactions and journal entries. AI tools, like predictive data analytics, can play a crucial role in analyzing complex data patterns and trends during risk assessments as these tools are adept at identifying anomalies, variations, and exceptional cases within areas such as account receivables with significant credit losses. Furthermore, they are instrumental in developing predictive models that can effectively pinpoint potential sales returns in transactional data. In addition, analyzing vast or full populations of transactions may lead to the identification of anomalies indicating to the auditor areas of risks for material misstatement (Seethamraju and Hecimovic 2020).

Regulators and standard setters however often caution auditors against solely or blindly relying on automated tools and techniques, encouraging them to apply an increased level of professional skepticism and professional judgment in assessing the implications of the identified risks (IAASB 2024; IRBA 2022). It is key for auditors to limit over-reliance on outcomes produced by these AI tools as they are not intended to substitute their professional competence, due care, and professional judgments. As a result, exercising professional judgment to validate the appropriateness of the financial accounts identified through the use of machine learning enhances overall audit quality.

Assessing the risk of fraud is another area of the audit process that can be enhanced by the use of AI tools during the audit process, especially considering possible difficulties in detecting fraud. Fraud in financial reporting is a worrying factor for various stakeholders worldwide and can cause significant damage to the financial markets, various stakeholders, and auditors alike, as seen from the likes of Enron and Steinhoff. Machine learning, through computer algorithms and trained data can learn behaviors and trends to identify unusual activities linked to fraudulent reporting of transactions (Bao et al. 2020a, 2020b), while, for example, *"Topic,"* a machine learning technique has the ability to analyze text and language to identify possible misrepresentations in disclosures (Brown et al. 2020). The tool *Topic* is useful and informative in predicting intentional and perceived opportunities for management to misguide in their financial reporting disclosures.

4 Gathering of Audit Evidence Stage (ISA 500)

4.1 Audit Evidence Defined

Audit evidence is the information used by the auditor to form an opinion on the fair presentation of financial statements and other information. The evidence is generally obtained from underlying records to support the accounting entries such as invoices, minutes of meetings, journal entries, confirmations, and reports among others.

4.2 Gathering Audit Evidence/Automation

A detailed audit plan per assertion normally set out the nature, timing, and extent of audit procedures to be performed for a specific class of transaction or account balance. Traditionally, the auditor's approach to preparing audit documentation was manually driven and labor-intensive. Manually capturing data on audit working papers is time-consuming, highly susceptible to human error and can result in limitations in the case of testing large populations. The advent of AI has been widely noted to bring value to the audit process through the substantial impact it has on the handling of large data, providing in-depth analysis of all transactions in an entities data set rather than analyzing samples (Seethamraju and Hecimovic 2020). In addition, it has been noted to reduce time spent on audits through automating routine tasks such as reviewing and capturing contractual information from data populations (Hasan 2022; Kommunuri 2022). ISA 500 recommends a principles-based approach to evaluate sources of information, and while it is not prescriptive on the use of AI in performing the procedures, it does require the auditor's attention to excising professional judgment in ensuring the reliability and relevance of information intended to be used as audit evidence.

An auditor can obtain audit evidence either through test of controls or substantive procedures as per the audit plan of that particular account balance or class of transactions. Test of controls are audit procedures designed to evaluate the operating effectiveness of controls in preventing and detecting misstatements while in contrast, substantive procedures are designed to detect material misstatements in the line items presented on financial statements.

Globally, audit quality inspections highlighted the potential use and value of automated tools and techniques in audits, particularly in performing substantive procedures and test controls (IRBA 2022). "The procedures for obtaining audit evidence, as set out in ISA 500 Audit Evidence, consist of inspection, observation, external confirmation, recalculation, reperformance, analytical procedures, and inquiry, continue to apply, regardless of whether those procedures are performed manually or using technology" (IAASB 2019). Below are further considerations of the impact of AI on each type of ISA 500 audit procedures.

4.3 Enquiries and Corroborations

In gathering audit evidence, an auditor is permitted to inquire from the personnel of the entity who are responsible for making decisions concerning transactions processed. This includes inquiries to obtain an understanding of various matters during the audit and requesting supportive audit evidence. It is widely acknowledged that AI's notable impact on audit is shifting focus away from repetitive tasks (Munoko et al. 2020). Looking ahead, it is evident that as AI technology continues to advance, it's highly probable that the task of inquiring with management to request supporting documentation will be seamlessly automated by AI. However, inquiries to obtain an understanding of audit work findings and other matters cannot be fully automated or completed without human interaction. The adoption of technology modifies audit approaches, reducing the need for physical presence but also carrying the risk of human isolation in executing the audit. This results from potentially reduced client-facing time and limited presence at client premises. Inquiries made with the intention of obtaining an understanding or clarity on significant matters of interest are often better conducted in person. Valuable information can be lost if inquiries are not conducted in person, as auditors may miss out on opportunities to observe non-verbal cues, such as the client's reaction to on-the-spot questioning, an element of unpredictability: this is increasingly important in the digital age, where there are more opportunities for fraud and error (Munoko et al. 2020). Overall, inquiries made to obtain an understanding of various audit matters are insufficient on their own and need to be corroborated with other supporting documentation, emphasizing the need for human involvement and judgment in the audit in the gathering of evidence.

4.4 Recalculations

Recalculating requires time to gather information from relevant source documents and to redo the client procedures and processing that were previously applied. This process can be time-consuming, especially when dealing with large data sets or populations that rely on multiple supporting documents, particularly if it is done manually.

AI has been proven to add value in this regard, with audit firms having observed increased efficiency through the use of natural language processing (NLP) technology to extract information and data from populations or samples and then transferring it to a platform for various other purposes which could translate to recalculations and reviews (Wiliams et al. 2024). A further example of the use of AI is in analyzing unstructured complex data utilized in a share-based payment valuation calculation, it is possible to uncover multiple sources with distinct characteristics, with these sources then being leveraged to conduct recalculations or to implement advanced algorithms to validate the accuracy of the calculation. For instance, consider the process of recalculating the total revenue generated by a hospital or medical center through the provision of medical procedures and services to patients. Advanced AI tools such as Nuance-DAX Copilot, a Microsoft AI technology, has the capability to seamlessly extract data from a variety of healthcare systems, converting it into a standardized format. These tools then leverage a multitude of downstream automations to conduct comprehensive recalculations on the entire population of hospital patients, leading to more efficient and accurate results: this has the value of enhancing audit quality.

Machine Learning excels in AI domains by ingesting large datasets and identifying intricate patterns that might be imperceptible to human analysis (Jejeniwa et al. 2024), proving to be a valuable tool for meticulously reviewing and analyzing supporting documents such as lease contracts, surpassing the precision levels of the average human reviewer. For leases, information on guaranteed versus unguaranteed residual values and interest rates inherent in the lease affect the measurement of leases in the financial statements and by using machine learning, an appropriate interpretation of the lease agreement can be made, using a consistent method on all lease contracts. In recalculating the value of investments, machine learning can analyze extensive sets of daily investment security pricing data, having the potential to uncover fluctuations in prices that may not have ordinarily been discerned through human observation. Robotic process automation can be helpful and instrumental in streamlining external confirmations for auditors, providing seamless access to crucial information for use in audit procedures. Traditionally, external confirmations to banks or lender were initiated via email or telephonically, while in the AI domain, due to technological advancements, bank confirmations can be easily accessed through confirmations.com, a robotic process automation tool connecting financial service providers in South Africa with their clients. This audit tool driven by technological advancements streamlines what used to be a highly manual and repetitive task in the audit procedures for the existence and valuations of bank and cash.

4.5   Inspection/Observations

"Inspection involves an examination (being physically present or using remote observation tools) of an asset or an examination of records or documents, whether internal or external, in paper form, digital form, or other media." —ISA 500.

The challenges with such procedures are even more significant when the audit is done manually, as sampling increases the risk of undetected material misstatements. Traditionally, inspections were easy to perform when applied to a handful of supporting documents. The auditor would inspect and draw conclusions on the selected few items resulting in increased bias and subjectivity. Using AI such as NLP, drawing conclusions on large volumes of unstructured and multiple sources can add significant effectiveness and value to the audit process. NLP is capable of extracting information from various sources and can assist analysts to derive meaningful insights, which can be particularly beneficial in the audit of aspects that have a high degree of uncertainty associated with complex estimates such as employee compensation schemes. Complex accounting estimates are by nature subjective due to the use of forward-looking data, incorporating various difficult-to-verify inputs and assumptions. In the modern-day audit environment auditors can leverage AI tools using algorithms to access a large data from multiple varying sources, which will strengthen the auditor's ability to evaluate the reasonability and appropriateness of the valuation of complex transaction and balances to support their audit work or their reliance on the work of experts. NLP can effectively analyze and understand human language by extracting specific information from contracts and legal documents and has, for example, the capability to review board minutes and identify noteworthy or potentially risky elements that might be on interest to the auditor.

The use of NLP poses unintended ethical challenges and risk, as the analysis of unstructured data involves transferring client information onto various technological platforms, and in the event that data is transferred without adequate safeguards or with minimal due diligence, the firm may be at risk of experiencing data breaches. The various implications of a breach can have a negative impact on the firm's reputation and non-compliances to data privacy legislation. As the auditor is entrusted with sensitive information during the audit process, it is imperative that this confidential information remains secure and protected. Disclosure to third parties is strictly prohibited without the client's explicit consent, unless mandated by legal or professional obligations. This commitment to confidentiality ensures a relationship of trust and integrity between the auditor and the client.

AI can be valuable in evaluating the design and implementation of control processes for the client. Controls over journal entries can be assessed by comparing individuals authorized to initiate or approve journal entries to the individuals processing the entries on the systems, which will reveal possible misstatement due to fraud. As a result, audit procedures where journals are inspected for preparer/reviewer signature could be improved if integrated with NLP to draw insights on possible abuse of power. This analysis will significantly enhance our comprehension of the specific characteristics and makeup of all journal entries, providing a more reliable indicator of operational effectiveness. Similarly, during the stock count process, auditors have the option to utilize drones for observing and monitoring their clients' inventory (IRBA 2022). Utilizing these technologies allows the auditor to ask more insightful questions and engage more effectively with executives, boards of directors and audit committees, proving the audit process to be valuable and of high quality.

The use of critical thinking and professional skepticism remains essential in evaluating the sufficiency, appropriateness, and reliability of the audit evidence generated by the automated tools. Furthermore, it is crucial to thoroughly scrutinize any conflicting audit evidence that has been gathered before making conclusions regarding the validity of the audit evidence obtained through the use of AI-driven audit tools.

4.6   Reperformance

Reperformance is an audit procedure where the auditor independently replicates an activity that the audit client has done as part of the client's internal control system. Gone are the days of laborious data and reconciliation processes performed by auditors which demanded extensive manual effort. AI-driven automation now enables auditors to reperform these processes with remarkable speed and precision by automating previously labor-intensive reconciliations. Traditionally the reconciliation process would involve manually sifting through spreadsheets containing hundreds of records and pivot tables, which consumed a significant amount of time, but with the implementation of automation, the reconciliation time is drastically reduced from many hours to just a matter of minutes, not only saving time but also increased operational efficiency (IRBA 2022). This efficiency gain translates into more streamlined auditing workflows, allowing the audit teams to allocate their time and expertise to higher-value activities such as exercising professional skepticism and judgment in analyzing output from the various AI tools employed during the audit process. The benefits encompass reduction in human errors and extend beyond as it allows for innovative mindsets to respond to changing business environments.

Overall, assurance professionals liberated from desktop tasks can significantly contribute to promoting stakeholder confidence, unlocking value through data-driven insights and efficiencies (Rkein et al. 2019).

5 Concluding and Reporting Stage (ISA 700)

Throughout the audit, the auditor designs audit procedures to respond to the risk of material misstatements. Due to advancements in technology, these procedures now involve obtaining audit evidence and performing testing that incorporates AI. Once audit evidence is gathered, the auditor is in a position to evaluate the sufficiency and appropriateness of the audit evidence as a basis for forming an opinion on the true and fair view of the information presented in the financial statements. Forming an opinion on the financial statements is encapsulated in the overall objectives of an audit, being the last step in the audit process referred to as concluding and reporting. This stage allows auditors to reflect on the audit by assessing whether the financial information is consistent with their knowledge of the business including IT related matters. The audit evidence obtained enables the auditor to form an opinion on the financial statements. The crucial part of this stage is issuing the client with an auditor's report and auditor's opinion.

5.1 Evaluating Misstatements

There are three categories of misstatements being factual, judgmental, and projected misstatements. The last type of misstatement, namely projected misstatements arise where the auditor did not test the full population but rather a selected a sample, and there being a misstatement in the selected sample. In this case, the auditor would have to extrapolate the error to estimate what the misstatement will be in the entire population. AI tools and techniques are used to extrapolate the error to the full population taking into account the different characteristics that could apply to the set of information the auditor is projecting. Data analytics and machine learning can improve projecting misstatements and ultimately fraud detection in the population by harnessing the power of data analytics to gain a deeper insight into the characteristics of the client's population (Mpofu 2023). This involves integrating data from various sources within the environment and operations, resulting in enhanced efficiency and accuracy of the auditors' projections of misstatements. Taking revenue as an example, if the auditor finds misstatements in revenue occurrence—where some transactions did not meet IFRS recognition requirements—data analytics employing deep learning can identify all other transactions with similar characteristics that the clients may have invalidly recorded.

5.2 Events after the Reporting Period

As part of the concluding and reporting process, the auditor carefully monitors any significant events that occur after the reporting period. This is done to ensure that all relevant developments are taken into account when issuing the audit opinion to stakeholders. The auditor can explore the potential use of machine learning for ongoing pattern recognition of transactions processed after the reporting period. Leveraging AI provides valuable support for continuous monitoring after the audit has been concluded but before the signing of the audit report.

5.3 Going Concern

In accounting, financial statements are prepared with the assumption that the entity is a going concern and will continue its operations for the foreseeable future. This is the basis on which the auditor issues the audit report unless indicated otherwise in the audit opinion and accordingly the auditor would thus need to consider the appropriateness of the going concern basis. Traditionally, management will present the auditors with their assessment of going concern for a period of at least 5 years into the future normally including both financial and non-financial data and analysis. Machine learning algorithms, leveraging techniques such as clustering and classification, can sift through vast amounts of financial data to uncover hidden correlations and trends. For example, by leveraging advanced data analysis techniques, we can accurately pinpoint specific trends in consumer spending behavior, fluctuations in the market, and inefficiencies in our operational processes (Hasan 2022). This not only enhances the reasonability checks on management's going concern assessment and analysis but also provides a deeper understanding of the factors influencing future performance. This can thus be used in assessing the appropriateness of the use of management's assumption that an entity is a going concern as defined in IFRS.

5.4 Timely Reporting for Group Audits

NLP has the capability to effectively categorize and group information and this can be particularly beneficial in the context of group audits, where multiple companies come together to form group entities. In group audits, communication is key between clients and competent auditors to allow for the ultimate signing and reporting on consolidated annual financial statements. Using visualization software can make auditing more efficient for groups or entities with multiple operating centers with the further use of software that can help improve communication with clients by creating control boards that present regular updates on the status of the audit. These dashboards utilize visualization software to display audit status data graphically, enabling component auditors and clients to visualize outstanding tasks or data and identify the responsible parties. Harnessing the power of dashboards provides real-time visualization of group audit progress and can assist in meeting crucial deadlines for issuing audit reports to stakeholders.

6   Conclusion

As we continue to operate in one of the most modern times where AI is revolutionizing industries with its speed and diverse applications, auditors must adapt to serve the public interest by continuing with robust audits to meet the requirements of the IAASB. Due to the increased use of AI to meet institutional objectives and strategies in the twenty-first century, auditors need to change traditional approaches of audit methodology and processes to continually provide appropriate and relevant value adding assurance services to their various clients. The most notable impact of AI is improved audit quality by enhancing anomaly and fraud detection, risk assessment, and enabling human workers to focus on more complex and high-risk areas. The impact of AI in audit processes extends beyond audit quality, it creates more well-rounded professionals that can work alongside technology and vastly increases auditors' engagement in their work as critical thinkers. Lack of clear policy guidelines, ethical and responsible use related to AI applications in audits remain a concern. Auditors should leverage their advanced technical skills and extensive expertise in accounting to streamline processes in a digitally enhanced environment to offer a top-tier audit experience.

Our study, through literature review, aims to facilitate the approach that auditors and academics adapt to unpack and understand how AI affects the audit process. The use of audit process stages as outlined by the ISAs is fundamental in aligning how an auditor could potentially respond to the adoption of AI by businesses. Our study points out that, in each stage of the audit, there are various components that could be affected by AI.

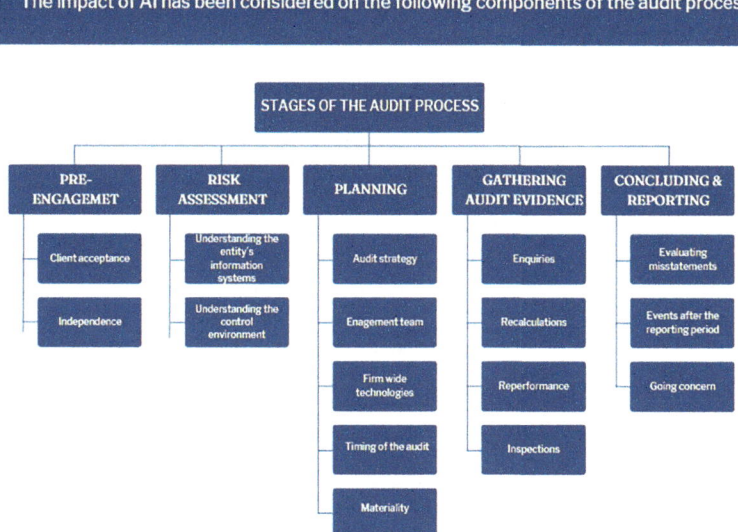

The impact of AI has been considered on the following components of the audit process

STAGES OF THE AUDIT PROCESS

PRE-ENGAGEMET	RISK ASSESSMENT	PLANNING	GATHERING AUDIT EVIDENCE	CONCLUDING & REPORTING

In order to be able to respond to the changing times ahead, audit practitioners and academics need to upskill on critical thinking and exhibit heightened professional skepticism due to the complexities of AI. As noted in its broad definition, AI is a formidable, interrelated computer technology encompassing speech-image recognition, language processing, and data mining. A future fit audit practitioner will not only be expected to exhibit proficiencies in accounting technical knowledge, but the related technologies used by businesses including AI. In the year 2023, the abilities to think analytically and creatively are vital skills for employees in various industries (World Economic Forum 2023). The Independent Regulatory Board for Auditors notes that audit firms have started to significantly invest in AI tools to enable them to offer relevant and best services to their clients (IRBA 2022). The future of the auditing profession relies heavily on Artificial Intelligence technologies. As technology evolves and new auditing approaches develop, the importance of a specific AI audit tool and technique and its relative advantages may change. The considerations provided in this study are not a comprehensive list of all possible implications of AI on the various elements of each stage of the audit process.

References

Agrawal A, Gans JS, Goldfarb A (2017, January 7). What to expect from Artificial Intelligence
Bao Y, Ke B, Li B, Yu JY, Zhang J (2020a) Detecting accounting fraud in publicly traded US firms using a machine learning approach. J Account Res 58:199–235

Bao Y, Ke B, Li B, Yu J, Zhang J (2020b) Detecting accounting fraud in publicly traded U.S. firms using a machine learning approach. J Account Res 58(1):199–235

Brown N, Crowley R, Elliott B (2020) What are you saying? Using topic to detect financial misreporting. J Account Res 58(1):237–291

Cooper L, Holderness K, Sorensen T, Wood D (2019) Robotic process automation in public accounting. Account Horiz 33(4):15–35

Coskun Arslan M, Demirkan S (2017) Auditing and assurance services. Journal of Accounting & Finance 128

Deloitte (2024) *Automating-audit-processes.* https://www2.deloitte.com/us/en/pages/about-deloitte/articles/automating-audit-processes

Elliott RK (1998) Assurance services and the audit heritage. Certified public accountant. The CPA Journal 68(6):40

EY (2024a) *How big data and analytics are transforming the audit.* https://assets.ey.com/content/dam/ey-sites/ey-com/en_gl/topics/assurance/assurance-pdfs/ey-reporting-big-data-transform-audit.pdf?download

EY (2024b) *How-an-ai-application-can-help-auditors-detect-fraud.* https://www.ey.com/en_ae/insights/assurance/how-an-ai-application-can-help-auditors-detect-fraud

Hasan AR (2022) Artificial intelligence (AI) in Accounting & Auditing: A literature review. J Bus Manag 10(1):440–465

International Auditing and Assurance Standards Board (2019) *isa-315-first-time-implementation-guide.* Retrieved from www.iaasb.org: https://www.iaasb.org/publications/isa-315-first-time-implementation-guide

IRBA (2022) Public inspections report. The Independent Regulatory Board for Auditors, Johannesburg

Issa H, Sun T, Vasarhelyi MA (2016) Research ideas for artificial intelligence in auditing: the formalization of audit and workforce supplementation. J Emerg Technol Account 13(2):1–20

Jejeniwa TO, Mhlongo NZ, Jejeniwa TO (2024) A comprehensive review of the impact of artificial intelligence on modern accounting practices and financial reporting. *Computer Science & IT Research 5*, 1031–1047. https://doi.org/10.51594/csitrj.v5i4.1086

Kend M, Nguyen L (2022) The emergence of audit data analytics in existing audit spaces: findings from three technologically advanced audit and assurance service markets. Qual Res Account Manag 19(5):540–563

Kommunuri J (2022) Artificial intelligence and the changing landscape of accounting: a viewpoint. Pac Account Rev 34(4):585–594

Kuo T-C, Smith S (2018) A systematic review of technologies involving eco-innovation for enterprises moving towards sustainability. J Clean Prod 192:207–220

Maroun W (2018) Modifying assurance practices to meet the needs of integrated reporting the case for "interpretive assurance". Account Audit Account J 31(2):400–427

Mpofu FY (2023) The application of artificial intelligence in external auditing and its implications on audit quality? A review of the ongoing debates. Res Bus Soc Sci 12(9):496–512

Munoko I, Brown-Liburd HL, Vasarhelyi M (2020) The ethical implications of using artificial intelligence in auditing. J Bus Ethics 167(2):209–234

PwC (2024, October 15) *How auditors combine tech know-how and finance skills to drive innovation.* https://www.pwc.com/us/en/tech-effect/automation/audit-technology-and-digital-skills.html

Quick R, Zaman M, Mandalawattha G (2023) Auditors' application of materiality: insight from the UK. Account Forum 47(1):24–46

Rkein H, Issa Z, Awada F, Hejase H (2019) Impact of automation on accounting profession and employability: A qualitative assessment from Lebanon. Saudi J Bus Manag Stud 4(2):372–385

Rosner RL, Comunale CL, Sexton TR (2006) Assessing materiality. CPA J 76(6):26

Schneider S, Leyer M (2019) Me or information technology? Adoption of artificial intelligence in the delegation of personal strategic decisions. Manag Decis Econ 40(3):223–231

Seethamraju R, Hecimovic A (2020) Impact of artificial intelligence on auditing—an exploratory study. In: Americas conference on information systems (AMCIS) 2020 proceedings. AIS Electronic Library, Sydney, p 8

Sobel P, Reding K (2004) Aligning corporate governance with enterprise risk management. Manag Account Q 5(2):29–37

The 2000–2001 Auditing Section Education Committee American Accounting Association (2003) Challenges to audit education for the 21st century, a survey of Curricula, Course Content and Delivery Methods. *Issues in Accounting Education*, 241–263

The International Auditing and Assurance Standards Board (2024) 2022–2023 public report: balancing effectiveness and timeliness in audit and assurance standard setting. Public Interest Oversight Board, New York

Williams E, Neha M, Matt G (2024, October 09) Using AI to unleash the power of unstructured government data https://www2.deloitte.com/content/dam/insights/us/articles/4815_AI-unstructured-data/DI_AI-unstructured-government-data.pdf

Wirtz BW, Müller WM (2019) An integrated artificial intelligence framework for public management. Public Manag Rev 21(7):1076–1100

World Economic Forum (2023) Future of jobs report. World Economic Forum, Geneva

Zemánková A (2019) Artificial intelligence and blockchain in audit and accounting: Literature review. wseas Transactions on Business and Economics, 16(1), pp.568–581

Integration of Artificial Intelligence into Taxation Processes

Adesanmi Timothy Adegbayibi and Mohammed Kayode Ajape

Abstract The growing complexity of tax regulations and the expanding volume of data have made traditional tax processes increasingly inadequate to address modern demands, even as artificial intelligence (AI) becomes globally integrated. Existing studies demonstrate that AI holds significant potential to enhance tax compliance, improve the accuracy of assessments, and streamline administrative functions. This chapter examines the integration of artificial intelligence (AI) and taxation, highlighting the transformative potential of AI technologies in enhancing tax administration and compliance. This chapter discusses how AI can be leveraged to streamline tax compliance, improve accuracy in tax assessments, and enhance fraud detection. This chapter adopts a conceptual methodological approach, featuring an extensive literature review of relevant studies on artificial intelligence (AI) and taxation. By analyzing current applications of AI in global tax systems, the chapter highlights the advantages of automation, predictive analytics, and machine learning in alleviating the administrative burden on both tax authorities and taxpayers. Additionally, it examines the challenges and ethical considerations related to AI implementation in tax practices, including data privacy and security, the risk of algorithmic bias, and the absence of regulatory frameworks governing AI usage in tax systems. Many tax authorities also encounter resistance to change, limited technological infrastructure, and a shortage of skilled personnel necessary for effectively utilizing AI tools. Therefore, there is an urgent need to explore effective strategies for integrating AI into taxation practices while addressing these challenges to promote a fair, efficient, and transparent tax system. This chapter concludes that the adoption of artificial intelligence (AI) in taxation will enhance efficiency while fostering greater transparency and trust in the tax system. This chapter seeks to contribute to the ongoing discourse regarding the significance of AI in tax processes, offering stakeholders a clearer understanding to proactively embrace these changes.

A. T. Adegbayibi (✉) · M. K. Ajape
Department of Accountancy, University of Johannesburg, Johannesburg, South Africa
e-mail: aadegbayibi@uj.ac.za; majape@uj.ac.za

© The Author(s), under exclusive license to Springer Nature
Switzerland AG 2025
M. Adelowotan, C. A. Leke (eds.), *Artificial Intelligence in Accounting, Auditing and Finance*, Contributions to Finance and Accounting,
https://doi.org/10.1007/978-3-031-87368-3_7

Keywords Artificial Intelligence · Taxation · Tax compliance · Fraud detection · Predictive analytics · Regulatory frameworks

1 Introduction

The taxation landscape has undergone significant changes in recent years, largely driven by technological advancements, particularly the integration of Artificial Intelligence (AI). The increasing complexity of tax regulations, the rise of digital transactions, and the expansion of data analytics have prompted a reevaluation of traditional tax processes (Adha et al. 2024; Belahouaoui and Attak 2024; Frommelt 2024; Kimani et al. 2024). Traditional tax administration, which relies heavily on manual processes and human oversight, often struggles to keep pace with the demands of a global economy. In this context, AI offers a promising solution by enhancing tax compliance, improving assessment accuracy, and streamlining administrative tasks, ultimately leading to a more efficient and transparent tax system (African Tax Administration Forum (ATAF) 2021).

The modern tax environment poses multifaceted challenges. Governments must ensure compliance among a diverse taxpayer base while managing vast amounts of financial data. The complexities of tax regulations, which vary across jurisdictions, hinder effective compliance monitoring and accurate assessments (Institute of Electrical and Electronics Engineers (IEEE) 2019). As businesses evolve and employ sophisticated financial strategies, robust and proactive tax administration mechanisms become essential. Additionally, the sheer volume of data generated today can overwhelm traditional tax systems that rely on human intervention. Tax authorities must adopt innovative solutions for real-time data processing, anomaly detection, and decision-making. Herein lies AI's promise: a technology capable of swiftly analyzing massive datasets and identifying patterns that may elude human oversight (PricewaterhouseCoopers (PwC) 2017).

1.1 Overview of Artificial Intelligence

Artificial Intelligence (AI) refers to the capability of a machine to imitate intelligent human behavior. AI encompasses a range of technologies that enable machines to perform tasks that typically require human intelligence, including learning, reasoning, problem-solving, perception, and language understanding (Adha et al. 2024; Popovič and Sábo 2021; Zaqeeba 2024). As the simulation of human intelligence processes by machines, particularly computer systems, AI covers a multitude of technologies, including machine learning, natural language processing, and robotics, each contributing uniquely to various sectors, including taxation. As these technologies evolve, their application extends to various fields such as healthcare, automotive, finance, and public administration (Fig. 1).

The evolution of artificial intelligence (AI) has significantly impacted taxation, progressing from the foundational concepts of the 1950s, where AI began emulating human intelligence, to the 1980s, which saw the rise of machine learning systems analyzing historical tax data for improved compliance. In the 2010s, deep learning introduced sophisticated neural networks capable of identifying patterns and detecting tax fraud. Currently, in the 2020s, generative AI is transforming the field by creating original insights and personalized tax solutions. This evolution highlights how AI enhances tax processes and decision-making in the modern era (IEEE 2019).

Machine learning, a key subset of AI, enables systems to learn from data patterns and improve performance over time without explicit programming, while natural language processing facilitates interactions between taxpayers and tax authorities (Coita et al. 2023; Strak and Tuszynski 2022). As tax authorities recognize AI's potential, innovations such as predictive analytics for compliance monitoring, fraud detection models, and chatbots for taxpayer inquiries have emerged, enhancing operational efficiency and enabling proactive responses to real-time changes. AI is reshaping various sectors by addressing inefficiencies and promoting a more equitable tax framework through data-driven decision-making, allowing for quick and accurate analysis of vast datasets. Predictive analytics helps identify high-risk sectors, improving enforcement strategies, and AI tools provide real-time assistance to taxpayers, fostering collaborative relationships with tax authorities. However, integrating AI into tax administration necessitates careful consideration of ethical implications and potential challenges.

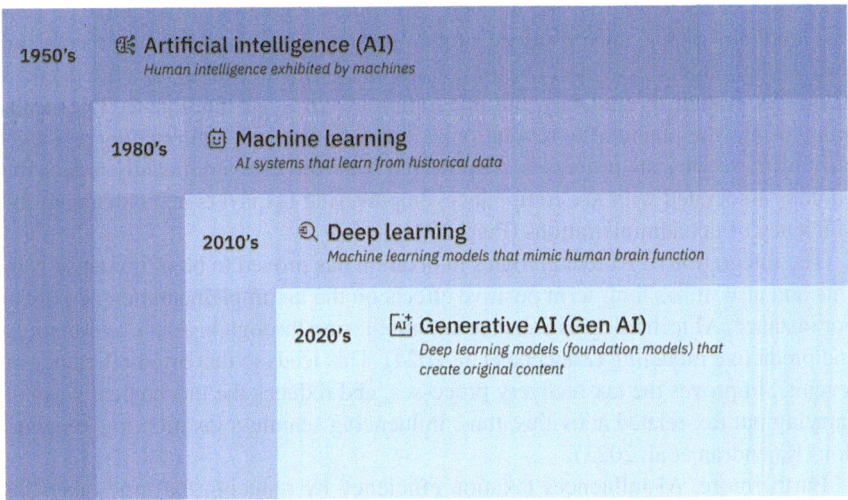

Fig. 1 Evolution of Artificial Intelligence: A timeline of key developments. *Source:* https://www.ibm.com/topics/artificial-intelligence

1.2   Significance of AI in Taxation

Taxation is a cornerstone of governance, providing essential revenue for public services and infrastructure. However, tax compliance faces challenges such as complex regulations, manual processing inefficiencies, and significant administrative burdens. In regions like Africa, where tax revenue is crucial for development but remains low, the adoption of technology, particularly AI, can drive substantial improvements. Yet, integrating AI into tax administration comes with challenges, including data privacy, algorithmic bias, and potential job displacement within tax agencies. For AI systems to be effective and equitable, they must be developed with a focus on ethics and accountability. Establishing clear regulatory frameworks based on global best practices is essential to mitigate these concerns (Deloitte 2020).

As governments in different parts of the globe seek to leverage AI's benefits in taxation, understanding its implications becomes increasingly urgent. This discussion examines how AI can streamline compliance, enhance accuracy in assessments, automate data processing, and create a more efficient, equitable tax environment (International Monetary Fund (IMF) 2021). By learning from global experiences and best practices, the potential for AI to transform taxation into a more effective governance tool can be fully realized (Deloitte 2020).

2   The Role of Artificial Intelligence in Tax Administration

Navigating the complexities of tax compliance can be a daunting task for both taxpayers and tax authorities. Traditional tax compliance often requires individuals and businesses to meticulously sift through convoluted regulations, manually process vast amounts of data, and ensure accurate reporting. This cumbersome process can lead to confusion, errors, and frustration, ultimately undermining the effectiveness of the tax system. Fortunately, the integration of Artificial Intelligence (AI) technologies has the potential to revolutionize tax compliance by automating and simplifying these intricate processes. AI-powered solutions can significantly reduce the burdens associated with tax compliance, empowering taxpayers and enhancing the efficiency of tax administrations (PwC 2021).

The integration of AI technologies in taxation has proved to be of immense benefits and also, it has long-term positive effects on the tax implementation activities. For instance, AI technologies enhance tax monitoring through big data, automation, and predictive modeling (Zaqeeba et al. 2024). This leads to increased efficiency of revenue, improves the tax recovery processes, and reduces the mechanical ways of carrying out tax-related activities, thus, influencing seamless taxation implementation (Rajendran et al. 2023).

Furthermore, AI influences taxation efficiency by reducing the time taken for tax-related activities. Thus, maximizing the tax time (Wang and Wang 2020). Activities are easily conducted within a limited time frame, and large tax-related activities for several individuals can be completed at minimum time. This reduces the time-based efficiency experienced by the traditional taxation structures which depends majorly on human activities.

2.1 Streamlining Tax Compliance

AI can streamline tax compliance through automated tools that help taxpayers understand and fulfill their obligations. Chatbots and virtual assistants provide real-time guidance, answering queries and simplifying complex regulations into easy-to-understand language, which aids in accurate return submissions (Smith 2023). AI algorithms analyze historical compliance data to identify patterns, enabling tax authorities to proactively flag potential non-compliance issues. By using predictive analytics, tax administrations can create targeted outreach programs for taxpayers at risk of non-compliance, enhancing voluntary compliance and building trust in the tax system (Johnson 2023).

Additionally, AI-driven data analysis offers insights into taxpayer behavior and compliance trends. By uncovering patterns in large datasets, AI helps tax authorities understand the motivations and challenges of different taxpayer segments, informing more effective compliance strategies. For example, analyzing payment histories allows authorities to identify taxpayers needing extra support. This targeted understanding enables tailored assistance programs, ensuring compliant taxpayers are not overburdened while helping those struggling to meet their obligations. The integration of AI-powered chatbots, virtual assistants, and predictive analytics can significantly improve the taxpayer experience, making it more efficient and reducing the administrative burden on both taxpayers and tax authorities (OECD 2021; World Bank 2020).

Moreover, AI enhances fraud detection and error reduction by automating data verification and integrating blockchain technology. Advanced analytics and machine learning techniques help tax authorities monitor, detect, and predict unethical behaviors. For example, profiling tools identify discrepancies in tax filings, enabling swift corrective actions (Zadeh et al. 2023). These tools promote compliance with constitutional regulations by reducing errors and curbing fraudulent activities (Pica 2021, 2024).

AI also contributes to fairness in tax calculations, ensuring tax laws are upheld while minimizing costs associated with compliance. By simplifying tax processes and offering real-time guidance, AI influences taxpayer decision-making and encourages adherence to tax obligations (Saragih et al. 2023). Personalized communication between tax authorities and taxpayers further enhances the experience, making compliance more efficient and user-friendly.

In summary, AI-driven innovations such as predictive analytics, blockchain integration, and real-time assistance tools significantly improve tax compliance by reducing administrative burdens, enhancing accuracy, and fostering trust between taxpayers and authorities.

2.2 Enhancing Accuracy in Tax Assessments

Accurate tax assessments are fundamental to a well-functioning tax system. However, traditional processes often rely on historical data and manual evaluations, which can introduce human error, bias, and inconsistencies (Li 2020). The integration of artificial intelligence (AI), particularly through machine learning models, offers transformative solutions to these challenges (Rajendran et al. 2023).

AI systems excel in analyzing large and complex datasets, quickly identifying anomalies and discrepancies that may signify errors or fraud (Siham and Mohammed 2024). Using advanced pattern recognition algorithms, these models detect subtle inconsistencies often missed during manual reviews, significantly improving the reliability of tax assessments. AI also mitigates issues such as discrimination and legal misinterpretation, ensuring fair application of tax laws across different societal segments (Peeters 2024). By bridging gaps created by human misjudgment, AI promotes fairness, upholding equitable treatment and contributing to a more just society.

In addition to enhancing accuracy, AI bolsters transparency within the tax system. Its ability to process extensive datasets enables comprehensive analyses of taxpayers' financial profiles and transaction histories, surpassing the limitations of traditional sampling methods. AI evaluates entire datasets, allowing tax authorities to prioritize audits effectively. This ensures compliant taxpayers are not unduly burdened while focusing efforts on high-risk cases (Smith 2023).

By reducing human bias in assessments, AI fosters trust in the tax system. Impartial evaluations enhance the credibility of tax administration, reinforcing the social contract between citizens and government. Furthermore, AI's capacity to ensure fairness and transparency strengthens taxpayer confidence, promoting voluntary compliance and improving the overall efficiency of tax governance (Yordanova 2024).

Therefore, AI represents a powerful tool for enhancing the accuracy, fairness, and transparency of tax assessments. By addressing limitations inherent in traditional processes, AI not only improves the reliability of tax evaluations but also reinforces public trust in the tax system.

2.3 Ethical Considerations and Responsible AI Implementation

As AI integration in tax administration accelerates, addressing ethical considerations and potential risks becomes essential. While AI can improve tax compliance and automate data processing, biases may arise from training data, algorithms, and developers' assumptions, leading to unfair treatment of specific taxpayer groups (Johnson 2022). To mitigate these risks, tax administrations should prioritize ethical AI frameworks focusing on transparency, accountability, and fairness. This includes involving diverse perspectives in AI design, conducting regular audits for bias, and providing clear explanations of how these systems operate to build taxpayer trust and reinforce the legitimacy of the tax system. Additionally, safeguarding taxpayer privacy and ensuring robust data security are critical as AI technologies handle sensitive financial information (Thompson 2023).

Collaboration between tax administrations and AI service providers is expected to grow, leveraging private sector expertise to develop innovative shared services and cross-border compliance solutions (Roberts 2022). As societies face twenty-first-century economic and social challenges, AI's role in tax administration will expand. By enhancing compliance processes, improving assessment accuracy, and promoting ethical AI practices, tax authorities can create a more equitable tax system. Furthermore, addressing AI's impact on the workforce through proactive engagement and upskilling programs will be vital in mitigating job displacement risks.

3 AI Applications in Taxation

Taxation is a fundamental aspect of any government's fiscal policy, providing the necessary resources to fund public services and drive economic growth. However, ensuring tax compliance has long been a challenge for tax administrations worldwide. In recent years, the emergence of advanced technologies, particularly predictive analytics, has transformed the landscape of tax compliance, enabling tax authorities to enhance their understanding of taxpayer behavior and proactively address the risk of non-compliance (Taylor 2023).

This section delves into the applications of predictive analytics in the realm of taxation, exploring how tax authorities can leverage historical data, statistical algorithms, and machine learning to forecast future compliance outcomes. The discussion highlights the benefits of this approach, the challenges involved, and the potential future directions in this rapidly evolving field.

3.1 Predictive Analytics for Tax Compliance

Predictive analytics plays a crucial role in modern tax administration by leveraging historical data and statistical algorithms to forecast future outcomes (Zaqeeba 2024). This approach enhances tax compliance and enables tax authorities to make informed decisions based on empirical evidence. By analyzing taxpayer behavior and identifying patterns that correlate with compliance risks, predictive analytics becomes a powerful tool for ensuring adherence to tax regulations and improving revenue collection (Johnson 2023). At its core, it involves collecting and analyzing data from various sources, including past tax filings, economic indicators, and demographic information. Utilizing advanced statistical techniques and machine learning algorithms, tax authorities can gain insights into taxpayer behavior, fore-casting which taxpayers are likely to comply and which may pose a risk of non-compliance.

The early detection of potential non-compliance is vital in tax administration. Predictive analytics tools allow tax authorities to systematically monitor filing behaviors and detect early signs of deviation from expected compliance patterns. For example, if a taxpayer suddenly changes their filing frequency or claims unusually large expenses, predictive models can flag these anomalies for further investigation. By identifying risks early, tax authorities can intervene proactively, providing support to taxpayers before issues escalate (Smith 2023).

3.2   Challenges and Considerations

Despite the benefits of predictive analytics, challenges arise in its implementation. One major challenge is the data collection and integration process. Tax authorities often face disparate data systems and varying data quality, necessitating standard-ized data management practices to ensure accuracy (Miller 2023). Additionally, ethical considerations around privacy and data protection must be addressed. The collection and analysis of taxpayer data should be transparent and responsible, adhering to legal standards. Fostering public trust is essential; agencies should clearly communicate their data practices and reassure taxpayers about the protec-tion of their personal information (Wong and Harris 2023a, 2023b, 2023c). Other challenges associated with AI and taxation are the regulatory gaps and a lack of adequate skilled personnel to operate the AI innovative technologies in taxation (Saragih et al. 2023). Poor implementation of the AI infrastructure is also a major challenge that might be encountered which affects the system integration structure and data readiness (Li and Zhu 2021).

3.3   Future Directions in Predictive Analytics
for Tax Compliance

Looking ahead, predictive analytics in tax compliance will likely evolve with advances in AI and data analytics technology. Future implementations may involve more sophisticated machine learning models capable of recognizing intricate pat-terns in taxpayer behavior, providing insights into motivations behind actions to develop effective outreach programs (Jones 2023). Collaboration between tax authorities and data scientists can enhance the precision of predictive analytics. By investing in data science talent and partnering with tech firms, tax agencies can improve their analytical capabilities, leading to innovative solutions for complex compliance issues.

Moreover, integrating real-time data analytics into tax compliance is a promising development. Improved technological infrastructure may enable tax authorities to continuously monitor transactions and taxpayer behaviors, allowing for swift responses to emerging compliance risks. Predictive analytics significantly enhances tax compliance by forecasting potential risks based on historical data and behavioral patterns. The South African Revenue Service's implementation of these strategies illustrates the profound impact of predictive analytics on compliance rates and taxpayer collaboration (South African Revenue Service (SARS) 2020). Despite challenges in data management and ethics, the future of predictive analytics in taxation appears promising. As technology advances, tax authorities that embrace these innovations will be better equipped to ensure compliance and optimize revenue collection (OECD 2021).

3.4   Chatbots and Virtual Assistants in Tax Services

In recent years, chatbots and virtual assistants have transformed taxpayer interactions with tax authorities by providing immediate support and guidance. These AI-driven tools, utilizing natural language processing (NLP), streamline communication by addressing common inquiries related to filing procedures, payment options, and eligibility for deductions, significantly reducing the workload on human tax officers. A notable example is the Canada Revenue Agency's (CRA) virtual assistant, "Emily," which facilitates real-time interaction and answers questions on various topics, improving responsiveness and accessibility, especially during peak tax season. The implementation of chatbots in tax services reflects a broader trend toward digital transformation in public administration, allowing tax authorities to streamline processes, reduce operational costs, and enhance overall efficiency (OECD 2020). Automated assistance enables tax officials to focus on strategic initiatives, such as analyzing compliance data and conducting risk assessments, which strengthens taxpayer relationships and encourages higher levels of compliance (PwC 2021; Deloitte 2020).

Despite their advantages, chatbots face challenges regarding the range of inquiries they can effectively address. While they excel at handling frequently asked questions, more nuanced inquiries requiring a deeper understanding of tax law may pose difficulties. To overcome this, tax authorities should continually update their chatbot algorithms and knowledge bases (Smith 2023). Ensuring user-friendly and accessible interfaces is also crucial to overcoming barriers related to language differences or disabilities. Future developments may involve integrating chatbots with technologies like machine learning and predictive analytics, enabling them to anticipate taxpayer needs and proactively provide information, thus enhancing satisfaction and fostering collaborative relationships (Johnson 2023).

4   Case Studies

The integration of artificial intelligence (AI) technologies into tax administration systems has emerged as a global trend, transforming the way tax authorities interact with data, identify patterns, and enforce compliance. This section explores several case studies that illustrate the successful implementation of AI in tax systems around the world. By closely examining the experiences of leading tax agencies, such as the Internal Revenue Service (IRS) in the United States, HM Revenue and Customs (HMRC) in the United Kingdom, the South African Revenue Service (SARS), the Australian Taxation Office (ATO), and the Federal Inland Revenue Service (FIRS) in Nigeria, we can gain invaluable insights into the best practices and strategies for effective AI adoption. Additionally, the chapter discusses the critical lessons learned from these case studies, highlighting the importance of data quality, interdisciplinary collaboration, continuous monitoring and evaluation, and transparent communication with taxpayers.

4.1   *United States—Internal Revenue Service (IRS)*

The Internal Revenue Service (IRS) in the United States has been increasingly embracing AI-enhanced data analytics to boost audit efficiency and improve compliance rates. Utilizing sophisticated algorithms to analyze tax return data in conjunction with external data sources, the IRS can identify and prioritize cases that warrant further examination. The agency's adoption of these cutting-edge technologies has been a game-changer, allowing them to streamline their operations and better target potential areas of non-compliance. "The AI systems we've implemented have been a real asset in our efforts to ensure that everyone pays their fair share," says the IRS Commissioner. "By automating certain tasks and identifying high-risk cases, we're able to allocate our resources more effectively and make the most of our limited budget" (Miller 2023).

4.2   *United Kingdom—HM Revenue and Customs (HMRC)*

Another leading example of AI implementation in tax administration can be seen with HM Revenue and Customs (HMRC) in the United Kingdom. HMRC has actively embraced AI solutions to enhance the accuracy of tax assessments and reduce fraudulent claims, particularly concerning Value Added Tax (VAT). "The ability to quickly analyze massive datasets and spot anomalies has been a game-changer for us," explains the HMRC Chief Data Officer. "By using machine learning algorithms, we've been able to catch more instances of VAT fraud and ensure that taxpayers are paying the right amount" (Jones 2023). The agency's ongoing investment in AI technologies has not only strengthened their enforcement capabilities but has also helped to streamline the tax filing process for compliant taxpayers.

4.3   South Africa—The South African Revenue Service (SARS)

In South Africa, the South African Revenue Service (SARS) has recognized the transformative potential of predictive analytics in tax administration. SARS has begun incorporating these sophisticated technologies to enhance compliance rates significantly. "We've seen a noticeable uptick in our ability to identify high-risk taxpayers and target our audits more effectively," says the SARS Commissioner. "The AI models we've developed can detect patterns and anomalies that our human auditors might have missed, allowing us to be more proactive in addressing non-compliance." The agency's commitment to leveraging data-driven insights has been crucial in its efforts to improve tax collection and fairness.

4.4   Australia—The Australian Taxation Office (ATO)

In Australia, the Australian Taxation Office (ATO) has successfully integrated machine learning techniques into its operational framework. By cross-referencing data from various sources, the ATO has significantly improved its capacity for fraud detection. "The ability to quickly analyze and connect data points from different systems has been a game-changer for us," explains the ATO's Chief Technology Officer. "We're now able to identify suspicious activities and potential fraud much more efficiently, which has helped us crack down on tax evasion and ensure that everyone is paying their fair share" (Wong and Harris 2023a, 2023b, 2023c). The ATO's embrace of AI-driven analytics has been a key component of its broader efforts to enhance compliance and maintain the integrity of the tax system.

4.5   Nigeria—The Federal Inland Revenue Service (FIRS)

In Nigeria, the Federal Inland Revenue Service (FIRS) has implemented AI-powered solutions to enhance tax compliance and fraud detection. By leveraging machine learning algorithms, FIRS can analyze taxpayer data patterns, identify potential discrepancies, and streamline the audit process (Johnson 2023). "The AI tools we've implemented have been a real asset in our fight against tax evasion," says the FIRS Executive Chairman. "We're now able to identify suspicious activities and target our resources more effectively, which has resulted in a significant increase in tax collections and a reduction in fraudulent claims" (Miller 2023). The FIRS's innovative use of AI technologies has been a crucial part of its broader strategy to modernize the country's tax administration system and improve overall compliance.

5 Challenges and Limitations in the Integration of AI in Tax Administration

The integration of artificial intelligence (AI) into tax administration represents a significant technological advancement that promises to enhance operational efficiency, improve compliance rates, and facilitate proactive engagement with taxpayers (OECD 2021). However, with these advancements come notable challenges and limitations that must be addressed for AI technologies to be successfully implemented within the complex landscape of tax systems. In this section, we delve into critical challenges related to data privacy and security concerns, algorithmic bias and fairness, and resistance to change within tax authorities. By examining these issues comprehensively, we can identify potential pathways for mitigating their impact and ensuring that the implementation of AI is both effective and ethical.

5.1 Data Privacy and Security Concerns

The integration of AI into tax administration raises significant concerns regarding data privacy and security, as tax authorities manage sensitive personal and financial information from millions of taxpayers, making them prime targets for cyberattacks (Smith 2023). A data breach could lead to severe consequences, including identity theft and financial fraud, undermining taxpayer trust in the system. Therefore, ensuring data protection must be a paramount consideration in AI implementation, as failing to secure personal information can deter compliance and provoke resistance from taxpayers (Jones 2023). Countries like South Africa have enacted comprehensive regulatory frameworks, such as the Protection of Personal Information Act (POPIA), which mandates transparency, accountability, and informed consent in data processing. In addition to these frameworks, tax administrations should implement strong cybersecurity measures, including advanced encryption, multi-factor authentication, and regular security assessments, while also training personnel on data security best practices (Kumar 2023). By prioritizing cybersecurity and legal compliance, tax authorities can better safeguard taxpayer information and promote greater trust in their systems.

5.2   Algorithmic Bias and Fairness

Algorithmic bias represents another critical concern in the application of AI within taxation. As AI systems become increasingly reliant on data-driven decision-making, the quality and composition of the data used to train these algorithms become paramount. If AI models are trained on biased or unrepresentative datasets, they may inadvertently perpetuate existing inequities within the tax system (Nguyen 2023). To effectively address algorithmic bias, tax authorities must continually audit and revise their AI algorithms. Establishing regular review processes that examine the data used for training AI models can help identify potential sources of bias. Moreover, actively seeking out diverse datasets for training initiatives is vital, as this can enhance the robustness and fairness of the resulting algorithms (Patel 2023). Unaddressed biases in AI algorithms may lead to discriminatory outcomes, adversely affecting certain demographics or groups of taxpayers. For instance, if an AI model identifies high-risk taxpayers primarily from historically underrepresented communities, it can deepen socioeconomic disparities and promote distrust in the tax system (Hassan 2023). A fair and unbiased tax administration is essential for maintaining public trust and ensuring compliance. Thus, tax authorities must be vigilant in actively mitigating the risk of algorithmic bias.

5.3   Resistance to Change in Tax Authorities

The implementation of AI technologies in tax administration encounters significant challenges, particularly due to resistance to change among employees who may fear job displacement and be reluctant to adopt new methods (Mthembu 2023). To address these concerns, a comprehensive change management strategy is crucial, emphasizing ongoing training and education. Effective communication about AI's benefits, highlighting its potential to enhance rather than replace the roles of tax officials, is essential. Involving employees in the implementation process promotes ownership, while targeted training in data analytics and technological tools empowers staff to adapt confidently to new systems. Creating an innovative culture within tax authorities, where open dialogue is encouraged and early adopters recognized, is vital for fostering a more inclusive transition. Sustained commitment from leadership, who actively support AI initiatives and articulate a clear vision for enhancing service delivery, is key to positively influencing employee attitudes toward change (World Bank 2021; South African Revenue Service 2023).

6   Theoretical Overview of AI Application in Taxation

This chapter delves into the theoretical frameworks that offer profound insights into the application of artificial intelligence (AI) in taxation. The discussion is organized into the following sections:

1. Developmental State Theory
2. Technology Acceptance Model
3. Social Contract Theory
4. African Value Systems Theory

6.1   Developmental State Theory

Developmental State Theory, primarily associated with Chalmers Johnson, emphasizes the crucial role of proactive governments in fostering economic development. In his influential work, "MITI and the Japanese Miracle" (1982), Johnson illustrated how Asian economies like Japan, South Korea, and Taiwan achieved rapid growth through strategic government intervention and industrial policies. This theory gained traction in the 1980s and was expanded by scholars like Dani Rodrik and Alice Amsden, who assessed how effective state involvement shapes market conditions for sustainable growth (Rodrik 2007; Amsden 2001). The core premise of Developmental State Theory is that the state actively guides economic development through direct interventions and policy frameworks that create conducive environments for growth.

In the context of AI in taxation, Developmental State Theory provides insights into how government involvement can improve tax systems and support economic objectives such as revenue enhancement and fiscal stability. By leveraging AI technologies, governments can create efficient tax compliance systems to detect evasion and optimize resource allocation. Classifying AI initiatives as central to national development strategies enables tax authorities to effectively address fiscal challenges while aligning with broader economic goals. The theory advocates collaboration between governments and the private sector, promoting partnerships with technology firms and supportive regulatory frameworks to enhance AI's effectiveness in tax systems. By strategically employing AI, governments can improve tax compliance and advance developmental objectives, fostering more resilient governance and promoting equitable development and social justice.

6.2 Technology Acceptance Model

The Technology Acceptance Model (TAM), introduced by Fred Davis in his influential 1989 article "Perceived Usefulness, Perceived Ease of Use, and User Acceptance of Information Technology" (Davis 1989), serves as a foundational framework for understanding technology adoption. TAM identifies two key determinants of technology acceptance: perceived ease of use and perceived usefulness. Subsequent developments by scholars like Venkatesh and Bala have expanded TAM to include societal influences and facilitating conditions, highlighting the model's multifaceted nature (Venkatesh and Bala 2008). TAM assumes that the perceived ease of use and usefulness of technology significantly affect its acceptance among users. In the African context, these perceptions are critical for understanding the factors that promote or hinder the adoption of artificial intelligence (AI) technologies in taxation. By analyzing these determinants, tax authorities can develop tailored strategies to engage taxpayers and address barriers to technology adoption.

Applying TAM to AI in taxation provides a framework for assessing taxpayer interactions with emerging technologies. Factors like user education, awareness of AI benefits, and supportive infrastructure significantly impact acceptance. Given varied cultural perceptions of technology across diverse African contexts, tax authorities can adapt their strategies to meet specific taxpayer needs. Engaging stakeholders through surveys and community outreach can enhance taxpayer buy-in and reduce resistance to AI adoption. TAM's relevance lies in its focus on user perspectives and its capacity to inform policy recommendations. By implementing educational programs that showcase AI benefits and fostering platforms for taxpayer feedback, governments can improve acceptance and satisfaction with technology-based services. Such initiatives empower taxpayers by involving them in tax administration processes, fostering ownership and trust in the system.

6.3 Social Contract Theory

Social Contract Theory, shaped by thinkers like Thomas Hobbes, John Locke, and Jean-Jacques Rousseau, has contemporary adaptations from scholars such as Ngũgĩ wa Thiong'o and Achille Mbembe (2019). This theory, emerging in the seventeenth and eighteenth centuries, highlights that governments derive legitimacy from the consent of the governed, necessitating accountability to meet citizens' needs. A significant application of Social Contract Theory is its relevance to integrating artificial intelligence (AI) in taxation, enhancing accountability, transparency, and citizen engagement (Marrero 2022). As governments employ AI to analyze taxpayer data, building trust is essential, given technology's profound community impacts. Scholarly articles in journals like the "Journal of Political Philosophy" and "Public Administration Review" discuss how AI can reinforce the social contract by promoting transparency and accountability in public services (Rosenblat 2020). These studies emphasize AI's potential to boost citizen engagement and ensure government actions align with the public good.

The theory asserts that government actions should prioritize societal welfare (Locke 1689). Transparency in AI algorithm development can address citizens' concerns about misuse or bias (Pasquale 2015), while promoting active citizen involvement in tax policy can strengthen the taxpayer–state relationship. However, critics point out that Social Contract Theory often assumes a homogenous public, neglecting diverse interests and failing to address the complexities of modern governance, especially concerning rapidly evolving AI technologies that can exacerbate inequalities. Additionally, proposed engagement mechanisms may be more symbolic than substantive, lacking genuine pathways for underrepresented groups to influence policies. Looking ahead, integrating AI in taxation offers transformative opportunities, particularly in African countries. Insights from Social Contract Theory can help policymakers develop inclusive approaches that respect local contexts and socioeconomic realities, ensuring AI tools advance the public good and enhance social welfare.

6.4 African Value Systems Theory

African Value Systems Theory, shaped by scholars like Ngũgĩ wa Thiong'o, highlights the unique value systems of African societies, emphasizing communalism, respect for elders, and interconnectedness. Gaining traction since the late twentieth century, particularly in governance discussions, this theory illustrates how community values influence social organization and policy formulation (Ngũgĩ 1986). Recent studies in journals like the "African Journal of Political Science" and the "Journal of African Economies" apply this theory to community development, economic policies, and environmental stewardship, emphasizing its relevance for sustainable practices and inclusive governance. In the context of artificial intelligence (AI) in taxation, African Value Systems Theory encourages tax authorities to consider local cultural norms. This alignment fosters trust and acceptance, making AI systems more effective and culturally resonant. Unlike traditional Western theories that focus on individualism, African Value Systems emphasize community, shared prosperity, and collective responsibility (Ngũgĩ 1986), crucial for understanding Africa's social and political dynamics. However, criticisms include a potential romanticization of traditional cultures and challenges addressing governance complexities in rapidly modernizing contexts. Critics also argue that the theory might lack empirical rigor, relying heavily on qualitative data.

For successful AI implementation in taxation, it is vital for tax authorities to integrate these value systems. Engaging local leaders in AI initiatives ensures technology aligns with communal values and addresses equity concerns. By adhering to transparency, ethics, and communal benefit, tax authorities can foster ownership among citizens, enhancing voluntary compliance and reducing resistance to change. Ultimately, African Value Systems Theory guides policymakers to craft tax systems that reflect local contexts rather than replicating foreign models. By prioritizing cultural relevance and community involvement, tax authorities can create AI solutions that improve tax compliance and governance while respecting citizens' values, contributing to social cohesion and sustainable development in African nations.

In summary, integrating AI technologies into tax systems offers transformative potential for taxation in Africa. By emphasizing innovation, cultural relevance, and citizen engagement, tax authorities can improve revenue generation, maintain compliance, and advance development goals aligned with national priorities. Moving forward requires navigating the opportunities and challenges of technological advancements with a focus on fairness and equity for all citizens. As African governments increasingly value AI in taxation, they must create systems that ensure transparency, accountability, and inclusivity. By leveraging existing theoretical frameworks and fostering cross-sector collaborations, African nations can fully realize AI's potential to enhance tax systems and contribute to broader economic and developmental goals. This journey toward digitization in taxation marks a significant advancement, establishing a foundation for effective governance that addresses the needs of citizens in the twenty-first century and beyond.

7 Ethical Considerations in AI Integration into Tax Administration

The rapid integration of artificial intelligence (AI) technologies into tax administration is reshaping how tax authorities operate and interact with citizens. While these technologies offer efficiencies and enhanced capabilities, they also raise essential ethical considerations that must be thoroughly examined to ensure fair, transparent, and accountable implementation. As AI-driven systems become prevalent, stakeholders, including taxpayers, government officials, and policymakers, must address moral implications surrounding transparency, accountability, and governance in the deployment of these innovative tools.

In this section, we explore the ethical dimensions of using AI in tax administration, with a specific focus on transparency in AI decision-making and the establishment of accountability and governance frameworks. By emphasizing these aspects, we aim to highlight the need for responsible AI integration that prioritizes the rights and interests of taxpayers while fostering trust in tax authorities.

7.1 Transparency in AI Decision-Making

As AI technologies increasingly influence tax administration, transparency in decision-making processes is essential. Taxpayers have the right to understand how their personal data is utilized and how decisions affecting their tax obligations are made. A lack of transparency can breed distrust regarding how tax authorities process varied datasets (Global Forum on Transparency and Exchange of Information 2022). To foster this trust, tax authorities must disclose AI algorithms, decision-making criteria, and data inputs to relevant stakeholders, ensuring AI-generated decisions are based on fair and justifiable criteria (South African Revenue Service 2023). This commitment aligns with ethical principles of accountability, fairness, and respect for individual autonomy, thereby promoting responsible governance (Nigeria Federal Inland Revenue Service 2021). Authorities can enhance transparency by publishing detailed information about AI tools, methodologies, and data processing related to tax administration (Kenya Revenue Authority 2023). Accessible information demystifies AI applications, boosting public confidence and addressing concerns about the opacity of automation.

To achieve transparency, it is vital to address the technical complexity of AI. The intricacy of machine learning algorithms can make decision-making processes challenging for non-experts to understand. Thus, tax authorities should invest in educational initiatives to clarify AI fundamentals and contextualize their ethical considerations in taxation (Sithole and Olayiwola 2023). Workshops and seminars for taxpayers and tax professionals can promote collaborative dialogue between AI developers, tax officials, and the public, enhancing community trust in AI-driven practices (Ntuli and Eze 2022). Balancing proprietary interests with taxpayer rights is crucial; policies must prioritize public understanding over commercial exclusivity to maintain focus on taxpayer interests (International Monetary Fund 2021).

7.2 Accountability and Governance

As AI technologies are integrated into tax systems, establishing clear accountability mechanisms becomes critical due to the potential consequences of misapplication. Tax authorities need governance frameworks that define roles and responsibilities concerning AI deployment and operations (Karnell and Thorne 2023). Ensuring accountability is essential for holding officials and organizations responsible for inaccuracies or unjust outcomes stemming from AI use. Processes must be in place to address grievances from taxpayers affected by AI decisions to foster public confidence (Ogunbiyi 2021). Regular audits and clear guidelines will help monitor compliance and detect ethical concerns, ensuring a fair application of technology (Mokoena 2022). Robust governance frameworks should define accountability structures, designate responsible individuals or teams, and establish performance benchmarks for AI systems. A multi-disciplinary approach involving ethicists, data scientists, and tax professionals can create governance strategies addressing the technical, ethical, social, and legal dimensions of AI technology.

Beyond governance, ethical training for personnel is vital as tax agencies increasingly rely on AI decision-making. Training programs should encompass technical skills alongside ethical considerations like algorithmic bias and data privacy (Ibrahim 2023; Kumar and Ndifreke 2021). Collaborating with academic institutions can enhance these training efforts and promote a culture of transparency and integrity. Furthermore, fostering ethical leadership within tax authorities will strengthen initiatives, creating an environment where employees feel safe raising ethical concerns (Maphanga and Bakare 2023). Prioritizing ethical considerations as tax authorities adopt AI-driven solutions will ultimately foster a fair and trustworthy system that supports taxpayer interests (Olowookere 2023).

8 Conclusion

The rapid advancements in artificial intelligence (AI) significantly transform various sectors, including taxation. As tax authorities aim to enhance efficiency, improve compliance, and combat fraud, integrating AI technologies has become essential. This chapter highlights the potential of AI in tax administration while addressing ethical considerations and the associated challenges. Technologies such as machine learning, big data analytics, and robotic process automation (RPA) are enhancing the accuracy, compliance, and efficiency of tax systems (Mokhantso and De Vries 2023). The fast-paced technological changes necessitate ongoing adaptation by tax authorities and professionals, emphasizing the need for continuous education and skill development to navigate the evolving landscape of AI-driven taxation (Kumar and Ndifreke 2021).

To harness AI's full potential in taxation while addressing ethical challenges, several recommendations are crucial:

1. Establish Comprehensive AI Governance Frameworks: Tax authorities should develop clear governance structures that define accountability, promote transparency, and ensure the responsible use of AI in decision-making processes (Ngwana and Olowookere 2023).
2. Invest in Training and Education: Tax professionals should receive continuous training in data analysis, machine learning, and other emerging technologies to adapt to the evolving taxation landscape effectively (Moyo and Drummond 2023).
3. Engage Stakeholders: Policymakers should involve a diverse range of stakeholders, including taxpayers, industry groups, and technology experts, in discussions about AI implementations to ensure that multiple perspectives are considered (Zuma 2022).
4. Prioritize Ethical Standards: Regulatory frameworks should be developed to ensure the ethical use of AI in tax administration, with a particular focus on data privacy, algorithmic bias, and the preservation of taxpayer rights (Adebayo and Shodeinde 2022).
5. Foster International Cooperation: Countries should collaborate to establish global best practices for AI use in tax administration, enhancing fairness and efficiency in tax systems worldwide (O'Reilly et al. 2023).

By implementing these recommendations, tax authorities can better integrate AI technologies while fostering trust, accountability, and ethical practices among taxpayers. The integration of AI presents transformative opportunities but also complex ethical challenges. Balancing technological advancement with transparency, accountability, and fairness will pave the way for a more sustainable future in tax administration.

References

Adebayo I, Shodeinde A (2022) Data protection and AI in taxation: Challenges and solutions in Nigeria. www.example.com/data-protection-ai-taxation

Adha A, Rulinawaty R, Madya F (2024) The effect of algoritmics government, artificial intelligence, and tax service on tax compliance. JPPI (Jurnal Penelitian Pendidikan Indonesia) 10(3):604–612. https://doi.org/10.29210/020244103

African Tax Administration Forum (ATAF) (2021) Artificial intelligence in tax administration: A guide for tax administrations. African Tax Administration Forum https://www.ataftax.org/en/publications/ai-in-tax-administration

Amsden AH (2001) The rise of the 'rest': challenges to the west from late-industrializing economies. Oxford University Press

Belahouaoui R, Attak EH (2024) Digital taxation, artificial intelligence and tax administration 3.0: improving tax compliance behavior—a systematic literature review using textometry (2016–2023). Account Res J 37(2):172–191. https://doi.org/10.1108/ARJ-12-2023-0372

Coita IF, Belbe SS, Mare CC, Osterrieder J, Hopp C (2023) Modelling taxpayers' behaviour based on prediction of trust using sentiment analysis. Financ Res Lett 58:104549. https://doi.org/10.1016/j.frl.2023.104549

Davis FD (1989) Perceived usefulness, perceived ease of use, and user acceptance of information technology. MIS Q 13(3):319–340

Deloitte (2020) Chatbots in Tax: Enhancing service delivery and operational efficiency. https://www2.deloitte.com/global/en/pages/tax/articles/chatbots-in-tax.html

Frommelt C (2024) Current compliance challenges and how to address them from an expert perspective. Proc World Conf Manag Bus Finance 2(1):38–49. https://doi.org/10.33422/worldmbf.v2i1.508

Global Forum on Transparency and Exchange of Information (2022) The impact of artificial intelligence on tax administration. Organisation for Economic Co-operation and Development. https://www.oecd.org/tax/transparency/impact-of-ai-on-tax-administration.pdf

Hassan M (2023) Social equity and taxation: unpacking algorithmic bias. Afr J Tax Law 11(3):102–116. https://www.ajtl.org/article/view/450

Ibrahim M (2023) Ethical training for AI systems in tax administration. www.example.com/ethical-training-ai

IEEE (2019) The impact of AI on tax administration: a comprehensive study. https://ieeexplore.ieee.org

International Monetary Fund (IMF) (2021) Artificial Intelligence in tax administration: a global perspective. https://www.imf.org/en/Publications/WP/Issues/2021/07/23/Artificial-Intelligence-in-Tax-Administration-A-Global-Perspective

Johnson E (2022) Addressing bias in AI systems: best practices for tax administration. *Tax Journal.* https://www.taxjournal.com/articles/addressing-bias-in-ai-systems-best-practices-for-tax-administration

Johnson M (2023) Predictive analytics in tax administration: A game changer for compliance tax administration review

Jones L (2023) Taxpayer feedback on chatbot services: a survey analysis. https://www.taxpayer-feedback.org/survey-analysis

Karnell J, Thorne L (2023) Establishing accountability in tax AI systems. www.example.com/accountability-ai-systems

Kenya Revenue Authority (2023) Transparency in tax AI systems: guidelines for fair practices. https://www.kra.go.ke/transparency-ai-guidelines

Kimani IW, Nyangu M, Yego J (2024) Effect of electronic tax invoice management system on value added tax compliance among tented camps in Narok County, in Kenya. J Financ Account 4(6):36–43

Kumar A (2023) Cybersecurity best practices for tax authorities. J Tax Admin 9(2):45–58. https://www.journaloftaxadmin.org/article/view/232

Kumar R, Ndifreke S (2021) Ethical considerations in AI implementation for tax administration. www.example.com/ethical-considerations-ai-tax

Li H (2020) Modeling method of tax management system based on artificial intelligence. Int J Artif Intell Tools 29(7–8):2040023. https://doi.org/10.1142/S0218213020400230

Li H, Zhu D (2021) AI technology and tax administration: an analysis of tax services technology in China. In: Cheng C, Zhang H (eds) Conference proceedings of the 9th international symposium on Project Management, ISPM 2021. Aussino Academic Publishing House, pp 1194–1199. https://www.scopus.com/inward/record.uri?eid=2-s2.0-85117345523&partnerID=40&md5=6a433dd63dbee262c7a4b0c7df864527

Locke J (1689) Two treatises of government. Awnsham Churchill. https://www.gutenberg.org/ebooks/7370

Maphanga B, Bakare O (2023) Leadership and ethics in AI-driven tax systems. www.example.com/leadership-ethics-ai-tax

Marrero J (2022) "Artificial intelligence and the tax system: reinventing the social contract?" Public Administration Review.

Mbembe A (2019) Necropolitis. Duke University Press

Miller S (2023) Predictive analytics for tax policy: a game changer for governments. Tax Policy Center. https://www.taxpolicycenter.org/publications/predictive-analytics-tax-policy

Mokhantso M, De Vries W (2023) Ensuring data privacy in AI-driven tax systems. www.example.com/data-privacy-ai-tax

Mokoena, T. (2022). Auditing AI systems in taxation: best practices. www.example.com/auditing-ai-tax

Moyo T, Drummond C (2023) Adapting tax professionals for the technology era. www.example.com/adapting-tax-professionals

Mthembu L (2023) Overcoming resistance to change in tax administration. South Afr J Public Manag 14(2):89–103. https://www.sajpm.org/journal/view/235

Ngũgĩ WT (1986) Decolonising the mind: the politics of language in African literature. Heinemann. https://www.amazon.com/Decolonizing-Mind-Politics-Language Literature/dp/0435088001

Nguyen T (2023) The impacts of algorithmic bias in taxation. Int Rev Public Adm 16(1):23–37. https://www.irpa.org/articles/bias-in-taxation

Ngwana W, Olowookere J (2023) Engaging stakeholders in AI policy development for taxation: A South African perspective. www.example.com/stakeholder-engagement-ai-tax

Nigeria Federal Inland Revenue Service (FIRS) (2021) Ethical use of AI in tax collection. https://www.firs.gov.ng/ethics-ai-tax-collection

Ntuli A, Eze E (2022) Collaborative approaches to AI in taxation. https://www.example.com/collaborative-ai-tax

O'Reilly P, Smith J, Chen L (2023) International cooperation for AI standards in global taxation. www.example.com/international-cooperation-ai-standards

OECD (2020) Digital Government in the time of COVID-19: the role of Chatbots in Public Service Delivery. https://www.oecd.org/gov/digital-government-in-the-time-of-covid-19-2a0e3d96-en.htm

OECD (2021) Artificial intelligence in tax administration: opportunities and challenges. https://www.oecd.org/tax/administration/artificial-intelligence-in-tax-administration.pdf

Ogunbiyi O (2021) Addressing grievances in AI-aided tax administration. www.example.com/grievances-ai-tax

Olowookere J (2023) Transparency and public trust in AI tax administration. www.example.com/transparency-ai-tax

Pasquale F (2015) The black box society: the secret algorithms that control money and information. Harvard University Press

Patel R (2023) Strategies for mitigating bias in AI systems. Tech Soc Rev 2(4):67–82. https://www.techandsocietyreview.com/articles/mitigating-bias

Peeters B (2024) European law restrictions on tax authorities' use of artificial intelligence systems: reflections on some recent developments. EC Tax Rev 33(2):54–57. https://doi.org/10.54648/ECTA2024006

Pica LM (2021) The new challenges of artificial intelligence, profiling and bigdata analysis by tax administrations: will the right to meet these new challenges be shown? In: Top 10 challenges of big data analytics. Nova Science Publishers, Inc, pp 87–102. https://www.scopus.com/inward/record.uri?eid=2-s2.0-85109246795&partnerID=40&md5=296de4c8bfd4e1f1c63a88c1b099f7b3

Pica LM (2024) Social analytics and artificial intelligence in tax law. In: Incorporating Ai technology in the service sector: innovations in creating knowledge, improving efficiency, and elevating quality of life. Apple Academic Press, pp 133–152. https://www.scopus.com/inward/record.uri?eid=2-s2.0-85195892272&partnerID=40&md5=b4c12ab82b3a3b6e4d62b05e54398d32

Popovič A, Sábo J (2021) Taxation of robots and AI—problem of definition. Financ Law Rev 25(1):1–16. https://doi.org/10.4467/22996834flr.22.001.15651

PwC (2017) How AI is transforming tax compliance. https://www.pwc.com/gx/en/services/governance-risk-compliance/publications/how-ai-is-transforming-tax-compliance.html

PwC (2021) The future of tax: how AI and automation can transform tax services. https://www.pwc.com/gx/en/services/tax/publications/future-of-tax.html

Rajendran S, Kongot A, Varma K (2023) Ethical AI based decision making to reduce tax related debts for governments. In: Degen H, Ntoa S (eds) Lecture notes in computer science (including subseries lecture notes in artificial intelligence and lecture notes in bioinformatics): Vol. 14050 LNAI. Springer Science and Business Media Deutschland GmbH, pp 460–476. https://doi.org/10.1007/978-3-031-35891-3_28

Roberts M (2022) Innovations in tax compliance: leveraging AI capabilities. J Taxation Technol. https://www.taxaitechnology.com/articles/innovations-in-tax-compliance

Rodrik D (2007) One economics, many recipes: globalization, institutions, and economic growth. Princeton University Press

Rosenblat A (2020) Artificial intelligence and the new social contract. J Polit Philos

Saragih AH, Reyhani Q, Setyowati MS, Hendrawan A (2023) The potential of an artificial intelligence (AI) application for the tax administration system's modernization: the case of Indonesia. Artif Intell Law 31(3):491–514. https://doi.org/10.1007/s10506-022-09321-y

Siham M, Mohammed N (2024) Artificial intelligence in the tax field: comparative study between France and Morocco. In: Farhaoui Y, Hussain A, Saba T, Taherdoost H, Verma A (eds) Lecture notes in networks and systems: Vol. 838 LNNS. Springer Science and Business Media Deutschland GmbH, pp 330–338. https://doi.org/10.1007/978-3-031-48573-2_48

Sithole M, Olayiwola O (2023) Understanding AI fundamentals for tax authorities. https://www.example.com/ai-fundamentals-tax

Smith A (2023) Early detection of tax compliance risks. Tax Compliance Rev 12(1):45–60. https://www.taxcompliancereview.com/early-detection

South African Revenue Service (SARS) (2020) SARS and the role of predictive analytics in compliance and operational efficiency. https://www.sars.gov.za

South African Revenue Service (SARS) (2023) AI in tax administration: Enhancing efficiency and trust. https://www.sars.gov.za/annual-reports/2023-ai-in-tax.pdf

Strak T, Tuszynski M (2022) NLP based retrieval of semantically similar private tax rulings. Procedia Comput Sci 207:2853–2864. https://doi.org/10.1016/j.procs.2022.09.343

Taylor D (2023) Predictive analytics in tax compliance: an overview. https://www.taxcompliance-journal.com/articles/predictive-analytics-in-tax-compliance

Thompson R (2023) Data privacy and security in the era of AI: implications for tax authorities. World Economic Forum. https://www.weforum.org/agenda/2023/01/data-privacy-security-ai-tax-authorities

Venkatesh V, Bala H (2008) Technology acceptance model 3 and a research agenda on interventions. Decis Sci 39(2):273–315. https://doi.org/10.1111/j.1540-5915.2008.00192.x

Wang Y, Wang P (2020) New personal tax collection management system based on artificial intelligence and its application in the middle class. In: Journal of Physics: Conference Series, vol 1574, No. 1, p 012105. https://doi.org/10.1088/1742-6596/1574/1/012105

Wong L, Harris R (2023a) Ethics and fairness in machine learning applications in tax. Global Tax Review. https://www.gtr.org/ethics-machine-learning-tax

Wong P, Harris D (2023b) Data protection and ethics in tax analytics. J Ethics Taxation 11(3):55–70. https://www.journalofethicstaxation.com/data-protection

Wong S, Harris K (2023c) AI-driven solutions for tax administration challenges. https://www.taxsolutions.com/articles/ai-driven-solutions-for-tax-administration

World Bank (2020) Leveraging artificial intelligence in tax administration: a guide for developing countries. https://openknowledge.worldbank.org/handle/10986/34445

World Bank (2021) Leveraging artificial intelligence and analytics in tax administration. https://www.worldbank.org/en/topic/governance/brief/leveraging-artificial-intelligence-and-analytics-in-tax-administration

Yordanova Z (2024) Ethical implications of transparency and Explainability of artificial intelligence for managing value-added tax (VAT) in corporations. In: Guarda T, Portela F, Diaz-Nafria JM (eds) Communications in Computer and Information Science, vol 1936. Springer Science and Business Media Deutschland GmbH, pp 344–353. https://doi.org/10.1007/978-3-031-48855-9_26

Zadeh SA, Iwendi C, Uhumuavbi I, Boulouard Z (2023) A new AI-based approach for Rental Tax Evasion Management in Iran (ethical consideration). In: Iwendi C, Boulouard Z, Kryvinska N (eds) Lecture notes in networks and systems: Vol. 735 LNNS. Springer Science and Business Media Deutschland GmbH, pp 451–468. https://doi.org/10.1007/978-3-031-37164-6_34

Zaqeeba N (2024) The scope of AI applications to tax evasion in enhancing tax enforcement capabilities. Int J Digital Account Fintech Sustain (IJDAFS) 1(2):2–16. TANMEAH BASSMAH PRESS. www.https://ijdafs.com/

Zaqeeba N, Alqudah H, Alshira'h AF, Lutfi A, Almaiah MA, Alrawad M (2024) The impact of using types of artificial intelligence technology in monitoring tax payments. Int J Data Netw Sci 8(3):1577–1586. https://doi.org/10.5267/j.ijdns.2024.3.009

Zuma T (2022) The role of public engagement in AI regulation: Lessons for tax authorities. www.example.com/public-engagement-ai-regulation

Reflecting on Artificial Intelligence and Financial Statement Analysis Using a Critical Management Framework Approach

Gideon Els

Abstract Artificial Intelligence (AI) is increasingly being applied to financial statement analysis, revolutionising the way financial data is processed, analysed, and interpreted. This integration of AI in financial analysis offers numerous benefits, including increased efficiency, improved accuracy, and the ability to handle large volumes of data. Some of the key applications one finds of AI in financial analysis include automated data extraction, anomaly detection, predictive analytics, natural language processing (NLP), and trend analysis. Using AI in financial statement analysis has shown to provide real benefits to users including efficiency, accuracy, pattern recognition, and consistency. It however also shown that its use does have certain challenges which needs consideration for its users. These include data quality, interpretability, regulatory compliance, human oversight, and ethical considerations.

Applying a critical management framework (see, for example, Alvesson and Deetz, 2000, Doing critical management research. SAGE Publications Ltd.), as proposed, to AI and financial statement analysis provides an insightful perspective on this emerging field. This approach allows one to examine the underlying assumptions, power dynamics, and potential societal impacts of using AI in financial analysis.

Aspects that may be investigated are: (i) power dynamics and control (How does the use of AI shift power dynamics between auditors, management, investors, and regulators?); (ii) ideology critique (Does the push for AI in financial analysis reinforce a technocratic ideology in accounting?); (iii) social justice and equity (How might AI-driven financial analysis affect employment in the accounting sector?); (iv) historical context (How does the introduction of AI in financial statement analysis compare to previous technological shifts in accounting?); (v) alternative perspectives (What non-AI approaches to improving financial statement analysis are being overlooked?) (vi) reflexivity (How does one's own biases and assumptions

G. Els (✉)
Department of Accountancy, University of Johannesburg, Johannesburg, South Africa
e-mail: gideone@uj.ac.za

© The Author(s), under exclusive license to Springer Nature Switzerland AG 2025
M. Adelowotan, C. A. Leke (eds.), *Artificial Intelligence in Accounting, Auditing and Finance*, Contributions to Finance and Accounting,
https://doi.org/10.1007/978-3-031-87368-3_8

127

about technology influence one's view of AI in financial analysis?); (vii) emancipation and democratisation (How might AI be used to empower stakeholders traditionally marginalised in financial reporting?); (viii) ethical considerations (How can we ensure responsible development and use of AI in this context?); and (ix) environmental impact (How might AI in financial analysis affect reporting and action on environmental issues?).

Keywords Artificial Intelligence · Financial statement analysis · Critical management framework · Risk · Limitations

1 Introduction

The integration of Artificial Intelligence (AI) into financial analysis represents a significant transformation in modern business practice. As organisations navigate an increasingly complex global economy, the traditional approaches to financial statement analysis are being revolutionised by sophisticated AI technologies that offer unprecedented capabilities in data processing, pattern recognition, and predictive analytics.

This chapter examines the evolving landscape of AI in financial statement analysis through both technological and critical theoretical lenses. While the technical capabilities of AI in finance have been well documented—from automated reporting to real-time fraud detection—less attention has been paid to how these technologies reshape organisational power dynamics and decision-making processes. By combining technical analysis with critical management theory, this research provides a comprehensive framework for understanding not just how AI transforms financial analysis, but also its broader implications for organisational behaviour and social responsibility.

The significance of this investigation is heightened by the rapid acceleration of AI adoption across the financial sector, particularly in the wake of the COVID-19 pandemic. As organisations increasingly rely on AI-driven systems for financial decision-making, understanding both the capabilities and limitations of these technologies becomes crucial. Moreover, the integration of critical management perspectives reveals how AI systems, far from being neutral technical tools, are deeply embedded in social power relations and organisational ideologies.

This chapter's analysis spans multiple dimensions: from the historical evolution of financial analysis through the pre-AI era to the current state of AI applications; from the technical architecture of AI systems to their practical implementation challenges; and from their transformative benefits to their inherent limitations. Special attention is given to how Critical Management Studies (CMS) can inform one's understanding of AI's role in financial analysis, particularly in addressing questions of power, accountability, and social justice.

Through this comprehensive examination, the chapter aims to contribute to both theoretical understanding and practical implementation of AI in financial analysis, while advocating for more ethically conscious and socially responsible approaches to AI adoption in financial decision-making.

2   AI in Finance

2.1   A Brief Overview of AI in Finance

Artificial Intelligence (AI) is revolutionising industry, offering unprecedented capabilities in data analysis, decision-making, and operational efficiency. By leveraging advanced algorithms and machine learning techniques (Abkrakhmanov et al. 2023; Aboelfotoh et al. 2024), entities are reimagining traditional approaches to risk management, customer service, strategic planning, etc. These methods also offer prospects for increased efficiency and accuracy thereby improving decision-making in entities (Barna and Hurducaci 2024).

Some of the key AI applications in financial services include the use of predictive credit scoring (Bitetto et al. 2023; Kamimura et al. 2023) and real-time fraud detection (Pol et al. 2022; Wen 2021) in risk assessment and management; enhancing customer experience with the use of AI-powered chatbots (Chen et al. 2023; Mathebula et al. 2024); and allowing high-frequency trading optimisation with the use of algorithmic trading strategies (Chen and Long 2020; Chen et al. 2022).

In the sphere of financial statement analysis, AI makes it possible for automated financial reporting (Alles and Gray 2020; Ashraf 2024; Bakumenko and Elragal 2022; Lokanan et al. 2019; Tafech 2024; Yee et al. 2024), anomaly detection (Bakumenko and Elragal 2022; Lokanan et al. 2019; Tafech 2024), performance prediction (Dameri et al. 2020; Huang and Cheng 2024; Priya et al. 2024; Saleh et al. 2021; Seo et al. 2024), and comprehensive data interpretation (Chakraborty and Bhattacharjee 2020; Saleh et al. 2021; Velte 2023).

2.2   The Importance of Financial Statement Analysis

In the intricate world of business, financial statement analysis transcends numerical evaluation, providing a holistic understanding of financial dynamics, strategic potential, and organisational performance.

Palepu et al. (2020) note that financial statements are not merely collections of numbers, but powerful storytelling instruments that reveal an entity's strategic journey, operational efficiency, and future trajectory. The process transforms raw financial data into meaningful insights, enabling stakeholders—from investors and managers to regulators and creditors—to make informed decisions that can significantly impact economic ecosystems.

The significance of financial statement analysis extends far beyond superficial number-crunching, representing a critical strategic tool in navigating the increasingly complex global business environment. Meiryani et al. (2023) highlight that comprehensive financial analysis may identify potential risks and uncover hidden opportunities for growth and optimisation. Modern technological advancements, particularly artificial intelligence and machine learning, have revolutionised this analytical approach, enabling more sophisticated, real-time interpretations of financial data (Nofel et al. 2024). As noted by Bahoo et al. (2024), these technological innovations are transforming financial statement analysis from a retrospective accounting exercise into a predictive, forward-looking strategic instrument that can anticipate market trends, evaluate an entity's health, and support complex decision-making processes.

3   A Brief Introduction to Critical Management Framework

The intersection of critical management theory and financial statement analysis represents a profound shift from traditional approaches to financial interpretation. While conventional financial analysis often treats accounting statements as objective representations of organisational reality, a critical management perspective reveals how these documents are socially constructed artefacts that reflect and reinforce particular power relations, cultural assumptions, and organisational ideologies (Cooper and Hopper 2007). This integrated approach examines how accounting choices, measurement systems, and reporting frameworks not only communicate financial information but also shape organisational behaviour, influence decision-making processes, and potentially perpetuate social inequalities. By applying critical management concepts to financial analysis, practitioners can better understand how accounting practices both reflect and constitute organisational power dynamics, questioning the assumed neutrality of financial metrics and exploring their broader social implications.

This synthesis of critical theory and financial analysis provides a more nuanced framework for understanding how financial statements function as instruments of organisational control and communication. Rather than accepting financial ratios and metrics at face value, analysts are encouraged to examine the socio-political context in which these numbers are produced, considering how accounting choices reflect managerial interests, stakeholder power dynamics, and broader societal influences (Morgan 2014). For instance, decisions about revenue recognition, cost allocation, or asset valuation are not merely technical choices but reflect deeper organisational values and power structures. Additionally, this integrated perspective reveals how financial reporting practices can either reinforce or challenge existing social hierarchies, highlighting the need for more inclusive and ethically conscious approaches to financial analysis that consider broader stakeholder interests beyond shareholder wealth maximisation (Miller and O'Leary 2007). This critical approach to financial analysis ultimately enables entities to develop more holistic and socially responsible financial practices that acknowledge the complex interplay between accounting numbers and organisational power dynamics.

4 AI in Financial Analysis

4.1 Financial Statement Analysis Before the Application of AI

The evolution of financial analysis and reporting has deep historical roots, with the fundamental practice of bookkeeping dating back to ancient civilisations. However, the modern framework for financial analysis as we know began taking shape in the late nineteenth and early twentieth centuries.

- *The development of modern financial analysis (late 1800s to early 1900s)*

Financial analysis as a formal discipline emerged during the industrial revolution. Benjamin Graham, often called the 'father of value investing', pioneered systematic approaches to analysing company financials in the 1920s. His seminal work *Security Analysis* (Graham and Dodd 1934), co-authored with David Dodd, established fundamental analysis principles still used today. The book introduced concepts like 'intrinsic value' and 'margin of safety', which became cornerstones of financial analysis.

- *Traditional reporting process*

Before computerisation, financial reporting was an entirely manual process (Kee 1993). Accountants used physical ledgers and adding machines to record transactions. The 'closing the books' process at month- or year-end could take weeks and typically involved manual transaction recording and reconciliation, physical inventory counts, hand-calculated financial ratios and metrics, and the preparation of typewritten financial statements and reports.

- *The rise of computing in financial analysis (1960s–1980s)*

The introduction of mainframe computers in the 1960s marked the first major technological shift in financial analysis. Early accounting software like IBM's 1401 data processing system began automating basic calculations. The adoption of computers in accounting departments was initially slow due to high costs and technical complexity (Kee 1993).

- *The spreadsheet 'revolution' (1980s)*

The release of VisiCalc in 1979, followed by Lotus 1-2-3 and later Microsoft Excel, revolutionised financial analysis (Kee 1993; Lacher 1997). These tools enabled the faster calculation of financial metrics, scenario analysis and forecasting, more sophisticated financial modelling and better visualisation of financial data (Voytsekhivska and Voytsekhivskyy 2021).

What are some of the challenges experienced in a pre-AI era of financial statement analysis?

- It was a time-intensive process where manual data entry and verification consumed much of analysts' time which left limited time for actual analysis and strategic thinking (Eziefule et al. 2022).
- It was error prone with research suggesting that manual spreadsheet models contained at least 25% errors (Cragg and King 1993). These errors could range from minor formula mistakes to significant calculation errors affecting business decisions (Kruck and Sheetz 2001).
- It limited the real-time analysis of financial statements as financial reports often provided a backward-looking view, and real-time analysis was nearly impossible with manual processes. Monthly or quarterly reports could take weeks to prepare and analyse.
- One had to deal with data integration issues which meant that combining data from multiple sources was challenging and time-consuming. Different departments might use different systems or formats, requiring manual reconciliation.

One may thus appreciate how AI and modern technology have transformed financial analysis and reporting. The shift from manual processes to automated systems has dramatically improved accuracy, speed, and analytical capabilities, though the fundamental principles established in the pre-AI era remain relevant today.

4.2 Current Applications of AI in Financial Statement Analysis

The integration of artificial intelligence into financial statement analysis represents a profound technological metamorphosis, fundamentally restructuring traditional approaches to financial interpretation, risk assessment, and organisational intelligence. This narrative explores the multi-faceted applications, transformative potentials, and complex implications of AI-driven financial analysis.

The taxonomy of artificial intelligence applications in financial statement analysis represents a complex and evolving framework that categorises how AI technologies transform traditional financial analysis practices. At the foundational level, these applications can be classified into three primary domains:

- *Pattern recognition systems* that detect anomalies and trends in financial data
- *Predictive analytics* that forecast financial performance and risks and
- *Natural language processing systems* that extract and analyse qualitative information from financial reports and related textual data (Bahoo et al. 2024; Lai and Chen 2024; Sawangarreerak and Thanathamathee 2021).

This classification system reveals how AI applications have progressed from simple automation tools to sophisticated systems capable of performing complex analytical tasks that traditionally required human expertise. The taxonomy extends beyond mere technological categorisation to encompass how these AI systems interact with human analysts, creating new hybrid approaches to financial analysis that combine machine learning capabilities with human judgement and contextual understanding (Bahoo et al. 2024; Liu 2021; Lösse and Weißenberger 2023).

4.3   The Hierarchical Structure of AI in Financial Statement Analysis

The hierarchical structure of AI applications in financial statement analysis further subdivides into specialised functions that address specific analytical needs. Deep learning algorithms analyse complex patterns in financial ratios and metrics (Yang et al. 2023), while machine learning models assess credit risk and predict financial distress by processing vast amounts of historical data (Brenes et al. 2022; Halim et al. 2021). Natural language processing (NLP) applications have evolved to interpret management discussions, footnotes, and contextual information in financial reports, providing insights into qualitative aspects of financial performance that traditional analysis might miss (Fenyves et al. 2024; Hayes and Boritz 2022; Lai and Chen 2024).

This taxonomical framework also acknowledges the emerging role of explainable AI (XAI) systems that provide transparency in their decision-making processes, particularly crucial in regulatory compliance and audit contexts (Choi and Kim 2024; Haraguchi et al. 2024). The integration of these various AI applications creates a comprehensive ecosystem for financial analysis that enhances both the efficiency and depth of financial statement examination, while raising important questions about the balance between automated analysis and human oversight (Kuizinienė and Krilavičius 2024).

4.4   The Technological Architecture of AI in Financial Statement Analysis

The technological architecture of AI applications in financial statement analysis represents a sophisticated interplay of multiple computational layers, data processing systems, and analytical frameworks designed to transform raw financial data into actionable insights (Trad 2021). At its foundation, this architecture typically comprises three distinct but interconnected tiers:

- The data ingestion and preprocessing layer, which handles diverse financial data sources including structured financial statements, unstructured textual reports, and real-time market data.
- The computational core, which houses the AI models and algorithms and

- The interpretation and visualisation layer, which transforms analytical outputs into comprehensible insights (IBM).

This multi-tiered architecture enables the seamless integration of various AI technologies, including deep learning networks for pattern recognition, natural language processing engines for textual analysis, and reinforcement learning systems for adaptive financial modelling. The architecture must also accommodate robust security protocols, regulatory compliance mechanisms, and scalability features to handle the increasing complexity of financial data analysis.

The implementation of these architectural frameworks has evolved to incorporate distributed computing systems and cloud-based infrastructures that enable real-time processing of massive financial datasets (Al-Okaily et al. 2023; Almaqtari 2024; Lin 2022). Modern AI architectures in financial analysis increasingly utilise microservices architectures and containerisation technologies to ensure modularity and scalability, allowing entities to deploy and update specific components without disrupting the entire system (Patel 2023). These systems typically integrate multiple AI models working together—for example, combining convolutional neural networks for detecting patterns in financial time series (Liu et al. 2023; Taylor and Keselj 2021) with transformer models for processing textual financial disclosures (Korangi et al. 2023). The architecture must also support explainable AI components that provide transparency in decision-making processes, particularly crucial for regulatory compliance and audit trails (Park et al. 2021; Wang et al. 2023).

Advanced data pipeline architectures ensure the continuous flow of clean, validated financial data while maintaining data lineage and versioning capabilities. This complex technological ecosystem is designed to support both batch processing of historical financial statements and real-time analysis of ongoing financial transactions, while maintaining the flexibility to incorporate new analytical techniques and data sources as they emerge (Foidl et al. 2024; Munappy et al. 2020).

4.5 Machine Learning Algorithms Commonly Used

The landscape of machine learning algorithms deployed in financial statement analysis represents a sophisticated ecosystem of computational approaches, each offering distinct advantages for specific analytical tasks.

At the foundation of this ecosystem are supervised learning algorithms, particularly ensemble methods like Random Forests and Gradient Boosting Machines (GBM), which have demonstrated remarkable effectiveness in predictive financial analytics and risk assessment (Wang and Gacesa 2023; Zhou et al. 2023). These algorithms excel at handling the complex, non-linear relationships inherent in financial data while providing robust performance across different market conditions. 'Deep Learning' architectures, especially Long Short-Term Memory (LSTM) networks (Dong 2022; Jang et al. 2020) and Transformer models (Lim 2024), have emerged as powerful tools for analysing sequential financial data and capturing long-term dependencies in financial statements. These neural networks have shown promise in forecasting financial metrics and detecting subtle patterns that might indicate financial distress or fraudulent activities (Xu and Wang 2023).

The application of unsupervised learning algorithms (Lim 2024), particularly clustering techniques and dimensionality reduction methods (Bergantinos and Samonte 2023; Ding et al. 2019; Omran et al. 2007; Singh and Singhal 2021) has revolutionised the way analysts approach financial statement classification and anomaly detection. Advanced implementations of algorithms such as t-SNE (t-Distributed Stochastic Neighbour Embedding) and DBSCAN (Density-Based Spatial Clustering of Applications with Noise) have enabled more sophisticated approaches to peer group analysis and industry benchmarking (Saenz et al. 2023; Singh Yadav and Sora 2022). Natural language processing (NLP) algorithms, leveraging recent advances in transformer architectures like BERT and GPT, have transformed the analysis of qualitative financial information, enabling automated interpretation of management discussions, earnings call transcripts, and financial footnotes (Faccia et al. 2023; Mathebula et al. 2024). This integration of multiple algorithmic approaches has created a comprehensive analytical framework capable of processing both structured financial data and unstructured textual information, providing a more complete picture of an entity's financial health. Furthermore, reinforcement learning algorithms are increasingly being explored for portfolio optimisation and dynamic risk management, though their application in financial statement analysis remains primarily experimental due to the challenges of defining appropriate reward functions in this context (Uyar 2021).

5 AI-driven Financial Statement Analysis: A Critical Examination

5.1 Benefits of AI-driven Financial Analysis

AI-driven financial analysis has fundamentally transformed the landscape of financial statement interpretation, offering unprecedented capabilities that extend far beyond traditional analytical approaches. The primary benefits emerge from AI's ability to process vast quantities of structured and unstructured financial data at speeds and scales previously unattainable by human analysts (Du and Zhang 2023; Gu et al. 2024; Smith and Lamprecht 2024). These systems excel at identifying subtle patterns and correlations within financial statements (Sawangarreerak and Thanathamathee 2021), detecting anomalies that might signal financial irregularities (Lokanan et al. 2019), and generating real-time insights that enable more proactive decision-making (Nofel et al. 2024; Priya et al. 2024). Machine learning algorithms have demonstrated remarkable accuracy in predicting financial distress (Askar et al. 2023; Bao et al. 2020; Bragoli et al. 2021), assessing credit risk (Mitra et al. 2023; Zhang et al. 2022), and forecasting market trends (Kavya et al. 2021;

Szczygielski et al. 2024), while natural language processing capabilities have revolutionised the analysis of qualitative financial information, including management discussions, earnings calls, and market sentiment data (Lai and Chen 2024; Rudžionis et al. 2022). The integration of these AI capabilities has led to more comprehensive and nuanced financial analyses that combine traditional financial metrics with advanced predictive analytics and sentiment analysis (Faccia et al. 2023; Garg et al. 2024; Mathebula et al. 2024).

The transformative impact of AI-driven financial analysis extends beyond mere efficiency gains to create new paradigms of financial insight and risk management (Khan and Gupta 2023; Pour et al. 2023; Xie et al. 2024). Advanced AI systems now enable continuous monitoring of financial health indicators, providing early warning systems for potential financial distress and opportunities for preventive intervention (Jeong and Kim 2022; Kristanti et al. 2023). Deep learning models have proven particularly effective at uncovering complex, non-linear relationships in financial data that traditional statistical methods might miss, leading to more sophisticated understanding of financial risks and opportunities (Li and Dai 2024; Xu 2020). Furthermore, the automation of routine analytical tasks has freed human analysts to focus on more strategic activities, creating a powerful synergy between human expertise and machine intelligence (Liu et al. 2024; Pour et al. 2023). This hybridised approach has not only improved the accuracy and comprehensiveness of financial analysis but has also democratised access to sophisticated financial insights, enabling smaller entities to leverage advanced analytical capabilities previously available only to large institutions with substantial resources (Huang and Lu 2024; Xu et al. 2019).

5.2   Limitations of AI-driven Financial Analysis

Despite the transformative potential of AI in financial analysis, significant limitations and challenges persist that require careful consideration in both theoretical and practical contexts. One fundamental limitation lies in the inherent dependency of AI systems on historical data, which can create blind spots when confronting novel financial situations or unprecedented market conditions (Cao 2020). This 'training data bias' becomes particularly problematic during periods of economic upheaval or structural market changes, where historical patterns may no longer serve as reliable predictors of future performance (Murikah et al. 2024; Peng and de Moraes Souza 2024; Varsha 2023). Additionally, AI systems often struggle with the interpretation of complex contextual factors that influence financial performance, such as changes in regulatory environments, geopolitical events, or subtle shifts in business strategies (Murikah et al. 2024). The challenge of incorporating these qualitative factors into quantitative models represents a significant limitation in AI's ability to provide comprehensive financial analysis, potentially leading to oversimplified or misleading conclusions when complex judgement calls are required (Al-Khulaidy Stine and Kavak 2023; Murikah et al. 2024).

Another critical limitation centres on the 'black box' nature of many advanced AI algorithms, particularly deep learning models, which poses significant challenges for regulatory compliance and stakeholder trust (Al-Khulaidy Stine and Kavak 2023; Murikah et al. 2024; Valencia et al. 2019; Varsha 2023). The lack of transparency in how these systems arrive at their conclusions can make it difficult to validate their findings or defend their recommendations in regulatory contexts. This opacity becomes particularly problematic in financial analysis, where the ability to explain and justify decisions is often as important as the decisions themselves (Karim et al. 2024; Oneshko et al. 2023; Rawashdeh 2023). Furthermore, AI systems can perpetuate and amplify existing biases present in financial data and traditional analytical approaches, potentially leading to systematic errors in financial assessment and decision-making (Murikah et al. 2024). The challenge of ensuring fairness and avoiding discriminatory outcomes in AI-driven financial analysis remains a significant concern, particularly in applications such as credit assessment and risk evaluation. These limitations underscore the continuing importance of human oversight and judgement in financial analysis, suggesting that the optimal approach lies in developing hybrid systems that combine AI capabilities with human expertise rather than pursuing full automation (Liu 2022; Murikah et al. 2024; Varsha 2023).

The COVID-19 pandemic dramatically transformed the accounting profession and accelerated the digital transformation of financial services (Coman et al. 2022). The crisis revealed significant challenges in traditional accounting practices which led to a rapid adoption of digital solutions.

The shift towards digitalisation involved implementing Industry 4.0 technologies like artificial intelligence and cloud computing that reshaped how companies operate both internally and externally (Hamundu et al. 2020). Cloud accounting emerged as a particularly important innovation, allowing real-time access to financial data from anywhere and automating many routine tasks. This technology helps companies maintain business continuity while improving efficiency and accuracy.

The role of professional accountants is evolving dramatically in this digital transformation. Rather than simply recording transactions, accountants are becoming business analysts, consultants, and strategists. Modern accounting professionals need new skills in data analysis, IT systems, and cybersecurity (Coman et al. 2022).

Research indicates that most accounting professionals now recognise the need to adapt to a more digital future (David and Cernușca 2020). Young entrepreneurs, particularly millennials, expect their accountants to provide real-time insights and strategic advice using modern digital tools. This represents a fundamental shift in the profession, moving from traditional bookkeeping to value-added business consulting supported by artificial intelligence and automation technologies (Coman et al. 2022).

AI technologies in accounting and auditing span multiple approaches, each serving different purposes. Expert Systems (ES), the most developed application, store expert knowledge and simulate reasoning processes for tasks like audit planning and risk assessment. Continuous Auditing enables real-time collection and analysis of electronic audit evidence in paperless accounting systems. Decision Support

Systems assist with non-structured management problems, while Neural Networks replicate human brain organisation for tasks like analytical review procedures (Hasan 2022).

The implementation of these technologies offers significant benefits: improved efficiency, better accuracy, enhanced decision-making, and the ability to redirect human resources to more complex, value-added tasks (Danylkiv et al. 2022; Moustafa Al et al. 2024; Ramachandran et al. 2023; Ziemba et al. 2023). However, these advantages come with notable risks and challenges. Organisations face high implementation costs, potential technological unemployment, and the challenge of maintaining systems as regulations change. There is also concern about the technology's limitations in areas requiring human judgment, professional scepticism, and emotional intelligence (de Almeida Patricia Gomes et al. 2021; Haq et al. 2020; Kannan and Garad 2021).

5.3   The Added Risk Challenges of AI Technology

The rise of artificial intelligence has introduced unprecedented challenges in cybersecurity and fraud prevention (Stewart et al. 2020). According to the Federal Trade Commission's 2023 report (Commission 2024), AI-enabled fraud has become increasingly sophisticated, with deepfake technology and AI-generated content being used to create highly convincing scams. Studies from the Association of Certified Fraud Examiners (ACFE) suggest that AI-powered fraud schemes are notably more successful than traditional methods, with success rates up to 40% higher in initial contact attempts (Staiger 2023).

The financial and societal implications of AI-enhanced fraud are far-reaching and severe. The World Economic Forum's Global Risks Report (World Economic Forum 2024) highlights how AI is being used to automate and scale fraudulent activities, potentially causing billions in annual losses across sectors. Cybersecurity firm McAfee reports that AI-driven fraud attempts are becoming more difficult to detect, as machine learning algorithms can adapt to security measures and create more convincing deceptions (McAfee 2024). The impact extends beyond direct financial losses—the Banque de France has documented how AI-enabled fraud erodes trust in digital communications and financial systems, potentially hampering legitimate digital commerce and communication (Brousse et al. 2024). The combination of AI's capability to learn from defensive measures and its ability to generate highly personalised scam attempts has created what security experts call a perpetual cat-and-mouse game between fraudsters and security professionals.

5.4   Some Strategic Approaches to Mitigate the Limitations of AI-driven Financial Analysis

The development of strategic approaches to mitigate the limitations of AI-driven financial analysis has emerged as a critical focus in both academic research and practical implementation. These mitigation strategies operate across multiple dimensions, incorporating technological, organisational, and human-centred solutions to address the inherent limitations of AI systems in financial analysis. A fundamental approach involves the implementation of hybrid intelligence frameworks that strategically combine human expertise with AI capabilities, creating systems that leverage the strengths of both while compensating for their respective weaknesses (Venigandla et al. 2024). These frameworks typically incorporate explicit feedback loops between human analysts and AI systems, allowing for continuous refinement of analytical models while maintaining critical human oversight. Additionally, organisations are developing sophisticated validation frameworks that employ multiple AI models with different architectural approaches, creating ensemble systems that can cross-validate findings and reduce the risk of systematic errors or biases inherent in any single approach (Correia et al. 2023).

The advancement of explainable AI (XAI) technologies represents another crucial strategic approach to addressing the transparency limitations of AI-driven financial analysis. Entities are increasingly implementing layered interpretability frameworks that combine traditional statistical methods with advanced machine learning techniques, enabling better understanding and validation of AI-generated insights (Hagras 2018; Varsha 2023). These frameworks are complemented by robust governance structures that establish clear protocols for model validation, regular performance assessment, and systematic bias detection. Furthermore, entities are adopting dynamic data integration strategies that combine traditional financial metrics with alternative data sources, including real-time market indicators, social media sentiment, and environmental, social, and governance (ESG) metrics, to create more comprehensive and contextually aware analytical systems (Lim 2024; Sorathiya et al. 2024). This multi-faceted approach to mitigation demonstrates an evolving understanding that overcoming AI limitations requires not just technological solutions but also organisational and procedural innovations that ensure responsible and effective deployment of AI in financial analysis.

6 The Critical Interpretative Dimensions of AI in Financial Statement Analysis

6.1 Critical Management Studies (CMS): Theoretical Framework and Conceptual Foundations

Critical Management Studies (CMS) represents a distinct approach to management scholarship that challenges traditional, mainstream management theory and practice by examining organisational phenomena through a critical theoretical lens. At its core, CMS questions the taken-for-granted assumptions, power relations, and institutional structures that underpin conventional management thinking and organisational practices (Alvesson and Deetz 2000; Alvesson and Willmott 2003). The field is characterised by its emancipatory agenda, which seeks to expose and transform oppressive institutional arrangements while promoting more sustainable and socially just forms of organisation.

The key theoretical components of CMS constitute a complex framework that fundamentally challenges mainstream management theory and practice while offering alternative ways of understanding organisational phenomena. At its core, CMS is built upon three interrelated theoretical pillars: denaturalisation, reflexivity, and anti-performativity (Fournier and Grey 2000). Denaturalisation involves questioning and exposing the supposedly 'natural' or 'inevitable' character of management practices and organisational arrangements, revealing their socially constructed and historically contingent nature. Reflexivity demands critical self-awareness about knowledge production processes and the role of power in shaping management theory and practice, while anti-performativity challenges the notion that organisational knowledge should be primarily oriented towards improving technical efficiency and control (Alvesson and Deetz 2000).

The framework also incorporates critical perspectives on identity and subjectivity, examining how organisational practices shape employee identities and experiences, while maintaining a strong commitment to emancipatory ideals that seek to expose and transform oppressive organisational arrangements (Fournier and Grey 2000).

The practical implications of CMS extend far beyond theoretical critique to offer tangible approaches for transforming organisational practices and management education. At the organisational level, CMS has fostered the development of alternative management practices that emphasise participatory decision-making, workplace democracy, and sustainable organisational or entity forms (Spicer and Alvesson 2024). These practical applications have led to the emergence of more inclusive leadership approaches that challenge traditional hierarchical structures and promote employee empowerment through critical dialogue and collective reflection.

In management education, CMS has revolutionised pedagogical approaches by introducing critical reflection exercises, problematisation of mainstream management theories, and emphasis on ethical decision-making frameworks that consider broader societal implications (Alvesson and Deetz 2000; Spicer and Alvesson 2024). The practical impact of CMS is particularly evident in its influence on corporate social responsibility practices, where entities increasingly adopt more substantive approaches to addressing social and environmental issues rather than superficial compliance-based strategies (Spicer and Alvesson 2024). Furthermore, CMS has contributed to the development of alternative performance metrics that go beyond financial indicators to include social justice, environmental sustainability, and employee well-being measures (Spicer and Alvesson 2024). These practical applications demonstrate how CMS's theoretical insights can be translated into concrete organisational changes that promote more equitable, sustainable, and socially responsible management practices while challenging the traditional profit-maximisation paradigm that has dominated organisational decision-making.

6.2   Critical Framework Theory: Applications in Financial Analysis

The reframing of financial intelligence represents a fundamental shift from viewing financial analysis as merely a technical exercise to understanding it as a complex, pragmatic social practice embedded within power relations and organisational meaning-making processes (Spicer and Alvesson 2024).

According to Thomas (1997), financial statements are not neutral representations of organisational performance, but sophisticated texts embedded with complex power dynamics, ideological constructions, and strategic representations of the entity's identity and its behaviour. The critical lens reframes financial analysis from a technical exercise into a nuanced exploration of how entities communicate their economic realities, challenging the seemingly objective facade of financial reporting (McIntyre 1975; Thomas 1997).

This reconceptualisation positions financial analysis at the intersection of technical expertise and social construction, where financial metrics and indicators are not merely objective measurements but are instead understood as narratives that both reflect and constitute organisational reality. The critical lens reveals how financial intelligence practices serve as sites of power negotiation, where various stakeholders compete to define and interpret financial 'reality' through their preferred metrics and analytical frameworks (Alvesson and Deetz 2000).

Through this critical perspective, financial intelligence emerges as an ideological meaning-making process that shapes organisational understanding and decision-making (Spicer and Alvesson 2024). The production and interpretation of financial information is recognised as inherently political, reflecting particular interests and power relations while simultaneously constructing the organisational reality it purports to merely describe (Lewis 2015; Sugiarto 2023). This reframing emphasises how financial metrics and analysis create powerful narratives about organisational performance, success, and value, which in turn influence behaviour, strategy, and resource allocation. These narratives are not neutral technical representations but are instead deeply implicated in the construction and maintenance of organisational power structures and ideological frameworks (Montagna 1986).

Critical theory's imperative in AI financial analysis emerges from the recognition that artificial intelligence systems, far from being neutral technical tools, are deeply embedded in social power relations and ideological frameworks that shape their development and implementation (Jungherr 2023; Rakowski and Kowaliková 2024). The critical perspective reveals how AI financial analysis systems both reflect and reproduce existing power structures within entities and financial markets, while simultaneously creating new forms of algorithmic authority and control (Bahoo et al. 2024; Jungherr 2023). This understanding becomes particularly crucial as AI systems increasingly mediate financial decision-making processes, raising important questions about whose interests are served by these technological implementations and how they reshape organisational power dynamics. The critical lens highlights how AI systems in financial analysis often encode and amplify existing biases and power relations, while their perceived objectivity and technical sophistication can mask the inherently political nature of their design choices and operational parameters (Bahoo et al. 2024; Guler et al. 2024; Jungherr 2023; Rakowski and Kowaliková 2024).

The integration of critical theory into AI financial analysis also reveals the profound epistemological implications of algorithmic decision-making in financial contexts. As entities increasingly rely on AI systems for financial analysis, critical theory provides essential frameworks for understanding how these systems construct and legitimise particular forms of financial knowledge while potentially marginalising alternative perspectives and interpretations (Alvesson and Deetz 2000). This critical examination extends to questioning how AI systems influence the very nature of financial expertise and professional judgement, potentially reshaping traditional power relations within entities (Huber and DiGabriele 2021; Sachan et al. 2024). Furthermore, the critical perspective emphasises the need for reflexive awareness about how AI systems in financial analysis contribute to the broader financialisation of organisational life and the potential social and ethical implications of this (Al-Okaily et al. 2023; Dzhereleiko et al. 2024; Nguyen et al. 2024; Winata and Soekarno 2024).

The emancipatory agenda of critical theory becomes particularly relevant in addressing the ethical and social justice implications of AI-driven financial analysis (Priya et al. 2024). Critical perspectives help reveal how algorithmic systems can perpetuate or exacerbate existing inequalities in financial decision-making while highlighting the importance of developing more inclusive and socially conscious approaches to AI implementation (Jungherr 2023; Rakowski and Kowaliková 2024). This critical framework emphasises the need for greater transparency and accountability in AI financial systems, advocating for approaches that acknowledge the socially constructed nature of both financial data and the algorithmic systems that interpret them. The integration of critical theory thus becomes essential for developing more ethically aware and socially responsible approaches to AI implementation in financial analysis (Bahoo et al. 2024; Jungherr 2023; Rakowski and Kowaliková 2024).

7 Conclusion

The integration of AI into financial statement analysis represents a transformative shift in how organisations understand and interpret their financial data. This evolution, from traditional manual analysis to sophisticated AI-driven systems, has fundamentally reshaped the landscape of financial intelligence while raising important questions about the nature of financial analysis itself.

The research demonstrates that AI technologies offer unprecedented capabilities in processing vast amounts of financial data, detecting patterns, and generating real-time insights that were previously unattainable. From machine learning algorithms that predict financial distress to natural language processing systems that analyse qualitative information, AI has expanded both the scope and depth of financial analysis.

However, this technological advancement comes with significant challenges and limitations. The 'black box' nature of many AI systems, their dependence on historical data, and potential biases in their algorithms raise important concerns about transparency, reliability, and fairness. The COVID-19 pandemic has further accelerated digital transformation while highlighting both the potential and limitations of AI-driven financial analysis.

Perhaps most significantly, viewing AI implementation through the lens of Critical Management Studies reveals that these systems are not merely neutral technical tools, but are deeply embedded in social power relations and organisational structures. This critical perspective emphasises that financial statements and their analysis are sophisticated texts that reflect and constitute organisational reality, carrying implicit power dynamics and ideological constructions.

Looking forward, the successful integration of AI in financial statement analysis will likely depend on developing hybrid approaches that combine the computational power of AI with human expertise and judgment. This integration must be guided by ethical considerations and an understanding of the broader social implications of AI implementation. Organisations will need to balance the drive for efficiency and accuracy with the need for transparency, fairness, and social responsibility.

AI in financial statement analysis is not merely a technological intervention but a profound reimagining of organisational intelligence. It represents a dynamic, evolving ecosystem where computational capabilities and human expertise continuously negotiate meaning, risk, and organisational understanding.

The future of financial statement analysis thus lies not just in technological advancement, but in developing more nuanced, ethical, and socially conscious approaches to AI implementation that acknowledge both its transformative potential and its limitations. This advancement requires ongoing dialogue between technical expertise, critical theory, and practical application to ensure that AI serves not just as a tool for financial analysis, but as a means to create more equitable and sustainable organisational practices.

References

Abkrakhmanov R, Elubaeva A, Turymbetov T, Nakhipova V, Turmaganbetova S, Ikram Z (2023) A novel 2D deep convolutional neural network for multimodal document categorization. Int J Adv Comput Sci Appl 14(7):720–728. https://doi.org/10.14569/ijacsa.2023.0140779

Aboelfotoh A, Zamel AM, Abu-Musa AA, Frendy F, Sabry SH, Moubarak H (2024) Examining the ability of big data analytics to investigate financial reporting quality: a comprehensive bibliometric analysis [article]. J Financ Report Account. https://doi.org/10.1108/JFRA-11-2023-0689

Al-Khulaidy Stine A, Kavak H (2023) 4 – Bias, fairness, and assurance in AI: overview and synthesis. In: Batarseh FA, Freeman LJ (eds) AI Assurance. Academic Press, pp 125–151. https://doi.org/10.1016/B978-0-32-391919-7.00016-0

Alles MG, Gray GL (2020) Will the medium become the message? A framework for understanding the coming automation of the audit process [article]. J Inf Syst 34(2):109–130. https://doi.org/10.2308/isys-52633

Almaqtari FA (2024) The role of IT governance in the integration of AI in accounting and auditing operations. Economies 12(8):199. https://doi.org/10.3390/economies12080199

Al-Okaily M, Alsmadi AA, Alrawashdeh N, Al-Okaily A, Oroud Y, Al-Gasaymeh AS (2023) The role of digital accounting transformation in the banking industry sector: an integrated model. J Financ Report Account 22(2):308–326. https://doi.org/10.1108/jfra-04-2023-0214

Alvesson M, Deetz S (2000) Doing critical management research. SAGE Publications Ltd. https://doi.org/10.4135/9781849208918

Alvesson M, Willmott H (2003) Studying management critically. SAGE Publications Ltd. https://doi.org/10.4135/9781446220030

Ashraf M (2024) Does automation improve financial reporting? Evidence from internal controls [article]. Rev Acc Stud 30(1):436–479. https://doi.org/10.1007/s11142-024-09822-y

Askar AH, Kovács E, Bolló B (2023) Prediction and optimization of thermal loads in buildings with different shapes by neural networks and recent finite difference methods. Buildings 13(11):2862. https://doi.org/10.3390/buildings13112862

Bahoo S, Cucculelli M, Goga X, Mondolo J (2024) Artificial intelligence in finance: a comprehensive review through bibliometric and content analysis. SN Bus Econ 4(2):23. https://doi.org/10.1007/s43546-023-00618-x

Bakumenko A, Elragal A (2022) Detecting anomalies in financial data using machine learning algorithms. Systems 10(5):130. https://doi.org/10.3390/systems10050130

Bao Y, Ke BIN, Li BIN, Yu YJ, Zhang JIE (2020) Detecting accounting fraud in publicly traded U.S. firms using a machine learning approach [article]. J Account Res 58(1):199–235. https://doi.org/10.1111/1475-679x.12292

Barna LEL, Hurducaci CC (2024) The impact of using artificial intelligence and ERP systems in the work of accounting professionals and auditors [article]. Ann Univ Oradea Econ Sci Ser 33(1):246–258. https://search.ebscohost.com/login.aspx?direct=true&AuthType=sso&db=bsu&AN=178933775&site=ehost-live&scope=site&custid=s6390179

Bergantinos KJA, Samonte MJC (2023) Clustering and classification analysis in financial reporting of Philippine government business enterprises. In: 2023 IEEE 15th International conference on humanoid, nanotechnology, information technology, communication and control, environment, and management, HNICEM 2023

Bitetto A, Cerchiello P, Mertzanis C (2023) Measuring financial soundness around the world: a machine learning approach [article]. Int Rev Financ Anal 85:102451. https://doi.org/10.1016/j.irfa.2022.102451

Bragoli D, Ferretti C, Ganugi P, Marseguerra G, Mezzogori D, Zammori F (2021) Machine-learning models for bankruptcy prediction: do industrial variables matter? [article]. Spat Econ Anal 17(2):156–177. https://doi.org/10.1080/17421772.2021.1977377

Brenes RF, Johannssen A, Chukhrova N (2022) An intelligent bankruptcy prediction model using a multilayer perceptron. Intell Syst Appl 16:200136. https://doi.org/10.1016/j.iswa.2022.200136

Brousse C, Fliche O, Joyez J, Uri J (2024) *Artificial intelligence challenges for the financial system* (FINANCIAL STABILITY REPORT: Assessment of risks and vulnerabilities in the financial system Issue. https://www.banque-france.fr/system/files/2024-10/Artificial_intelligence_challenges_for_the_financial_system.pdf

Cao L (2020) AI in finance: a review. SSRN Electron J. https://doi.org/10.2139/ssrn.3647625

Chakraborty B, Bhattacharjee T (2020) A review on textual analysis of corporate disclosure according to the evolution of different automated methods. J Financ Report Account 18(4):757–777. https://doi.org/10.1108/jfra-02-2020-0047

Chen BB, Long SJ (2020) A novel end-to-end corporate credit rating model based on self-attention mechanism. IEEE ACCESS 8:203876–203889. https://doi.org/10.1109/ACCESS.2020.3036469

Chen Y-C, Kuo S-M, Liu Y, Wu Z, Zhang F (2022) Improving returns on strategy decisions through integration of neural networks for the valuation of asset pricing: the case of Taiwanese stock. Int J Financ Stud 10(4):99. https://doi.org/10.3390/ijfs10040099

Chen B, Wu Z, Zhao R (2023) From fiction to fact: the growing role of generative AI in business and finance. J Chinese Econ Bus Stud 21(4):471–496. https://doi.org/10.1080/14765284.2023.2245279

Choi I, Kim WC (2024) Practical forecasting of risk boundaries for industrial metals and critical minerals via statistical machine learning techniques [article]. Int Rev Financ Anal 94:103252. https://doi.org/10.1016/j.irfa.2024.103252

Coman DM, Ionescu CA, Duică A, Coman MD, Uzlau MC, Stanescu SG, State V (2022) Digitization of accounting: the premise of the paradigm shift of role of the professional accountant. Appl Sci 12(7):3359

Commission U. S. F. T. (2024) Annual Report-Fiscal Year 2023. https://www.ftc.gov/system/files/ftc_gov/pdf/FTC_Annual_Report_FY2023_5.15.24.pdf

Cooper DJ, Hopper T (2007) Critical theorising in management accounting research. Elsevier

Correia A, Grover A, Schneider D, Pimentel AP, Chaves R, de Almeida MA, Fonseca B (2023) Designing for hybrid intelligence: a taxonomy and survey of crowd-machine interaction. Appl Sci 13(4):2198. https://www.mdpi.com/2076-3417/13/4/2198

Cragg PB, King M (1993) Spreadsheet modelling abuse: an opportunity for OR? J Oper Res Soc 44(8):743–752. https://doi.org/10.2307/2583886

Dameri RP, Garelli R, Resta M (2020) Neural networks in accounting: clustering firm performance using financial reporting data [article]. J Inf Syst 34(2):149–166. https://doi.org/10.2308/isys-18-002

Danylkiv K, Dropa Y, Petyk M, Teslya S (2022) The use of innovative blockchain technology in the public finances of Ukraine in the conditions of the formation of the digital economy. VUZF Rev 7(3):101–112. https://doi.org/10.38188/2534-9228.22.3.10

David D, Cernuşca L (2020) The perception of professional accountants regarding the future of the accounting profession in the digital era. CECCAR Bus Rev 1(7):3–10

de Almeida Patricia Gomes R, dos Santos Carlos D, Farias Josivania S (2021) Artificial intelligence regulation: a framework for governance. Ethics Inf Technol 23(3):505–525. https://doi.org/10.1007/s10676-021-09593-z

Ding K, Peng X, Wang Y (2019) A machine learning-based peer selection method with financial ratios [article]. Account Horiz 33(3):75–87. https://doi.org/10.2308/acch-52454

Dong H (2022) Stock Price prediction using ARIMA and LSTM. In: Proceedings −2022 6th annual International conference on data science and business analytics. ICDSBA 2022

Du MR, Zhang ZQ (2023) Modeling selection for credit risk measurement: based on meta path features. TEHNICKI VJESNIK-TECHNICAL GAZETTE 30(2):545–554. https://doi.org/10.17559/TV-20221107051221

Dzhereleiko S, Borisova V, Konieva I, Yakovenko O, Zinchenko A (2024) Innovative approaches to financial risk mitigation: insights for digital business and accounting systems. Financ Credit Activity-Problems Theory Pract 4(57):67–79. https://doi.org/10.55643/fcaptp.4.57.2024.4411

Eziefule AO, Adelakun BO, Okoye IN, Attieku JS (2022) The role of AI in automating routine accounting tasks: efficiency gains and workforce implications. Eur J Account Audit Finance Res 10(12):109–134

Faccia A, McDonald J, George B (2023) NLP sentiment analysis and accounting transparency: a new era of financial record keeping. Computers 13(1):5. https://doi.org/10.3390/computers13010005

Fenyves V, Tarnóczi T, Orbán I (2024) Application of text mining in analysing notes to financial statements: a Hungarian case. J Int Stud 17(3):205–225. https://doi.org/10.14254/2071-8330.2024/17-3/11

Foidl H, Golendukhina V, Ramler R, Felderer M (2024) Data pipeline quality: influencing factors, root causes of data-related issues, and processing problem areas for developers. J Syst Softw 207:111855. https://doi.org/10.1016/j.jss.2023.111855

Fournier V, Grey C (2000) At the critical moment: conditions and prospects for critical management studies. Hum Relat 53(1):7–32. https://doi.org/10.1177/0018726700531002

Garg A, Ghanshala KK, Sharma S (2024) A hybrid model of integrating sentiment analysis and key market indicators for IPO listing trend prediction. Int J Math Eng Manag Sci 9(4):902–913. https://doi.org/10.33889/ijmems.2024.9.4.047

Graham B, Dodd DLF (1934) Security analysis. McGraw-Hill Book Company

Gu ZY, Lv JY, Wu BY, Hu ZH, Yu XW (2024) Credit risk assessment of small and micro enterprise based on machine learning. HELIYON 10(5):e27096. https://doi.org/10.1016/j.heliyon.2024.e27096

Guler N, Kirshner SN, Vidgen R (2024) A literature review of artificial intelligence research in business and management using machine learning and chat GPT. Data Inform Manag 8(3):100076. https://doi.org/10.1016/j.dim.2024.100076

Hagras H (2018) Toward human-understandable, explainable AI [article]. Computer 51(9):28–36. Article 8481251. https://doi.org/10.1109/MC.2018.3620965

Halim Z, Shuhidan SM, Sanusi ZM (2021) Corporation financial distress prediction with deep learning: analysis of public listed companies in Malaysia. Bus Process Manag J 27(4):1163–1178. https://doi.org/10.1108/bpmj-06-2020-0273

Hamundu FM, Husin MH, Baharudin AS, Khaleel M (2020) Intention to adopt cloud accounting: a conceptual model from Indonesian MSMEs perspectives. J Asian Finance Econ Bus 7(12):749–759

Haq I, Abatemarco M, Hoops J (2020) The development of machine learning and its implications for public accounting: certified public accountant. CPA J 90(6):6–9. https://www.proquest.com/scholarly-journals/development-machine-learning-implications-public/docview/2420173544/se-2?accountid=13425

Haraguchi K, Tamba Y, Ikeda D, Abe S (2024) Does accrual information impact municipal bond prices? Evidence from Japan using AI [article]. Public Money Manag:1–12. https://doi.org/10.1080/09540962.2024.2392731

Hasan A (2022) Artificial intelligence (AI) in Accounting & Auditing: a literature review. Open J Bus Manag 10:440–465. https://doi.org/10.4236/ojbm.2022.101026

Hayes L, Boritz JE (2022) Classifying restatements: an application of machine learning and textual analytics [article]. J Inf Syst 35(3):107–131. https://doi.org/10.2308/ISYS-19-003

Huang C-K, Cheng Y-H (2024) Assessing firm performance in digital transformation: a preliminary analysis using financial indicators. Manag Financ 50(9):1641–1661. https://doi.org/10.1108/mf-02-2024-0081

Huang L, Lu H (2024) Design of intelligent financial data management system based on higher-order hybrid clustering algorithm. PeerJ Comput Sci 10:e1799. https://doi.org/10.7717/peerj-cs.1799

Huber D, DiGabriele JA (2021) Financial statement fraud and the failure of corporate financial statement fraud prediction. J of Acco And Fina 21(4):30–41. https://www.proquest.com/scholarly-journals/financial-statement-fraud-failure-corporate/docview/2573031842/se-2?accountid=13425

Jang Y, Jeong I, Cho YK (2020) Business failure prediction of construction contractors using a LSTM RNN with accounting, construction market, and macroeconomic variables [article]. J Manag Eng 36(2):1–15. https://doi.org/10.1061/(asce)me.1943-5479.0000733

Jeong J, Kim C (2022) Comparison of machine learning approaches for medium-to-Long-term financial distress predictions in the construction industry. Buildings 12(10):1759. https://doi.org/10.3390/buildings12101759

Jungherr A (2023) Artificial intelligence and democracy: a conceptual framework. Soc Media Soc 9(3):20563051231186353. https://doi.org/10.1177/20563051231186353

Kamimura ES, Pinto ARF, Nagano MS (2023) A recent review on optimisation methods applied to credit scoring models [article]. J Econ Finance Admin Sci 28(56):352–371. https://doi.org/10.1108/jefas-09-2021-0193

Kannan KSP, Garad A (2021) Competencies of quality professionals in the era of industry 4.0: a case study of electronics manufacturer from Malaysia [Competencies of quality professionals]. Int J Qual Reliab Manag 38(3):839–871. https://doi.org/10.1108/IJQRM-04-2019-0124

Karim S, Shafiullah M, Naeem MA (2024) When one domino falls, others follow: a machine learning analysis of extreme risk spillovers in developed stock markets [article]. Int Rev Financ Anal 93:103202. https://doi.org/10.1016/j.irfa.2024.103202

Kavya M, Silvester R, Anand A (2021) Forecasting the prominent, fluctuating and declining stock prices using a numerical approach. Turkish J Comput Math Educ 12(10):1289–1296. https://www.proquest.com/scholarly-journals/forecasting-prominent-fluctuating-declining-stock/docview/2623612246/se-2?accountid=13425

Kee R (1993) Data processing technology and accounting: a historical perspective. Account Hist J 20(2):187–216. http://www.jstor.org/stable/40698121

Khan S, Gupta S (2023) Using a hermeneutic phenomenological approach to twitter content: a social network's analysis of green accounting as a dimension of sustainability. Qual Res Financ Mark 15(4):672–692. https://doi.org/10.1108/qrfm-02-2022-0031

Korangi K, Mues C, Bravo C (2023) A transformer based model for default prediction in mid-cap corporate markets. Eur J Oper Res 308(1):306–320. https://doi.org/10.1016/j.ejor.2022.10.032

Kristanti FT, Safriza Z, Salim DF (2023) Are Indonesian construction companies financially distressed? A prediction using artificial neural networks [article]. Invest Manag Financ Innov 20(2):41–52. https://doi.org/10.21511/imfi.20(2).2023.04

Kruck SE, Sheetz SD (2001) Spreadsheet accuracy theory. J Inf Syst Educ 12(2):93–108. https://aisel.aisnet.org/jise/vol12/iss2/6

Kuizinienė D, Krilavičius T (2024) Balancing techniques for advanced financial distress detection using artificial intelligence. Electronics 13(8):1596. https://doi.org/10.3390/electronics13081596

Lacher J (1997, May 1) The power of spreadsheets: from columnar pad to silicon chip. J Account. https://www.journalofaccountancy.com/issues/1997/may/spread.html

Lai Y-W, Chen M-Y (2024) Using natural language processing with explainable AI approach to construct a human-centric consumer application for financial climate disclosures. IEEE Trans Consum Electron 70(1):1112–1121. https://doi.org/10.1109/tce.2023.3326953

Lewis JM (2015) The politics and consequences of performance measurement. Polic Soc 34(1):1–12. https://doi.org/10.1016/j.polsoc.2015.03.001

Li T, Dai X (2024) Financial risk prediction and management using machine learning and natural language processing. Int J Adv Comput Sci Appl 15(6). https://doi.org/10.14569/ijacsa.2024.0150623

Lim T (2024) Environmental, social, and governance (ESG) and artificial intelligence in finance: State-of-the-art and research takeaways. Artif Intell Rev 57(4):76. https://doi.org/10.1007/s10462-024-10708-3

Lin FP (2022) Computing technology for financial service. In: Encyclopedia of finance, third edition, pp 1869–1899. https://doi.org/10.1007/978-3-030-91231-4_81

Liu XC (2021) Empirical analysis of financial statement fraud of listed companies based on logistic regression and random forest algorithm. J Math 2021:9241338. https://doi.org/10.1155/2021/9241338

Liu M (2022) Assessing human information processing in lending decisions: a machine learning approach [article]. J Account Res 60(2):607–651. https://doi.org/10.1111/1475-679x.12427

Liu H, Li L, Ye Y, Pan C, Yang G, Chen T, Zhang T, Wang J, Qiu C (2023) A deep learning neural network method using linear eigenvalue statistics for schizophrenic EEG data classification. Mathematics 11(23):4776. https://doi.org/10.3390/math11234776

Liu LX, Sun Z, Xu K, Chen C (2024) AI-driven financial analysis: exploring ChatGPT's capabilities and challenges. Int J Financ Stud 12(3):60. https://doi.org/10.3390/ijfs12030060

Lokanan M, Tran V, Vuong NH (2019) Detecting anomalies in financial statements using machine learning algorithm: the case of Vietnamese listed firms [article]. Asian J Account Res 4(2):181–201. https://doi.org/10.1108/AJAR-09-2018-0032

Lösse LJ, Weißenberger BE (2023) Using interpretable machine learning for accounting fraud detection—a multi-user perspective. Die Unternehmung 77(2):113–133. https://doi.org/10.5771/0042-059x-2023-2-113

Mathebula M, Modupe A, Marivate V (2024) ChatGPT as a text annotation tool to evaluate sentiment analysis on south African financial institutions. IEEE ACCESS 12:144017–144043. https://doi.org/10.1109/ACCESS.2024.3464374

McAfee (2024) Artificial Intelligence and winning the battle against deepfakes and malware. https://www.mcafee.com/ai/news/artificial-intelligence-and-winning-the-battle-against-deepfakes-and-malware/

McIntyre EV (1975) Communicating through financial reports: an empirical study. J Bus Commun (1973) 12(3):9–15. https://doi.org/10.1177/002194367501200302

Meiryani M, Fahlevi M, Robbani AI, Winoto A, Salim G, Purnomo A, Lusianah L (2023) Factors affecting the integrity of financial statements [article]. Corp Gov Organ Behav Rev 7(3):211–227. https://doi.org/10.22495/cgobrv7i3p17

Miller P, O'Leary T (2007) Mediating instruments and making markets: capital budgeting, science and the economy. Acc Organ Soc 32(7):701–734. https://doi.org/10.1016/j.aos.2007.02.003

Mitra R, Dongre A, Dangare P, Goswami A, Tiwari MK (2023) Knowledge graph driven credit risk assessment for micro, small and medium-sized enterprises. Int J Prod Res 62(12):4273–4289. https://doi.org/10.1080/00207543.2023.2257807

Montagna P (1986) Accounting rationality and financial legitimation. Theory Soc 15(1/2):103–138. http://www.jstor.org/stable/657177

Morgan G (2014) Images of organization. Sage

Moustafa Al N, Mohamed Gaber G, Mahboub R, Nakhal B (2024) The role of artificial intelligence in eliminating accounting errors. J Risk Financ Manag 17(8):353. https://doi.org/10.3390/jrfm17080353

Munappy AR, Bosch J, Olsson HH (2020) *Data pipeline management in practice: challenges and opportunities* product-focused software process improvement: 21st International conference, PROFES 2020, Turin, Italy, November 25–27, 2020, Proceedings, Turin, Italy. https://doi.org/10.1007/978-3-030-64148-1_11

Murikah W, Nthenge JK, Musyoka FM (2024) Bias and ethics of AI systems applied in auditing – a systematic review. Sci Afr 25:e02281. https://doi.org/10.1016/j.sciaf.2024.e02281

Nguyen PT, Kend M, Le DQ (2024) Digital transformation in Vietnam: the impacts on external auditors and their practices. Pac Account Rev 36(1):144–160. https://doi.org/10.1108/par-04-2023-0051

Nofel M, Marzouk M, Elbardan H, Saleh R, Mogahed A (2024) Integrating Blockchain, IoT, and XBRL in accounting information systems: a systematic literature review. J Risk Financ Manag 17(8):372. https://doi.org/10.3390/jrfm17080372

Omran MGH, Engelbrecht AP, Salman A (2007) An overview of clustering methods. Intell Data Anal 11(6):583–605. https://doi.org/10.3233/ida-2007-11602

Oneshko S, Nazarenko A, Koval O, Yaremko I, Pysarchuk O (2023) Accounting and financial reporting in the IT sphere of Ukraine: opportunities of Artificial Intelligence. Financ Credit Act: Probl Theory Pract 5(52):79–96. https://doi.org/10.55643/fcaptp.5.52.2023.4151

Palepu KG, Healy PM, Peek E (2020) Business analysis and valuation: IFRS edition. Cengage Learning

Park MS, Son H, Hyun C, Hwang HJ (2021) Explainability of machine learning models for bankruptcy prediction. IEEE Access 9:124887–124899. https://doi.org/10.1109/ACCESS.2021.3110270

Patel K (2023) Big data in finance: an architectural overview. Int J Comput Trends Technol 71(10):61–68

Peng Y, de Moraes Souza JG (2024) Chaos, overfitting and equilibrium: to what extent can machine learning beat the financial market? [article]. Int Rev Financ Anal 95:103474. https://doi.org/10.1016/j.irfa.2024.103474

Pol S, Hudnurkar M, Ambekar SS (2022) Predicting credit ratings using deep learning models—an analysis of the Indian IT industry [article]. Australas Bus Account Finance J 16(5):38–51. https://doi.org/10.14453/aabfj.v16i5.04

Pour PD, Ahmed AA, Nazzal MA, Darras BM (2023) An industry 4.0 technology selection framework for manufacturing systems and firms using fuzzy AHP and fuzzy TOPSIS methods. Systems 11(4):192. https://doi.org/10.3390/systems11040192

Priya PS, Shah JA, Aarawal A, Kalra R, Kadam S, Sontakke KA (2024) Machine learning enabled financial statements in assessing a Business's performance. In: Proceedings of 9th international conference on science, technology, engineering and mathematics: the role of emerging technologies in digital transformation. ICONSTEM 2024

Rakowski R, Kowaliková P (2024) The political and social contradictions of the human and online environment in the context of artificial intelligence applications. Humanit Soc Sci Commun 11(1):289. https://doi.org/10.1057/s41599-024-02725-y

Ramachandran D, Mubarak A, Hussain A, Abbas Q (2023) Enhancing cloud-based security: a novel approach for efficient cyber-threat detection using GSCSO-IHNN model. Systems 11(10):518. https://doi.org/10.3390/systems11100518

Rawashdeh A (2023) A deep learning-based SEM-ANN analysis of the impact of AI-based audit services on client trust. J Appl Acc Res 25(3):594–622. https://doi.org/10.1108/jaar-10-2022-0273

Rudžionis V, Lopata A, Gudas S, Butleris R, Veitaitė I, Dilijonas D, Grišius E, Zwitserloot M, Rudzioniene K (2022) Identifying irregular financial operations using accountant comments and natural language processing techniques. Appl Sci 12(17):8558. https://doi.org/10.3390/app12178558

Sachan S, Almaghrabi F, Yang J-B, Xu D-L (2024) Human-AI collaboration to mitigate decision noise in financial underwriting: a study on FinTech innovation in a lending firm [article]. Int Rev Financ Anal 93:103149. https://doi.org/10.1016/j.irfa.2024.103149

Saenz JV, Quiroga FM, Bariviera AF (2023) Data vs. information: using clustering techniques to enhance stock returns forecasting. Int Rev Financ Anal 88:102657. https://doi.org/10.1016/j.irfa.2023.102657

Saleh MMA, Jawabreh OAA, Al Om R, Shniekat N (2021) Artificial intelligence (AI) and the impact of enhancing the consistency and interpretation of financial statement in the classified hotels in Aqaba, Jordan [article]. Acad Strateg Manag J 20(SpecialIssue3):1–18. https://www.

scopus.com/inward/record.uri?eid=2-s2.0-85107822725&partnerID=40&md5=35caaafcf131 d7384c56f766636a17e5

Sawangarreerak S, Thanathamathee P (2021) Detecting and analyzing fraudulent patterns of financial statement for open innovation using discretization and association rule mining. J Open Innov: Technol Mark Complex 7(2):128. https://doi.org/10.3390/joitmc7020128

Seo W, Kim B, Bang S, Kang Y (2024) Identifying key financial variables predicting the financial performance of construction companies [article]. J Constr Eng Manag 150(3):04024007. https://doi.org/10.1061/JCEMD4.COENG-13959

Singh S, Singhal S (2021) Implementation and analysis of the clustering process in the enhancement of manufacturing productivity. J King Saud Univ – Eng Sci 33(7):482–490. https://doi.org/10.1016/j.jksues.2020.06.005

Singh Yadav AK, Sora M (2022) Unsupervised learning for financial statement fraud detection using manta ray foraging based convolutional neural network. Concurr Comput: Pract Exp 34(27). https://doi.org/10.1002/cpe.7340

Smith L, Lamprecht C (2024) Identifying the limitations associated with machine learning techniques in performing accounting tasks. J Financ Rep Account 22(2):227–253. https://doi.org/10.1108/jfra-05-2023-0280

Sorathiya A, Saval P, Sorathiya M (2024) Data-driven sustainable investment strategies: integrating ESG, financial data science, and time series analysis for alpha generation. Int J Financ Stud 12(2):36

Spicer A, Alvesson M (2024) Critical management studies: a critical review. *J Manag Stud* 62(1):446–483. https://doi.org/10.1111/joms.13047

Staiger A (2023, October 2023) AI's double-edged sword: how fraudsters are Weaponizing intelligence. ACFE Insights Blog. https://www.acfe.com/acfe-insights-blog/blog-detail?s=how-fraudsters-are-weaponizing-artificial-intelligence

Stewart C, Armentrout T, Shorstein D, Giesen K (2020) Managing risk through innovation. J Gov Financ Manag 69(2):56–58. https://www.proquest.com/scholarly-journals/managing-risk-through-innovation/docview/2428567741/se-2?accountid=13425

Sugiarto I (2023) Strategic financial intelligence in the digital age: harnessing advanced data analytics for informed decision-making amidst complex business landscapes. Int J Econ Lit 1(3):293–304

Szczygielski JJ, Charteris A, Bwanya PR, Brzeszczyński J (2024) Google search trends and stock markets: sentiment, attention or uncertainty? [article]. Int Rev Financ Anal 91:102549. https://doi.org/10.1016/j.irfa.2023.102549

Tafech A (2024) Anomaly detection and categorization for a data quality management framework in financial regulatory reporting. Lecture notes in business information processing.

Taylor S, Keselj V (2021) Predicting the distress of financial intermediaries using convolutional neural networks. In: Proceedings – 2021 IEEE 23rd conference on business informatics, CBI 2021 – main papers

Thomas J (1997) Discourse in the marketplace: the making of meaning in annual reports. J Bus Commun (1973) 34(1):47–66. https://doi.org/10.1177/002194369703400103

Trad A (2021) The business transformation framework and Enterprise architecture framework for managers in business innovation [article]. Int J Serv Sci Manag Eng Technol 12(1):142–181. https://doi.org/10.4018/IJSSMET.20210101.oa1

Uyar M (2021) The role of business analytics in transforming management accounting information into cost performance. Ege Akademik Bakis (Ege Acad Rev) 21(4):373–389. https://doi.org/10.21121/eab.1015665

Valencia C, Cabrales S, Garcia L, Ramirez J, Calderona D, McMillan D (2019) Generalized additive model with embedded variable selection for bankruptcy prediction: prediction versus interpretation [article]. Cogent Econ Finance 7(1):1–10. https://doi.org/10.1080/2332203 9.2019.1597956

Varsha PS (2023) How can we manage biases in artificial intelligence systems—a systematic literature review. Int J Inf Manag Data Insights 3(1):100165. https://doi.org/10.1016/j.jjimei.2023.100165

Velte P (2023) Automated text analyses of sustainability & integrated reporting. A literature review of empirical-quantitative research. J Glob Responsib 14(4):530–566. https://doi.org/10.1108/jgr-09-2022-0090

Venigandla K, Vemuri N, Vemuri N (2024) Hybrid intelligence systems combining human expertise and AI/RPA for complex problem solving. Int J Innov Sci Res Technol(IJISRT) 9(3):2066–2075. https://doi.org/10.38124/ijisrt/IJISRT24MAR2039

Voytsekhivska I, Voytsekhivskyy I (2021, November 1) Journal-entry testing using excel. J Account. https://www.journalofaccountancy.com/issues/2021/nov/journal-entry-testing-excel.html

Wang F, Gacesa M (2023) Semi-strong efficient market of bitcoin and twitter: an analysis of semantic vector spaces of extracted keywords and light gradient boosting machine models [article]. Int Rev Financ Anal 88:102692. https://doi.org/10.1016/j.irfa.2023.102692

Wang D, Chen Z, Florescu I, Wen B (2023) A sparsity algorithm for finding optimal counterfactual explanations: application to corporate credit rating [article]. Res Int Bus Financ 64:101869. https://doi.org/10.1016/j.ribaf.2022.101869

Wen Y (2021) Research on the improvement path of financial report based on XBRL. In: Journal of Physics: Conference Series, vol 1756, No. 1. IOP Publishing, p 012018. https://doi.org/10.1088/1742-6596/1756/1/012018

Winata RK, Soekarno S (2024) Literature review on digitalization and financial performance [article]. J Econ Bus 7(3):148–165. https://doi.org/10.31014/aior.1992.07.03.601

World Economic Forum (2024) The global risks report 2024 – insight report. https://www3.weforum.org/docs/WEF_The_Global_Risks_Report_2024.pdf

Xie Q, Fang T, Rong X, Xu X (2024) Nonlinear behavior of tail risk resonance and early warning: insight from global energy stock markets [article]. Int Rev Financ Anal 93:103162. https://doi.org/10.1016/j.irfa.2024.103162

Xu X (2020) Risk factor analysis combined with deep learning in the risk assessment of overseas investment of enterprises. PLoS One 15(10):e0239635. https://doi.org/10.1371/journal.pone.0239635

Xu K, Wang W (2023) Limited information limits accuracy: whether ensemble empirical mode decomposition improves crude oil spot price prediction? [article]. Int Rev Financ Anal 87:102625. https://doi.org/10.1016/j.irfa.2023.102625

Xu YZ, Zhang JL, Hua Y, Wang LY (2019) Dynamic credit risk evaluation method for e-commerce sellers based on a hybrid artificial intelligence model. Sustainability 11(19):5521. https://doi.org/10.3390/su11195521

Yang S, Ding Y, Xie B, Guo Y, Bai X, Qian J, Gao Y, Wang W, Ren J (2023) Advancing financial forecasts: a deep dive into memory attention and Long-distance loss in stock Price predictions. Appl Sci 13(22):12160. https://doi.org/10.3390/app132212160

Yee A, Gepp A, Kumar K, Todd J, Vanstone B (2024) Detecting financial statement fraud: an alternative evaluation of automated tools using portfolio performance [article]. J Forensic Investigative Account 16(1):45–57. https://search.ebscohost.com/login.aspx?direct=true&AuthType=sso&db=bsu&AN=178990452&site=ehost-live&scope=site&custid=s6390179

Zhang W, Yan S, Li J, Tian X, Yoshida T (2022) Credit risk prediction of SMEs in supply chain finance by fusing demographic and behavioral data [article]. Transp Res Part E: Logist Transp Rev 158:102611. https://doi.org/10.1016/j.tre.2022.102611

Zhou LR, Duan YL, Wei W (2023) Research on the financial data fraud detection of Chinese listed enterprises by integrating audit opinions. KSII Trans Interest Inf Syst 17(12):3218–3241. https://doi.org/10.3837/tiis.2023.12.001

Ziemba P, Becker J, Becker A, Radomska-Zalas A (2023) Framework for multi-criteria assessment of classification models for the purposes of credit scoring. J Big Data 10(1):94. https://doi.org/10.1186/s40537-023-00768-7

Artificial Intelligence Tools and Use Cases in Corporate Finance

Mohammed Kayode Ajape and Adesanmi Timothy Adegbayibi

Abstract Sourcing funds to finance an organization's activities is one of the most critical strategic decisions every organization must make, as it constitutes the fulcrum which propels organizational growth and survival. This aspect of an organization is fundamental, strategic, and comprehensive, requiring concerted efforts from management, especially in the modern, technology-driven environment where businesses operate. Inappropriate financing decisions could mar corporate progress and deter it from achieving the very objective the organization was incorporated to pursue. On the other hand, artificial intelligence has assumed a pervasive dimension sweeping virtually every facet of corporate and individual lives. AI tools have proven to be effective in carrying out tasks which were hitherto done by humans and are worthy and dependable allies in navigating through some of the strategic decision-making duties of corporate managers. In this chapter, the concepts of corporate finance and artificial intelligence were copiously examined through the lens of the Modigliani and Miller, pecking order, and technology acceptance model theories. Also, we analyze the place of artificial intelligence tools in shaping corporate financing decisions. Specifically, the impervious role of AI tools in each corporate finance aspect, including capital budgeting, capital structure, dividend policy, financial planning and analysis, merger and acquisition decision, working capital management, portfolio management, and investor relations, was examined. The chapter highlighted a few organizations that have deployed AI in their corporate finance activities and concluded with some of the limitations of AI applications in corporate finance.

Keywords Corporate finance · AI · Financing decision · Risk management · Automation

M. K. Ajape (✉) · A. T. Adegbayibi
Department of Accountancy, University of Johannesburg, Johannesburg, South Africa
e-mail: majape@uj.ac.za; aadegbayibi@uj.ac.za

© The Author(s), under exclusive license to Springer Nature   153
Switzerland AG 2025
M. Adelowotan, C. A. Leke (eds.), *Artificial Intelligence in Accounting, Auditing and Finance*, Contributions to Finance and Accounting,
https://doi.org/10.1007/978-3-031-87368-3_9

1 Introduction

Corporate managers are charged with realizing the various corporate objectives, including maximizing shareholders' wealth. This objective and other goals of the organization are usually achieved through optimizing corporate human and financial resources. Corporate finance is an important activity that maximizes shareholders' value through short- and long-term financial planning and implementing various strategies. However, traditional financial approaches frequently need help quickly and effectively handling vast data and deriving valuable insights.

The development of revolutionary digital technologies and applications in artificial intelligence (AI) has propelled an unparalleled pace of technological advancement in the first two decades of the twenty-first century (Bahoo et al. 2024). The discipline of computer science, known as artificial intelligence, develops intelligent machines that can carry out cognitive functions that have historically been thought of as human, such as speech recognition, learning, reasoning, and action (Frankenfield 2021). Integrating AI tools into corporate finance has offered a paradigm shift by facilitating automated data analysis, pattern recognition, and modelling future trends, allowing finance professionals to make data-informed decisions quickly and precisely (Rane et al. 2024).

The adoption of AI in corporate finance has witnessed a significant increase due to AI's capacity to automate routine tasks, provide predictive analytics, enhance accuracy and efficiency and complex strategic financial decision-making. Gartner's (2022) report listed anomaly and error detection, cash collections, demand and revenue forecasting, decision support, and percentage of completion (POC) revenue forecasting as some of the areas of AI use in financial planning and analysis (FP&A). Mckinsey (2024) reported that about 72% of corporate organizations have integrated AI into corporate finance activities. KPMG (2024) revealed how generative AI has been used to automate and improve forecast budgeting and reporting. Therefore, artificial intelligence has become a true game changer within the world of finance and has redefined its landscape by driving innovation and efficiency across the industry.

This chapter develops as follows: the next section provides a detailed overview of corporate finance and artificial intelligence and traces the historical evolution of both concepts. Further, in the ensuing section, Modigliani and Miller trade-off, pecking order, and technology acceptance model theories were discussed vis-à-vis AI adoption. The next section explores the various AI tools used in corporate finance and examples of corporate organizations that have integrated the AI tools. The ultimate section identifies some challenges of integrating AI into corporate finance activities and concludes the chapter.

1.1 Overview of Corporate Finance

The topic of corporate finance is still critical and is becoming more and more popular in the discipline of financial management, which deals with how businesses manage their capital structure, investment possibilities, and funding sources. Promoting business success and sustainability entails experts, executives, and financial managers making well-informed judgements. Corporate finance refers to the financial decisions and actions taken by businesses to maximize shareholder value and accomplish corporate objectives. Capital budgeting, capital structure, funding, dividend policy, risk management, financial analysis, financial planning, mergers and acquisitions, working capital management, and investor relations are just a few areas it covers.

The primary goal of corporate finance is to increase shareholder value through the execution of numerous projects and long- and short-term financial planning. Specifically, the goals include maximizing shareholder value, allocating resources as efficiently as possible, minimizing expenses and risks, maintaining liquidity and solvency, and fostering strategic growth and expansion.

Strategic business decisions that impact an organization's stability and financial success are part of corporate finance. Financial, investment, and dividend policy considerations are the three main categories of essential decisions in this context. Each of these facets of decisions is briefly explained thus:

Financing Decision This entails determining the best method for funding investment projects. An organization may decide to use external money or internal resources to finance investments. Retained earnings and other reserves are examples of internal resources. Obtaining funds from outside investors may be accomplished by debt (bonds and debentures), equity sales, or the issuance of other financial products (derivatives, options, futures, forward, and leases). Principal and interest (the cost of borrowing) must be repaid to secure debt. This debt raises the company's level of exposure (gearing/leverage level). In essence, divesting shares entails selling off a piece of the company's equity. Ownership of a fractional stake in the business is represented by equity or shares. Financial assets or liabilities may result from the use of financial instruments.

Thus, corporate managers must maintain an appropriate mix of debt, equity, and other financial instruments to finance the company's investment projects, considering the cost of capital and its potential impact on the firm's statement of financial position.

Investment Decision Choosing how to allocate an organization's resources to assets that have the potential to generate the maximum returns for the business over a specific time frame is known as an investment choice. Choosing which asset to invest in will provide the greatest benefit to the business. A common term for this is capital budgeting. Investments may be categorized using several criteria, such as:

(a) Project size: small or large projects

(b) Accruable benefits: less risk, more cash flow, or other indirect advantages
(c) Dependency level: complimentary (A raises return of B), substitutes (A lowers return of B), or mutually incompatible (project X or Y)
(d) Degree of statistical dependence—positive, negative, or statistical independence and
(e) Cash flow type: non-conventional or conventional (one cash flow change)

Analysing an investment risk and possible return is part of the decision-making process. Making the best investment choices requires balancing the company's short- and long-term objectives and combining short- and long-term investment opportunities. In the short term, when an organization needs money to pay for expenses, loan repayment, and so on, it might have to hoard money, preventing investment. However, if the organization invests a portion of its funds in long-term projects, it might not be able to meet its immediate obligations and could be forced out of business.

The risk and return associated with various investment ventures vary. Thus, choosing which project to take on is a crucial investment choice that must be made to separate "expected return". Additionally, each investment opportunity's payback period and current value must be carefully evaluated.

Any investment that is considered needs to maximize the firm's worth and be sufficiently financed; otherwise, the money will have to be returned to shareholders.

Dividend Policy Decision The amount of earnings left over after taxes, which are given to the company's owners, is known as a dividend. It serves to compensate shareholders for their equity investment in the business. Dividends are a significant source of passive income for many investors. In addition to attracting potential investors and boosting shareholder trust, regular dividend payments also reflect solid financial performance and the company's long-term viability.

On the other hand, the dividend policy is the procedure that the company's management uses to decide how to ultimately divide the company's profits between cash dividend payments to shareholders and retention (reinvestment). Decisions over dividend policies, therefore, centre on striking a balance between the demands of business expansion and shareholders' need for speedy payouts. It displays the level of caution in the business's financial administration. These choices include determining how much of the company's revenues should be kept for internal reinvestment vs. how much should be distributed as dividends to shareholders.

Decisions on a company's dividends impact on its expansion, diversification, mergers, and future prospects. It is also affected by market conditions (macroeconomic factors), growth/investment potential, liquidity, and profitability (income stability).

The origin of corporate finance (CF) can be found in the early 1900s. Adam Smith's well-known 1776 work, "The Wealth of Nations", established the groundwork for the contemporary CF. Irving Fisher popularized the idea of the time value of money by 1930. Modern portfolio theory was invented by Harry Markowitz in 1952. Modern CF has its roots in the capital structure theory of Modigliani and

Miller (1958) and William Sharpe's Capital Asset Pricing Model (CAPM) (1964). As financial engineering, risk management, and international finance emerged in the 1970s and 1980s, the field of CF advanced steadily. In the 1990s and 2000s, behavioural finance, information asymmetry, and agency theory also gained popularity.

In summary, CF has evolved in four different stages (Table 1):

1.2 Overview of Artificial Intelligence

The goal of the extensive discipline of computer science known as artificial intelligence (AI) is to build machines that can do jobs that normally call for human intelligence. These activities cover perception, learning, cognition, problem-solving, and natural language comprehension. Numerous techniques and technologies that have made considerable strides in recent years are included in artificial intelligence.

Since OpenAI released ChatGPT in November 2022, artificial intelligence has revolutionized how businesses conduct their financial processes. AI is a disruptive catalyst in the financial industry and is not just a trendy term. The corporate finance sector is undergoing radical change due to four significant elements of artificial intelligence. These include efficiency to enhance procedures, accuracy by lowering human error, predictive analytics to guide decisions, and automation of repetitive chores.

Machine learning, neural networks, deep learning, natural language processing (NLP), robots, and computer vision are some of the subfields that make up artificial intelligence. AI has advanced quickly due to several factors, including advancements in algorithms, computer power, and the availability of large datasets.

Machine Learning (ML) This area of artificial intelligence focuses on creating algorithms that enable computers to learn from data and form opinions or predictions. Supervised, unsupervised, semi-supervised, and reinforcement learning are all included in this learning process. In addition to helping organizations boost and transform large data sets to gain valuable insights, machine learning (ML) can help businesses forecast financial implications and make data-driven, well-informed

Table 1 Stages of corporate finance evolution

Stage	Period	Key development
1	1950s	Corporate finance becomes a distinct field, with scholars like Modigliani, Miller, and Markowitz contributing foundational theories
2	1960s	CAPM and efficient market hypothesis gain acceptance.
3	1970s–1980s	Financial economics and corporate finance intersect, influencing practice and research.
4	1990s–2000s	Advances in risk management, behavioural finance, and international finance expand the field.

Source: Compiled by the Authors (2024)

decisions about pricing, risk management, and investments (Jordan and Mitchell 2015). It can also help with proactive risk management and strategic planning. Regression analysis, time series analysis, and neural networks are examples of machine learning approaches that are very good at predicting financial variables like cash flow, expenses, and revenue. These models can produce accurate forecasts of future financial performance by including past data and external variables such as market movements and economic indicators (Rane et al. 2024). As a result of this foresight, businesses may predict difficulties, improve tactics, and maximize results. Additionally, Gu et al. (2020) study uses machine learning to forecast market returns, indicating that artificial intelligence (AI) could enhance financial decision-making by seeing patterns in massive datasets. Other examples of ML algorithms include TensorFlow and PyTorch.

Neural Networks These computer models, made up of networked nodes or neurons that process information in layers, are modelled after the structure of the human brain. Applications like language translation, autonomous driving, and gaming use it. Deep learning driven by neural networks has transformed computer vision and speech recognition, according to LeCun et al. (2015).

Deep Learning Deep neural networks, a subject of machine learning, are neural networks with several layers that can learn from vast amounts of data. Applications like language translation, autonomous driving, and gaming use it. In the game of GO, AlphaGo, an AI machine, has been found to outperform human champions, demonstrating the effectiveness of deep learning in complex professions (Silver et al. 2016).

Natural Language Processing (NLP) This area of artificial intelligence focuses on natural language communication between people and machines. Among natural language processing (NLP) applications are ChatGPT, Google Gemini, financial chatbots, sentiment analysis, text categorization, financial document summarization, entity recognition, information retrieval, language translation, and customer feedback analysis. Bidirectional encoder representations from transformers (BERT), a pre-trained language model presented by Devlin et al. (2018), significantly raised the bar for several NLP tasks. NLP technologies facilitate extracting valuable information from unstructured data sources, including news articles, social media, and regulatory filings, enabling organizations to make informed decisions regarding corporate governance and sustainability (Rane et al. 2024). IBM Watson and CoreNLP are a few other examples of NLP.

Robotics In this area of artificial intelligence, robots that can interact with the natural environment are designed and built. By automating repetitive tasks like data input, reconciliation, and reporting, robotic process automation (RPA) increases operational efficiency, optimizes workflows, and ensures regulatory compliance (Rane et al. 2024). RPA provides several benefits to financial professionals. By automating routine operating tasks, RPA frees finance teams to focus on value-added activities like data analysis and strategic decision-making. It also streamlines accounting procedures in corporate finance departments, improves the accuracy and efficiency of financial forecasting and planning activities, and lowers the risk of errors and fraud while ensuring adherence to internal controls and regulatory standards. This allows finance professionals to focus on strategic initiatives. RPA has also transformed corporate finance, changing how financial processes are executed and managed (Kokina and Blanchette 2019; Doguc 2021).

RPA could use predictive analytics and historical data to produce more accurate forecasts, which would help organizations make well-informed decisions about investment strategies and resource allocation. It could also automate risk management, make scenario planning and stress testing more accessible, and enable organizations to evaluate the effects of different risk factors on their financial health. RPA promotes operational efficiency, cost savings, and scalability while driving significant transformative changes in corporate finance operations (Met et al. 2020; Devarajan 2018; Thekkethil et al. 2021).

Manufacturing, healthcare, and driverless cars are its main application areas. The deep reinforcement learning study by Mnih et al. (2015) shows how robots can learn to complete tasks by interacting with their surroundings, demonstrating advances in autonomous systems. UiPath and Automation Anywhere are other RPA tools.

Computer Vision A branch of artificial intelligence that allows computers to evaluate and draw inferences from visual inputs from their environment. It is frequently utilized in autonomous driving, medical image analysis, and facial identification. Empirical Study: Residual Networks (ResNets) was developed by He et al. (2016) and significantly improved image recognition systems' accuracy.

Because AI technologies offer priceless insights that were previously unattainable, they are becoming an increasingly important component of trading, risk management, and financial research. As artificial intelligence (AI) continues to grow, its transformative methods—such as machine learning, neural networks, deep learning, natural language processing (NLP), robots, and computer vision—have stimulated innovation and improved productivity, precision, and decision-making in a wide range of industries.

In conclusion, artificial intelligence has seen significant development over time, from its initial conception in the 1940s to its actual birth at the 1956 Dartmouth Conference. Due to a lack of financing, processing power, and attention from pertinent stakeholders, AI development saw a significant backlash of retrogression between the early 1970s and 1990s. However, in 1997, 2012, and 2016, AI computer programs outperformed human champions in several challenging computer-enabled games, marking a breakthrough in the decision-usefulness of AI. Table 2 summarizes the evolution of AI from complex computer algorithms to an integrative and interactive decision-making paradigm.

Table 2 Stages of AI development

Stage	Period	Main development	Source
Early concept	1940s–1950s	Proposal for a model of artificial neurons by McCulloch and Pitts (McCulloch and Pitts 1943) Publication of "Computing Machinery and Intelligence" by Turing (1950).	McCulloch and Pitts (1943), Turing (1950)
The birth of AI	1956–1970s	Official birth of AI at the Dartmouth Conference (1956) Development of ELIZA, a natural language processing program that stimulates conversation (1966)	McCarthy et al. (1956), Weizenbaum (1966)
The first AI winter	1970s–1980s	1970s witnessed slow progress in AI due to low computing power, funding, and interest Introduction of expert systems like MYCIN	Buchanan and Shortliffe (1984)
The rise of machine learning	1980s–1990s	Backpropagation popularized by Geoffrey and others (1986) Defeat of world chess champion by IBM's Deep Blue (1997)	Rumelhart et al. (1986), Campbell et al. (2002).
The second AI winter and revival	1990s–2000s	Late 1990s is a period of reduced funding and interest in AI Big Data and AI resurgence in the 2000s	Domingos (2012)
The deep learning revolution	2010s– present	AlexNet won ImageNet competition in 2012 AlphaGo, developed by Google defeated GO champion in 2016	Krizhevsky et al. (2012), Silver et al. (2016).
Current and future trends	2020s– onwards	2020s witnessed advancements in natural language processing, autonomous systems, and ethical AI considerations AI integration into everyday applications	Bostrom and Yudkowsky (2014).

Source: Compiled by the Author, 2024

2 Theoretical Background

In discussing how the emergence of AI and its tools affects corporate financing decisions, three (3) theories underlining this relationship are advanced in this sub-section.

2.1 Modigliani–Miller Theorem

The financing alternatives available to businesses, particularly the decision between debt and equity, are the focus of MM theory (Giglio 2022). The idea, developed in the 1950s by economists Franco Modigliani and Merton Miller, suggests that a firm's worth is independent of its financing in a perfect market free from taxes, bankruptcy expenses, and asymmetric knowledge. The idea, also known as the capital structure irrelevance principle, contends that a company's market value is unaffected by its capital structure and that, under specific presumptions, the amount of debt has no bearing on the total worth of the business. Jaros and Bartosova (2015) interpreted the theory to mean that the firm's internal and external sources are not worthy of any business consideration and that the capital structure composition of the company has no bearing on the company's value. According to the MM model, the amount on the assets side of the Statement of Financial Position—rather than the debt-to-equity ratio—determines the firm's worth. However, in cases where no tax assumptions are loosened, the amount of debt positively correlates with the company's worth since interest on debt acts as a tax shield and raises firm value. The trade-off, pricing order, and market timing theories all derived from this theory.

Accordingly, the use of AI may not directly affect a company's value, but indirectly, by reducing the risks associated with financial decisions and optimizing cash flows, AI can enhance decision-making, reduce costs, boost operational effectiveness, and increase the firm's value. For instance, AI can speed up financial forecasting, risk assessment, and fraud detection, leading to more accurate and timely financial management.

2.2 Pecking Order Theory

According to this hypothesis created by Myers in 1984, businesses would rather use internally generated funds, such as retained earnings, to fund their operations than to issue debt and equity (external financing). In other words, businesses prioritize their funding sources based on the least effort or least resistance concept, initially giving preference to internal financing, followed by debt, and, last, equity issuance. By adhering to a specific funding hierarchy, the pecking order theory suggests minimizing the firm's insider-outsider problems associated with information asymmetry (Jahanzeb et al. 2014).

According to this theory, management prioritizes using retained earnings. They decide to issue debt if they don't have enough of these. Finally, stock is offered when issuing more debt isn't a good idea. On the one hand, Pecking Order Theory backs up the notion that highly successful businesses would finance their operations via short-term, collateral-free financing, followed by long-term debt and equity issues (Bistrova et al. 2011).

AI can play a big role in this hierarchy and make internal finance more appealing by improving the accuracy and reliability of internal financial data. By enhancing data analytics and predictive modelling, artificial intelligence (AI) helps organizations better understand their financial health and future demands, reducing their need on outside finance. By providing insights into when it is most advantageous to issue new debt or restructure existing commitments, AI can also enhance debt management.

2.3 Technology Acceptance Model (TAM)

An information systems theory called the Technology Acceptance Model (TAM), developed in 1989 by Fred Davis, focuses on how people embrace and utilize technology (Marikyan and Papagiannidis 2024). According to TAM, the main forces behind the adoption of technology are users' perceptions of its utility (PU) and ease of use (PEOU). The fundamental principle is that the more users believe a certain programme would improve their performance and the less work it takes to use, the higher the adoption rate will be (Fiorini et al. 2018).

According to Liu et al. (2015), Fiorini et al. (2018), and Marikyan and Papagiannidis (2024), over the years, TAM has been expanded to include additional factors that determine technology acceptance, such as users' willingness to try new technology (behavioural intention, or BI), their effective reaction to using it (attitude towards using, or ATU), actual system use (ASU), or the belief of important others that they should utilize the technology (social influence, or SI); the presence of technical and organizational infrastructure to support adoption (facilitating conditions, or FC); and users' previous experiences using comparable technologies and adoption status (experience and voluntariness, or E&V).

According to TAM, the perceived benefits of AI solutions—such as precise financial forecasts, the ability to automate repetitive processes, and insightful information—as well as their ease of integration into existing operations—such as their intuitiveness and low training requirements—are the main factors that influence financial professionals' decisions to employ them in corporate finance. Furthermore, the adoption of AI tools can be facilitated by the availability of technical assistance, training programmes, and a strong IT infrastructure, provided that senior management and industry leaders support the usage of AI.

Financial analysts may therefore find AI solutions useful if they believe they could improve the accuracy of their financial projections or make complex data processing tasks easier. If AI solutions are user-friendly and seamlessly integrate with existing financial apps, financial professionals are more likely to use them.

When these theories are combined, it becomes clear that AI plays a variety of roles in corporate finance such as enhancing operational effectiveness and decision-making, to raise corporate value (M&M theory); improving debt management and make internal financing more feasible (pecking order theory); and emphasizing how crucial perceived utility and usability are to the integration of AI technologies in financial processes (TAM theory). In line with the tenets of these fundamental theories of corporate finance, businesses can use AI to improve risk management, financial forecasting, and overall financial performance.

3 Artificial Intelligence Application in Corporate Finance

The demand for improved efficiency, risk management, and decision-making has led to a global increase in interest in the use of AI tools in corporate financial operations. The business community can predict many more innovative advancements in the financial and other sectors as AI advances.

Artificial intelligence, in corporate finance, refers to the machine imitation of human behaviour and consciousness to accomplish financial goals by using technology tools and resources that enable digital systems to carry out tasks often performed by intelligent individuals (Lim 2024).

Corporate finance is a highly regulated domain and has complex requirements for transparency and traceability of decision-making processes. As such, corporate managers may face challenges such as a lack of specific guidelines on how to apply AI tools in finance in a way that complies with the law (Weber et al. 2024). As a result, organizations and regulators would need to work assiduously to balance innovation with compliance and private concerns (Nweze et al. 2024). The intersection of AI and finance has revolutionized many aspects of the financial industry and resulted in significant advancements, including new solutions for a variety of financial tasks (Lee et al. 2024). The advanced predictive powers of AI, including risk assessment and scenario planning, have the potential to alter strategic financial choices drastically.

AI's convergence with other technologies, such as blockchain and the Internet of Things (IoT), may open new financial administration and reporting possibilities. For example, AI may examine blockchain data to increase security and transparency, automate smart contracts, and offer personalized financial services. AI can also exploit IoT data for real-time financial forecasting, risk management, and ESG reporting (Lim 2024). This convergence enables reliable data for informed decision-making, adaptable business models, and efficiency gains.

Some of the examples of AI tools use cases in corporate finance are:

1. Risk Management: The act of identifying, evaluating, and mitigating possible risks and hazards that could lower the firm's value is known as risk management in corporate finance. By identifying patterns and correlations, artificial intelligence (AI) can monitor market trends, economic variables, and organizational financial data to spot warning signs of financial difficulties or breaches (Rane et al. 2024). Additionally, AI might model a variety of risk situations, assisting businesses in getting ready for upcoming difficulties.

These various risks include:

(a) Liquidity and Refinancing Risk: Even if a business is successful, it may not be solvent. Liquidity risk occurs if a business cannot meet its immediate cash needs. Therefore, the hallmark of managing liquidity and refinancing risk is making sure the business can meet its short-term obligations and refinance its debt when necessary.

(b) Interest Rate Risk: Corporate managers work hard to keep a proper capital structure by weighing the benefits of borrowing money against the drawbacks of employing equity. When an organization chooses debt over equity, interest rates signify the financial weight they must face. Controlling how changing interest rates affect a company's financial performance is paramount in corporate finance.

(c) Foreign Exchange Risk: This includes measures taken to reduce the risks associated with currency fluctuations, particularly for companies that conduct business internationally. It describes the losses resulting from currency changes in an overseas financial transaction. Other names for this risk are currency, exchange rate, and FX risks.

(d) Credit Risk: The likelihood that debtors will default is called credit risk. To reduce the danger of default, corporate managers evaluate vast amounts of financial data using AI algorithms to determine a potential borrower's credit risk. This helps financial institutions make well-informed lending decisions, especially in areas with poor credit records. Additionally, in order to stop and restrict fraudulent activity, machine learning algorithms are used to identify odd patterns and anomalies in financial transactions. AI aids in risk management by processing enormous volumes of data to identify potential dangers and risks. It can monitor market patterns, economic indicators, and internal financial data to provide early warnings of financial downturns or breaches. AI-driven solutions might be able to simulate various risk scenarios, assisting businesses in getting ready for potential problems and decreasing the possibility of financial fraud.

2. Investment Decision-Making: By allocating the organization's limited resources to lucrative endeavours, managers aim to optimize the return for shareholders. To forecast market indicators and optimize firms' portfolios, an understanding of market historical data, past performance, and trends is necessary to achieve the ideal investment portfolio.

Asset managers can optimize investment portfolios with the use of AI-driven analytics. Artificial intelligence (AI) can make risk-adjusted investing recommendations by analysing past data and market trends. Making better investing decisions can be facilitated by using AI algorithms to analyse market data and forecast changes in stock prices and other market indicators.

3. Operational Efficiency: Optimizing operations and attaining efficiency through revenue maximization and expense reduction are one of corporate finance's objectives. Data entry, reconciliation, and reporting are examples of repetitive operations that could be streamlined through process automation using Robotic Process Automation (RPA) and other AI solutions. By doing this, human error is

reduced, and resources are freed up for more strategic endeavours. Additionally, by automating some operational tasks, AI tools may help reduce operating costs, which is important for businesses in cost-sensitive markets. AI helps firms cut costs and prevent errors by standardizing corporate financial procedures, such as payroll processing, cost management, and accounts payable and receivable.

4. Customer Engagement and Service: AI-powered real-time customer support using chatbots and virtual assistants can answer questions, complete simple transactions, and improve customer pleasure and experience. Artificial intelligence (AI) tools analyse client data to tailor financial products and services to each person's needs, improving customer satisfaction and retention.

5. Regulatory Compliance: By searching for legislative requirements and making sure financial activities adhere to legal regulations, AI could assist management in regulatory compliance. This is especially important when handling the various regulatory frameworks. This is accomplished by automating audits and compliance checks and by keeping an eye on documents and transactions for regulatory compliance to avoid penalties resulting from non-compliance.

6. Strategic Planning and Forecasting: AI tools assist in forecasting economic and financial trends, enabling businesses to take preventive measures and make well-informed strategic choices. AI systems could model many economic situations using scenario analysis to find workable outcomes for business operations and financial impacts.

7. Financial Planning and Analysis (FP&A): AI solutions could help in financial planning and analysis by automating data gathering, processing, and analysis. Using machine learning algorithms, insights from big databases, threat detection, and financial trend prediction are all possible. This enables more accurate planning and forecasting, which enables businesses to allocate resources more effectively.

8. Liquidity and Working Capital Management: AI solutions could help in financial planning and analysis by automating data gathering, processing, and analysis. Using machine learning algorithms, insights from big databases, threat detection, and financial trend prediction are all possible. This enables more accurate planning and forecasting, which enables businesses to allocate resources more effectively.

9. Mergers and Acquisitions (M&A) Due Diligence: Due diligence is a time-consuming process that involves reviewing vast amounts of financial data in M&A discussions. AI can speed up this process by automating benchmarking and transaction review.

AI can quickly compare a company's financial performance to that of its competitors in the market and identify trends in development. This significantly reduces the time needed to perform early assessments and produces more accurate insights.

4   AI Use Case in Corporate Organizations

Finance professionals have myriads of AI tools at their disposal. These tools, according to Corporate Finance Institute (2024) include ChatGPT, Datarails FP&A (e.g. Adaptive Anaplan), Domo, Stampli, Vena Insights, Planful Predict, Macroaxis, Trullion, Nanonets Flow, and Booke.ai. In addition, predictive analytics software like SAS and R, AI-powered chatbots (such as Microsoft Bot Framework, Dialogflow), data visualization tools (e.g. Tableau and Power BI), and blockchain and distributed ledger technology (DLT). These tools, either individually or by combining two or more tools, have been employed by top business organizations across the globe to attain corporate goal of sound financial management. Brief examples of AI use cases in corporate financing across the world are:

JPMorgan Chase   JPMorgan Chase utilizes AI to enhance its financial projections. The bank uses machine learning algorithms to improve its investing strategy, credit risk assessment and predict market trends. This aids the company in making wise financial decisions.

HSBC   HSBC uses artificial intelligence (AI) to detect fraudulent transactions. By monitoring transaction patterns, AI technology may be able to spot questionable activities in real time, significantly reducing the likelihood of fraud.

KPMG   Clara, an AI-powered tool developed by KPMG, expedites the auditing procedure. Analysing financial data and producing audit reports will help Clara become more accurate and efficient.

General Electric   AI's real-time insights and analytics enable finance teams to make data-driven decisions. This could lead to improved strategic planning and financial performance. For example, General Electric (GE) employs AI to analyse financial data and offer decision-making insights. This aids GE in strengthening its financial strategy and increasing overall efficiency.

Siemens   Siemens uses AI to automate the payment process for its accounts. This has significantly reduced the cost and time involved in processing invoices. Thus, artificial intelligence has been utilized to streamline financial operations by automating the processing of invoices and the administration of expenses.

BlackRock   BlackRock, the top global asset management, has adopted artificial intelligence to monitor market trends and direct investment plans. Their AI technology, Aladdin, helps with risk management and investment portfolio structuring. This aids companies in maximizing profits while making prudent investment choices.

Deutsche Bank   Artificial intelligence is used by the Deutsche Bank to ensure that financial regulations are followed. The AI system ensures compliance with regulatory requirements through automated reporting processes by monitoring transactions and producing compliance reports.

Goldman Sachs uses predictive analytics for trading, **Microsoft** uses AI-driven financial planning and analysis, while **Amazon** leverages AI-powered cash flow forecasting.

The above examples illustrate AI tools' growing adoption and wider acceptability in corporate finance, enabling organizations to enhance corporate efficiency, accuracy, and strategic decision-making.

5   Challenges of Using AI Tools for Financial Analysis

While there are many benefits/advantages of using AI tools in corporate finance for financial analysis and other finance-related issues, there are yet several challenges that corporate organizations would have to take into consideration in employing AI (Goodell et al. 2021; Shanmuganathan 2020; Polak et al. 2020). Some of these obstacles are outlined below.

5.1   Cybersecurity Risks

Corporate AI-enabled financial systems are vulnerable to a range of cybersecurity risks, such as hostile assaults and data breaches. Strong cybersecurity procedures are necessary to protect these systems. Therefore, finance professionals must exercise caution when entering sensitive financial data into any financial AI technologies, even when these tools are used to help with safety and compliance. This is because posting sensitive private information online can expose the organization to cybersecurity danger.

5.2   Lack of Human Connection, Empathy, and Emotional Intelligence

In complex corporate financial decision-making and strategic planning, human judgement and supervision are still crucial despite the AI's ability to automate tasks. Even though AI-powered financial products can respond to consumer enquiries and provide customer service, a lot of people still prefer speaking with assistance or responses from real humans. This is particularly true when private data is at stake. Further, financial AI tools need more human emotions, and this could result in some clients feeling ignored or misunderstood when they can only communicate with AI. Thus, there is need for periodic and/or regular human intervention in reviewing clients' interactions with AI. Finance managers would need frequent face-to-face interactions with relevant stakeholders to assess the progress of the AI-enabled systems. There must be explicit rules for human supervision and involvement in AI decision-making, especially when the risks are high.

Responsible AI implementation requires the complementary role of human skills. When making critical decisions, finance managers must utilize both human and AI-driven systems to achieve optimal financing decisions. Combining AI technologies with well-established business financial infrastructure, such as enterprise resource planning (ERP) systems, can be challenging. Data silos and compatibility problems could appear, requiring careful preparation and implementation.

5.3   Bias and Discrimination

Sometimes, the prejudices of their programmers are reflected in AI financial analysis systems. These prejudices can then sustain discrimination, racism, and prejudice. Besides, AI-driven financial systems could reinforce prejudices embedded in past data, which could result in unfair outcomes, especially in relation to employment, credit scoring procedures, or lending decisions. Thus, it becomes critical that human beings continue to oversee any jobs that AI technologies perform. Doing this would ensure maintenance of moral principles, uphold equity, and reduce biases of AI systems in corporate finance.

5.4   Over-Reliance on AI

Despite their intelligence, AI financial analysis tools are not human. Therefore, they are unable to provide the kinds of critical thinking and interpersonal skills unique to human intellect. Finance professionals should avoid becoming so dependent on AI that they might lose the ability to think analytically for themselves. Although AI helps with risk assessment and mitigation, there are serious concerns associated with relying too much on these models without being aware of their limitations. Inadequate risk assessment can lead to regulatory fines or significant monetary penalties.

5.5   Data Availability, Quality, and Models Interpretability

The functionality of AI systems and integrity of its output depend wholly on the corporate data fed into it. In corporate finance, organizational data may be inconsistent, fragmented, lacking or dispersing across multiple systems. This makes it difficult to build precise models, therefore ensuring the availability, quality, sensitivity, confidentiality, and security of data are crucial. This calls for precise data governance standards that specify how AI algorithms gather, keep, and use data in addition to strict cybersecurity safeguards.

Moreover, stakeholders may need help understanding how decisions are made using AI models. In corporate finance, this opaqueness may make it more difficult to maintain confidence and adhere to regulatory requirements. Financial markets are also dynamic, and AI models that can adjust to changing circumstances must provide reliable forecasts and suggestions.

5.6 Required Investment

Creating and implementing AI systems in corporate finance requires a large investment. Significant initial cost outlay on software and hardware, including necessary investment to upgrade existing corporate systems to be AI compliant. Data management skills, computing infrastructure, and qualified staff are also required. The need for upskilling and development of AI competence in finance managers becomes imperative. This might pose some difficulties for small and medium-sized businesses with little funding.

6 Conclusion

In this chapter, we have explored how artificial intelligence is revolutionizing corporate finance. AI will have major economic consequences when integrated into corporate financial systems. By automating labour-intensive business processes, AI may considerably decrease operating expenses. Decision-making may be improved by AI-driven insights, which will increase the business's overall competitiveness and financial success. Moreover, AI's capacity to manage risks can improve businesses' resilience and economic viability. By automating repetitive operations, boosting decision-making, and increasing reporting precision, artificial intelligence (AI) has the potential to revolutionize the financial industry. Mid-size businesses may fully utilize AI and set themselves up for success in an intensely competitive marketplace by tackling problems like data quality, expenses, and cultural resistance. AI can be a potent instrument for improving financial performance and fostering long-term success with the correct preparation and tactics. Nevertheless, the chapter highlighted some of the obstacles to implementing AI which managers of corporate organizations should take cognizance of while integrating AI tools into corporate finance activities. As a result, the chapter encouraged policymakers in establishing more specific regulations and prerequisites for using AI-based systems in corporate finance.

In a whole, AI has a wide range of effects on business financial processes. By implementing AI technologies, organizations can enhance their financial operations, make more intelligent choices, and accomplish strategic goals. This change encourages productivity and profitability and prepares businesses to meet the demands of evolving financial environments.

References

Bahoo S, Cucculelli M, Goga X, Mondolo J (2024) Artificial intelligence in finance: a comprehensive review through bibliometric and content analysis. SN Bus Econ 4(23). https://doi.org/10.1007/s43546-023-00618-x

Bistrova J, Lace N, Peleckiene V (2011) The influence of capital structure on Baltic corporate performance. J Bus Econ Manag 12(4):655–669

Bostrom N, Yudkowsky E (2014) *The ethics of artificial intelligence* in Cambridge handbook of artificial intelligence. Cambridge University Press, pp 316–334

Buchanan BG, Shortliffe EH (1984) Rule-based expert systems: the MYCIN experiments of the Stanford heuristic programming project. Addison-Wesley

Devarajan Y (2018) A study of robotic process automation uses cases today for tomorrow's business. Int J Comput Techniq 5(6):12–18

Devlin J, Chang M, Lee K, Toutanova K (2018) BERT: Pre-training of deep bidirectional transformers for language understanding. arXiv:1810.04805v2 [cs.CL], https://doi.org/10.48550/arXiv.1810.04805

Doguc O (2021) Applications of robotic process automation in finance and accounting. Beykent Üniversitesi Fen ve Mühendislik Bilimleri Dergisi 14(1):51–59

Domingos P (2012) A few useful things to know about machine learning. Commun ACM 55(10):78–87

Fiorini PD, Seles BMRP, Jabbour CJC, Mariano EB, Jabbour ABLD (2018) Management theory and big data literature: from a review to a research agenda. Int J Inf Manag 43:112–129

Frankenfield J (2021, March 8). Artificial Intelligence (AI). Retrieved from https://www.investopedia.com/terms/a/artificial-intelligence-ai.asp

Gartner Inc. (2022). Gartner identifies 5 top use cases for AI in corporate finance. Available at Gartner Identifies 5 Top Use Cases for AI in Corporate Finance

Giglio F (2022) The capital structure through the Modigliani and Miller model. Int Bus Res 15(11):11–16. https://doi.org/10.5539/ibr.v15n11p11

Goodell JW, Kumar S, Lim WM, Pattnaik D (2021) Artificial intelligence and machine learning in finance: identifying foundations, themes, and research clusters from bibliometric analysis. J Behav Exp Financ 32:100577

Gu S, Kelly B, Xiu D (2020) Empirical asset pricing via machine learning. Rev Financ Stud 33(5):2223–2273. https://doi.org/10.1093/rfs/hhaa009

He K, Zhang X, Ren S, Sun J (2016) Deep residual learning for image recognition. *arXiv:1512.03385v1 [cs.CV]*, https://doi.org/10.48550/arXiv.1512.03385

Jahanzeb A, Saif-ur-Rehman, Bajuri NH, Karami M, Ahmadimousaabad A (2014) Trade-off theory, pecking order theory and market timing theory: a comprehensive review of capital structure theories. Int J Manage Commer Innov (IJMCI) 1(1):11–18

Jaros J, Bartosova V (2015) To the capital structure choice: Miller and Modigliani model. Proc Econ Finance 26:351–358. https://doi.org/10.1016/S2212-5671(15)00864-3

Jordan MI, Mitchell TM (2015) Machine learning: trends, perspectives, and prospects. Science 349(6245):255–260. https://doi.org/10.1126/science.aaa8415

Kokina J, Blanchette S (2019) Early evidence of digital labour in accounting: innovation with robotic process automation. Int J Account Inf Syst 35:100431

KPMG (2024). Why finance should lead the adoption of generative AI. Available at Why finance should lead the adoption of generative AI

Krizhevsky A, Sutskever I, Hinton GE (2012) ImageNet classification with deep convolutional neural networks. Adv Neural Inf Proces Syst 25

LeCun Y, Bengio Y, Hinton G (2015) Deep learning. Rev Insight 521:436–444. https://doi.org/10.1038/nature14539

Lee DKC, Guan C, Yu Y, Ding QA (2024) Comprehensive review of generative AI in finance. Fintech 3:460–478. https://doi.org/10.3390/fintech3030025

Lim T (2024) Environmental, social, and governance (ESG) and artificial intelligence in finance: state-of-the-art and research takeaways. Artif Intell Rev 57:76

Liu F, Dedehayir O, Katzy B (2015) Coalition formation during technology adoption. Behav Inform Technol 34:1186–1199

Marikyan D, Papagiannidis S (2024) Technology acceptance model: A review. In S. Papagiannidis (Ed), TheoryHub Book. Available at https://open.ncl.ac.uk / ISBN: 9781739604400

McCarthy J, Minsky ML, Rochester N, Shannon CE (1956) A proposal for the Dartmouth summer research project on artificial intelligence

McCulloch WS, Pitts W (1943) A logical calculus of the ideas immanent in nervous activity. Bull Math Biophys 5:115–133

McKinsey (2024) The state of AI in early 2024: Gen AI adoption spikes and starts to generate value. Available at The State of AI in early 2024 | McKinsey

Met İ, Kabukçu D, Uzunoğulları G, Soyalp Ü, Dakdevir T (2020) Transformation of business models in the finance sector with artificial intelligence and robotic process automation. Digital Business Strategies in Blockchain Ecosystems: Transformational Design and Future of Global Business, 3–29

Mnih V, Kavukcuoglu K, Silver D et al (2015) Human-level control through deep reinforcement learning. Nature 518:529–533. https://doi.org/10.1038/nature14236

Modigliani F, Miller M (1958) The cost of capital, corporation finance and the theory of investment

Nweze M, Avickson EK, Ekechukwu G (2024) The role of AI and machine learning in fraud detection: enhancing risk management in corporate finance. Int J Res Publicat Rev 5(10):2812–2830

Polak P, Nelischer C, Guo H, Robertson DC (2020) "Intelligent" finance and treasury management: what we can expect. AI & Soc 35:715–726

Rane NL, Choudhary SP, Rane J (2024) Artificial intelligence-driven corporate finance: enhancing efficiency and decision-making through machine learning, natural language processing, and robotic process automation in corporate governance and sustainability. Stud Econ Bus Relat 5(2):1–22. https://doi.org/10.48185/sebr.v5i2.1050

Rumelhart DE, Hinton GE, Williams RJ (1986) Learning representations by back-propagating errors. Nature 323(6088):533–536

Shanmuganathan M (2020) Behavioural finance in an era of artificial intelligence: longitudinal case study of robo-advisors in investment decisions. J Behav Exp Financ 27:100297

Silver D, Huang A, Maddison CJ, Guez A, Sifre L, Van Den Driessche G et al (2016) Mastering the game of Go with deep neural networks and tree search. Nature 529(7587):484–489

Thekkethil MS, Shukla VK, Beena F, Chopra A (2021) Robotic process automation in banking and finance sector for loan processing and fraud detection. In: In 2021 9th international conference on reliability, infocom technologies and optimisation (trends and future directions) (ICRITO). IEEE, pp 1–6

Turing AM (1950) Computing machinery and intelligence. Mind 59(236):433–460

Weber P, Carl KV, Hinz O (2024) Applications of explainable artificial intelligence in finance-a systematic review of finance, information systems, and computer science literature. Manage Rev Q 74:867–907

Weizenbaum J (1966) ELIZA—a computer program for the study of natural language communication between man and machine. Commun ACM 9(1):36–45

The Benefits and Challenges of Utilising Artificial Intelligence in Enterprise Risk Management

Justine Gomolemo Nkobane

Abstract The world we live in is one where Artificial Intelligence (AI) is being embraced by society at large as well as businesses, operating in the public and private sectors. COVID-19 heightened the utilisation of AI in business processes, which has competitive and innovative advantages, and this chapter will mainly focus on the AI used in Enterprise Risk Management (ERM) process. Therefore, the purpose of this study is to investigate and identify the benefits and challenges of utilising AI technologies in ERM. Through a content analysis of the most recent Integrated Reports of the Top 5 JSE (Johannesburg Stock Exchange)-listed companies based on market capitalisation and a systemic review of literature, this study will investigate the benefits and challenges of utilising AI in ERM. The results revealed that AI is changing how businesses manage their risks using various tools, e.g. AI algorithms can monitor risks, find patterns and predict risks. AI also aids companies resolve issues and mitigate risks. Furthermore, AI ensures that tasks are done automatically which makes sure employees are efficient in utilising their time. The study further revealed that if risks are not assessed, then AI might cause greater issues resulting in expensive implementation without the business benefiting. The study concluded that the future of ERM is one where AI, automation and human expertise complement each other. This study is important for small and medium-sized (SME) South African companies who are not yet fully embracing AI within their ERM processes to see how beneficial it can be so that they can embrace it and also invest in it.

Keywords Automation · Artificial intelligence · Enterprise risk management

J. G. Nkobane (✉)
Department of Accountancy, University of Johannesburg, Johannesburg, South Africa
e-mail: jgnkobane@uj.ac.za

© The Author(s), under exclusive license to Springer Nature
Switzerland AG 2025
M. Adelowotan, C. A. Leke (eds.), *Artificial Intelligence in Accounting, Auditing and Finance*, Contributions to Finance and Accounting,
https://doi.org/10.1007/978-3-031-87368-3_10

1   Introduction

We are living in an ever-changing world at where companies are embracing this change worldwide and incorporating AI in their ERM programmes daily. Various countries such as China and the United States of America are prioritising AI and making it a national priority (Cave and ÓhÉigeartaigh 2018). AI has gained popularity as it is being used in multiple sectors and across various fields and disciplines. Therefore, ERM is no exception as companies in South Africa must use and manage AI to remain competitive and innovative within their respective sector.

AI is the result of successful applications of big data and ML (Machine Learning) technologies to understand the past and predict the future based on enormous data (Yu et al. 2018). ML and AI play a very important role in magnifying and increasing the capabilities of business analytics (Bharadiya 2023). They allow companies to extract valuable insights from vast amounts of data, automate processes and make accurate predictions (Bharadiya 2023). The use of AI-powered chatbots and virtual assistants leverages natural language processing techniques to understand and respond to customer queries. ML enables companies to improve their responses over time by learning from customer interactions.

ML algorithms are used to analyse historical data and identify patterns and trends. This has allowed companies to make accurate predictions about future outcomes (Bharadiya 2023). According to Bharadiya (2023) accurate predictions for optimising operations and mitigating risks, predictive analysis also allows for organisations to optimise operations by forecasting demand and using this information to improve their supply chain management and inventory cycle (Bharadiya 2023). It aids in identifying potential risks and taking proactive measures to mitigate them. Therefore, AI can assist with leveraging predictive analytics to help with identifying potential risks and taking proactive measures to mitigate risks.

Rakipi et al. (2021) study found a positive correlation between data analytics use and internal audit functions' (IAF's) involvement in the assurance of ERM, fraud detection and IT risk audit activities. Another study done by Ribeiro et al. (2021) indicated that the current 4IR (Fourth industrial revolution) we are experiencing today lives on the fusion of the Internet of Things, intelligent automation, intelligent devices and processes and cyber-physical systems, where automation is used to improve business processes (Ribeiro et al. 2021). Lastly, a study done by Parker and Appel (2021) showed that the introduction of Robotic Process Automation (RPA) in businesses removed the repetitiveness of tasks for employees and the overall productivity of teams increased; it further allows for businesses to rethink their business model and create more value.

There has been an evolution from risk management to ERM and Enterprise Integrated Risk Management (EIRM) (Nikolova 2019). Risk management considers only the individual risk, for example, credit, business, financial as individual independent risks and is aimed at managing each risk separately. However, with ERM, the risks are considered within the individual structural and functional departments, according to circumstances (Nikolova 2019). The integration of all risks into a single enterprise management system determines the EIRM where the risks of the external environment, for example, financial crises, natural disasters, risk of epidemics, etc., are already part of it (Nikolova 2019). In recent years, ERM has evolved into what was previously labelled as EIRM and is now known and described by businesses as what is defined above as EIRM. EIRM is legislated and largely structured as a result.

There are various risk and risk management standards that have been adopted in different fields worldwide. Risk standards are used by managers and practitioners, and they are implemented and integrated in the documents and strategies in enterprises in both the financial and non-financial sector (Nikolova 2019). The most recognisable standards are those of the international Organization for Standardization (ISO) (Nikolova 2019). There are various frameworks being utilised and rationalised by management; some of these are COSO ERM—Integrated Framework and ERM integrating with strategy and performance.

How well AI technologies are used affects how systems are able to generate instant benefits for companies and multiple stakeholders through logicality wins, larger autonomy and new business strategies (Wamba-Taguimdje et al. 2020). AI has the potential to alter the way businesses operate, drive innovation and improve the lives of millions of people across Africa (Gikunda 2023). Africa plays a very crucial role in the development of AI systems, by contributing natural resources, labour and skills although the advantages have not yet materialised in Africa instead, they benefit Big Tech companies in the Global North and China along with those that can afford the daily conveniences offered by utilising AI (Gikunda 2023). In South Africa, AI is being embraced by larger enterprises and less by smaller enterprises.

There are many things that can contribute towards barriers to acquisition of AI in southern Africa SME's (Uwagaba et al. 2023). Some of the reasons could be very little availability to technology, limited funding as well a reduction of professional expertise (Devine and Kiggundu 2019). SME's have a huge role in the economy of Africa. International Finance Corporation (IFC) reported that 80% of jobs in Africa are from SMEs (IFC 2022). However, South Africa has a failure rate of start-up companies, which ranges between 50% and 90% depending on the industry (IFC 2022). Some African countries like Egypt, Mauritius and Rwanda are ahead of the rest and have published national AI strategies which may result in other African counties following suit.

This paper is motivated by the need for companies to maintain quality ERM programmes and utilising AI to do so to remain competitive globally. It was estimated in 2021 that AI will create a market well above $35 billion by 2025 and multiply annual economic growth rates (Schoeman et al. 2021). In South Africa, AI has been embraced by many entities; however, plenty of work remains as South Africans like many other developing countries believe that embracing AI will eliminate their jobs and worsen the current income inequalities that exist (Schoeman et al. 2021).

The research question that results from the review of the above literature is that although large companies in South Africa are embracing AI, there seems to be reservations as well as concerns from smaller entities and this paper seeks to resolve these reservations and concerns and show smaller companies that investing in AI is beneficial. The objective of the research is to highlight the benefits and understand the challenges of utilising AI in companies in South Africa to allow smaller companies such as SME's to start embracing AI more in their ERM programmes and reach global standards for utilisation of AI as this could significantly improve the performance of these companies.

2   Literature Review

Governments all over the world have recognised the potential of digital transformation to improve business operations and, consequently, this realisation has led them to formulating strategies that emphasise the role of digital transformation in expediting economic variegation ensuring happiness of citizens and advancing sustainability (Fryer 2020). In 2012, the South African government launched the South African National Development Plan 2030 which highlights the way ICT will support the development of more inclusive and flourishing economies as well as an information connected society. However, this vision has been hampered by the lack of experienced network engineers to enable the development of Internet infrastructure as it is critical for the unlocking of the country's full potential in the utilisation of the 4IR technologies (Fryer 2020). South Africa is also finding it difficult to fully deploy the 4IR technologies because the country has been struck by premature de-industrialisation, which is the relative shrinking of the production structure and lack of diversity leading to the slow and uneven adoption and spreading of digital technologies (Andreoni and Avenyo (2021).

Despite the constraints cited above, a survey of 516 South African firms by Andreoni and Avenyo (2021) in manufacturing, chemicals industry and engineering, among others indicated that some industries such as mining have increased the efficiency of their processes as well as reducing waste. Furthermore, these mining industries have predictive maintenance that employs data analysis to pick out potential problems that might fail production. AI is being employed in the metal-machinery value chains by some mills for predicting sub-surface defects as well as reducing internal scrap and rates of reworking thereby reducing energy consumption, increasing competitiveness as well as promoting environmental sustainability (Andreoni and Avenyo 2021). It was also noted that some producers in the agricultural sector are employing digital technologies like radio frequency identification tags and blockchain to enable the low temperature-controlled supply chain which can give them a competitive advantage in exporting quality fresh farm products. The same survey established that majority of the 516 firms still employed manual and semi-automated technologies with a few being fully automated and information and communication technology (ICT) enabled thus supporting the sentiments that the adoption of advanced digital technologies remains very restricted in South Africa. Examples of industries with limited adoption of digital technologies include customer–client relationships, product development, supplier relationships and production management among others. Therefore, it is those engineering and related services as well as manufacturing sectors that have adopted digital system-enabled technologies (Gaffley and Pelser 2021). According to Magwentshu et al. (2019), leading players in the South African banking sector have also started implementing AI to improve services as well as reducing operational costs.

AI has many different definitions. AI has changed the way in which the world operates and specifically the world of business (Ali et al. 2022). According to Zhou (2021), AI is defined as a theory, method, technology and the application system that makes use of a computer or a machine to acquire knowledge or to utilise knowledge to acquire results. Accenture defined AI as different technologies that can be combined in different ways to sense, comprehend, act and learn. AI is a broad concept of creating intelligent systems that can stimulate human-like intelligence (Bharadiya 2023). Accenture has identified three factors that enable AI to flourish in recent years: the first being quantum leaps in computing power, driven by growth of cloud computing, second being an increase in big data which has in turn increased the annual growth rate as more devices have become connected (Schoeman et al. 2021). Lastly there needs to be a significant investment in research and development (R&D) of basic AI technologies (Schoeman et al. 2021).

Artificial Intelligence (AI) is associated with increased and improved quality and efficiency of systems and operations, by allowing computer systems to extract, analyse and predict large masses of data across multiple industries (Boobier 2020). Robots are also now submerged in organisational systems so that they could be adapted to the work environment (Cascio and Montealegre 2016). Three key trends that have been identified from Accenture's technology division are an adaptive work force, ecosystem power plays and AI as the UI (User interface) (Schoeman et al. 2021). The current ecosystem power plays are that more businesses are making use of service providers to perform other non-core functionalities, and these seem to be unlocking strategic growth as well as value chains (Schoeman et al. 2021). AI is becoming the face of a company's digital brand by ensuring it aligns itself with the needs and wants of customers, employees, etc.

South Africa has been forced to change the ways of doing business and how people live and work because of the COVID-19 pandemic. The scenario before the outbreak of COVID-19 was widespread concerns about job losses due to the employment of robotics and automation and hence a clarion call was made to protect jobs in labour-intensive industries (Sutherland, 2020). South Africa, just like any other developing country, was thrown in at the deep end by the COVID-19 pandemic and found themselves embracing the much-feared 4IR technologies (Jegede 2021). 'The new normal' as it was labelled during the beginning of the COVID-19 saw even the 4IR sceptical people beginning to appreciate the 4IR technologies as the use of these technologies became the way to go.

Suddenly there was rapid increase in the use of previously technology-supported services such as online ordering of fast foods, groceries, clothing, medicine and other household goods by individuals for their households as well as by organisations. Organisations intensified the use of Zoom and Microsoft Teams for meetings among other online platforms, institutions of learning employed Learner Management systems such as Blackboard to offer online teaching and learning, and academic conferences were also hosted virtually. Religious meetings also went online. It is the employment of 4IR technologies such as IoTs, mobile applications, augmented and virtual reality, drones and 3D printing, robotics, blockchain and artificial intelligence among others that enabled people to carry on with life during the Covid-19. One can confidently say that the Covid-19 expedited the embracing of 4IR not only in South Africa but also in all other developing countries that were lagging in terms of adopting 4IR.

AI is expected to have a positive impact on the economy; firstly, it is expected to assist existing labour to be more productive by supporting them with the use of machines. Secondly, it is expected to inspire innovation and creativity. As per Schoeman et al. (2021), economic growth forecast without AI is 3.5 percent and with AI is 4.5% in South Africa. AI system solutions (AISS) are perplexing socio-technical solutions that result in increased business risks due to fast and unexpected behaviours, and their combination with the manual user and the environment (McGrath 2022). A study found that intensifying a companies' ERM approach to include managing the dynamic ethical risks resulting from the creation and use of AISS was a valid approach (McGrath 2022). New AI solutions are compound and add both new risks and new opportunities (McGrath 2022). This is not only because of AI capabilities (e.g. self-learning potential, intelligent capabilities and inscruta-bility) but also because of AI's combinations and dependence with physical users which establishes a system that involves both manual human intervention and intel-ligence (Asatiani et al. 2021; Makarius et al. 2020; Seeber et al. 2020).

The utilisation of AISS in companies requires business process to change in a similar way and so this research proposes an approach that appropriately engages businesses and Information Technology departments to make use of the concept of ERM (McGrath 2022). To perform well in business, a dynamic ERM programme is required as the standard risk management approach falls short in this regard. New legislation has been released called the European Union AI Act which is being used in many countries worldwide (Du and Xie 2021).

Although companies use AI to replace manual tasks and infrastructure there is minimal evidence that using AI results in a reduction in employment (Bonney et al. 2024). The best way to allow AI to thrive in an organisation is to ensure staff is trained, developing new workflows, purchasing cloud services/storage and chang-ing data management/collection practices (Bonney et al. 2024). The most widely used AI tools are marketing automation, virtual agents, natural language processing and data/text analytics and the use of these is expected to continue increasing (Bonney et al. 2024).

ERM is when firms choose to address all their risks comprehensively and coher-ently instead of managing them on an individual basis. Initially risk management was done on an individual basis; however, stakeholders required more of corporate governance and hence the move to ERM. The use of AI in ERM in business is evi-dence of the benefits being achieved using technologies (Wamba-Taguimdje et al. 2020). In a study by Uwagaba et al. (2023), it was found that more and more SMEs in Africa are at present utilising AI to better their businesses and continue maintaining fierce advantage and there is more potential for implementing AI.

It is clear from the literature review that 4IR technologies and AI are being embraced in South Africa, and this was largely because of Covid-19. However, to what extent AI is being used in ERM and how companies are disclosing this information still are in question and this will be answered under the Results Section of the Study.

3   Methodology

This study is a descriptive study that explores secondary data. This study makes use of a desk review to investigate the challenges as well as the benefits of utilising AI in ERM. A desk review is defined as secondary research that summarises and collates information that was previously collected (Travis 2016). A systematic review of literature will be done to explore the challenges as well as the benefits of AI being utilised in ERM. Various data from Google Scholar database and the Integrated Reports of the Top 10 JSE-listed entities based on market capitalisation will be dissected using a content analysis.

3.1   Data Collection

When there is a large amount of information for a given topic a desk review entails a strategic way of systematically gathering information (Aaron 2008). As a result, company websites of the Top 5 JSE-listed companies were inspected for Integrated Reports and these were downloaded for the latest available year being 2024 for Naspers Ltd., FirstRand and Capitec Bank and 2023 for Standard Bank Group Ltd. and Gold Fields Ltd. and inspected using a key word search of AI, ML and ERM. Secondly, applicable articles and journals on AI and ERM in South Africa and globally were inspected. Peer-reviewed studies published during the last 10 years, media stories, reports on benefits and challenges of AI and ERM and Internet blogs discussing trends in ERM were among the literature sources we used. Some of the documents consulted are summarised in Fig. 1.

Fig. 1 Documents consulted in the systematic literature review. *Source: Authors interpretation of literature*

4   Results

4.1   The Review of Integrated Reports

As per the Gold Fields (2023), the company strives to integrate and automate cyber technologies and controls to offer a unified view of the cyber estate, safeguarding all Gold Fields digital assets. With regard to cybersecurity, Gold Fields utilises threat intelligence to inform the Groups cybersecurity posture. Gold Fields implements cutting-edge technologies, tools and solutions to enhance cybersecurity defences and ensures protection of digital assets (Gold Fields 2023). They maintain a robust third-party risk assessment capability that enables Group continuous monitoring of digital attack surface and implementing appropriate risk mitigation strategies within their security operations centre (Gold Fields 2023). Various cybersecurity simulations are conducted by Gold Fields throughout the year such as real-time attack simulation, incident response, disclosure management simulation and external reviews to verify the effectiveness of the Groups cybersecurity posture (Gold Fields 2023). In the risk management disclosures of Gold Fields, the company is not explicit regarding how AI is being utilised within their ERM programme; however, what has been emphasised is how they are utilising technologies and how automated the continuous monitoring within their risk management process is and it is anticipated that the 2024 Integrated Report will have more disclosures.

The FirstRand Group (2024) follows an ongoing risk management process. The FirstRand Groups focus on continuous monitoring to mitigate potential risks like liquidity and other risks to ensure stability (FirstRand, 2024). Although FirstRand did not disclose a lot of information regarding the use of AI in their ERM system, responses were gathered from an interview with the head of ERM Magla Moodley which showed that at FNB, a subsidiary of FirstRand, AI is being utilised extensively within the ERM system. FNB uses AI chatbots and a very automated ERM process with very little manual intervention to mitigate and manage the risks faced by the bank. FNB like all the other Big 4 Banks is embracing AI within their systems to give them a competitive advantage, and FNB has been a leader amongst the banks in South Africa with regard to technological advancements.

Capitec Bank (2024) follows an ongoing ERM process, and risks are reviewed continuously to take count of the face changing environment in which it operates. Capitec referred to generative AI being a pertinent forward-looking emerging risk. Capitec Bank noted that there was a promotion of the European Act on AI being adopted has resulted in stricter governance and risk management on AI utilisation (Capitec Bank 2024). It is important to note that although the legislation is not yet implemented in South Africa, South African does tend to follow and will most likely have a similar act in future. Capitec Bank ensures it is on top of the ball with regard to ensuring continuous monitoring of developments, as well as proactive mitigation measures during the development and implementation of Capitec's current and future ML and AI capabilities and models utilised (Capitec Bank 2024). Capitec has also stated that their human capital makes use of AI to deliver services to clients. E.g. Client repayment risk is captured within the statistically validated granting models (Capitec Bank 2024). Granted models are regularly monitored and, when deemed necessary, dynamically adapted to improve performance by leveraging both machine learning solutions as well as forward-looking perspectives (Capitec Bank 2024). To mitigate financial crime risk, Capitec uses ML to scale their efforts and improve the efficiency of their prevention and detection mechanisms (Capitec Bank 2024). In the past year, Capitec Bank has increased the numerous models used as well as the difficulties of the usage of ML models, as part of model risk management (Capitec Bank 2024). Like all the other big banks in South Africa Capitec is embracing AI within their business process.

Naspers utilises a continuous evaluation process with regard to ERM (Naspers 2024). Due to Prosus (a subsidiary of Naspers) being a tech company AI is essential, globally to the group, and Prosus ensures that the Group remains competitive and up to date with technological advancements. Prosus has a strategy what is dedicated to using data, AI and ML in a responsible manner to ensure that they are able to support corporate governance. PayU accelerated the adoption of data and AI across its credit and payments business, and this is the core of running each business, delivering growth targets and controlling risks (Naspers 2024). Naspers is using AI responsibly in monitoring by auditing for accountability, bias and cybersecurity such as adopting tools for bias check as part of model development practices or introducing feedback loops for GenAI tools (Naspers 2024). Naspers has begun promoting awareness on implication of the European AI Act for subsidiaries that intend to start operating in Europe to ensure their compliance with the Act.

Standard Bank (2023) has a medium-term priority to continue maturing in their risk management and a long-term priority to leverage data in their digitisation journeys to mature their risk management. Standard Bank noted that in 2024, a key theme that will receive heightened focus will be emerging technologies and AI (Standard Bank, 2023). Therefore, although Standard Bank did not have many insights into how AI is currently utilised, it is evident from the statements made that the 2024 Integrated Reports will have more insights to offer.

4.2   Results from a Review of Literature

Results from the review of literature highlight that since the Covid-19 lockdown in South Africa, audit firm's employees were forced to adapt a hybrid work environment that allowed them to work from home to complete audits and only meet when necessary.

Although utilising AI is positive for businesses, there are some unintended consequences of employees being retrenched by an algorithm that does not require manual human labour or has a negative impact on the company, its reputation and its stakeholders (McGrath 2022). The following are some advantages of AI; firstly, AI has no personal biases that a human would have so there would be less motivation for fraud, and work efficiency does not decline based on a person being physically tired (Zhou 2021). The study by Uwagaba et al. (2023) also found that the advantages of AI implementation for smaller companies include better process productivity, lower costs and greater openness to markets. In the traditional sense if overtime labour was required, this would cost more; however, with AI this will not cost more even if the technology is used after hours when necessary. Another advantage is with the use of AI, human error is eliminated because if the AI is programmed appropriately there will be a huge advantage of accuracy and as a result greater efficiency and work output (Zhou 2021).

One of the principal barriers facing SMEs in Southern Africa is the shortage of access to funding and resources to invest in technology as many of these companies operate on minimal expenditure (Uwagaba et al. 2023). This then ultimately affects the investment in AI by companies. Furthermore, many SMEs in Southern Africa have scare technical skills to properly use technologies (Uwagaba et al. 2023).

AI technologies and systems assist with organisational efficiencies and can potentially improve the quality and process of operations, which are ideal for organisational performance (McGrath 2022). There are many initiatives with a focus on promoting the implementation of technology in smaller southern African companies, among these initiatives are Digital Impact Alliance, the United Nations Children's Fund and many more whose aim is to improve the usage of digital technologies to make people's lives better (Uwagaba et al. 2023). AI usage is especially high in larger firms. AI applications such as Generative AI are appealing to the youth and SMEs as they do not involve large costs (Czarnitzki et al. 2023).

Despite AI being embraced and making waves it is relatively in the early stages and as some companies do not yet see the tangible benefits of utilising AI it is still advancing.

5   Findings

A review of the latest available year being 2024 for Naspers Ltd., FirstRand Group Ltd. and Capitec Bank Ltd. and 2023 for Standard Bank Group Ltd. and Gold Fields Ltd. Integrated Reports of the 5 JSE listed companies as of 18 October 2024 revealed that AI integration into business corporations is an emerging theme, and larger companies are using AI within their business processes and within their ERM process. All the companies have highly automated and integrated processes. AI legislation available in Europe will most likely be followed due to other companies within the group. Cyber security risks are being managed via ERM processes and, in future years, it is anticipated that there will be more disclosures in the Integrated Reports regarding AI implementation with business operations.

Like anything worth having the 4IR comes with challenges that need to be overcome such as income inequality, cybersecurity and ethical dilemmas. The results from the review of literature show that AI is being embraced in South Africa largely because it eliminates human error and promotes the advantage of accuracy and efficiency. The benefits and challenges of utilising AI in ERM as per literature review are summarised below in Table 1.

6   Conclusion

This chapter presented the concept of AI and ERM as well as the utilisation of AI in South African Companies. AI has several definitions, and this chapter explored the benefits as well as the challenges of utilising AI in ERM. The chapter noted that the development of AI brings about both opportunities and challenges to ERM

Table 1 Benefits and challenges of utilising AI in ERM

Benefits	Challenges
AI technologies can extract valuable information from big data sets and compare variances in documents, perform forecasts allowing ERM to be performed more efficiently.	Use of AI in ERM process brings about new challenges to businesses being security risks and cybersecurity risks and possible manipulation by phishers.
No personal biases that a human would have so there would be less motivation for fraud to occur.	Reliance and use of AI technologies require professionals who know how to use the systems and tools appropriately.
Different data can be collected using intelligence systems, robots and software, e.g. images, videos and recordings to be used in the mitigating of risks within the ERM process. AI technologies and systems assist with organisational efficiencies and potentially increase the level and consistency of operations, which are perfect for organisations' bottom line.	Staff constantly needs to be trained to be able to use AI technologies that are utilised.
AI technologies can assist with saving time costs and labour costs for ERM teams.	Some employees believe that embracing AI technologies will result in job losses for them. There is a lack of necessary skills to allow for better usage of technologies.
Many costs involved in developing AI systems are largely one-off costs that will result in growth in profit.	There is a scarcity of funding to allow investment in technology.

Source: Authors review of literature

processes of companies. Businesses should continue integrating and developing new AI theories and improve the application of big data and cloud computing to continue improving operations' quality and efficiency.

Some of the key benefits of using AI and automation are the efficiency it brings to business, for example, through enabling quicker and bigger extracts of data and tools like variances analysis, forecasts and comparisons, allowing for the real-time processing and live learning to mitigate risks. Furthermore, no personal biases that a human would have so there would be less motivation for fraud to occur. AI technologies can assist with saving time costs and labour costs for ERM teams. The key challenges due to utilising automation and AI are security risks and manipulation by phishers that need to be managed. There is insufficient access to funds and resources that can allow a buy into technology. Using AI requires trained professionals managing it and training staff members gradually to keep up with the changes. Lastly, employees' buy-in and loss of morale are major challenges.

The following are emerging AI technologies: computer vision, audio processing, natural language processing, machine learning and expert systems.

7 Limitations of the Study

The limitation of the study is that the data utilised is secondary information as per the Integrated Reports of the Top 5 JSE-listed companies as per Appendix 1 as this information is historic. Secondly, the information was also limited to a systematic literature review and not tracked in real time.

8 Future Research

Future research can be focused on tracking the magnitude of how AI is utilised in business processes. In certain businesses, the magnitude of AI usage is already huge; therefore, the potential of tracking in real time the AI usage will be important for business processes.

Appendix 1

Top 20 companies based on market Capitalisation

Number	Name	Market capitalisation in Billions	Share price
1.	Naspers	€39.28	44.22 €
2.	FirstRand	€23.77	4.24 €
3.	Standard Bank group	€20.56	12.45 €
4.	Capitec Bank	€18.00	155.46 €
5.	Gold Fields	€13.11	14.65 €
6.	Vodacom	€10.96	5.67 €
7.	AngloGold Ashanti	€10.50	24.97 €
8.	Sanlam	€9.23	4.48 €
9.	MTN Group	€8.51	4.71 €
10.	Shoprite	€8.16	15.02 €
11.	Bid Corp	€7.53	22.47 €
12.	Nedbank	€7.19	15.40 €
13.	Harmony Gold	€6.19	9.75 €
14.	Discovery Limited	€5.74	8.68 €
15.	The Bidvest Group	€5.00	14.71 €
16.	Clicks Group	€4.79	20.14 €
17.	Pepkor	€4.52	1.23 €
18.	Impala Platinum	€4.48	4.98 €
19.	Remgro Limited	€4.41	7.95 €
20.	Aspen Pharmacare	€4.36	9.83 €

https://companiesmarketcap.com/eur/south-africa/largest-companies-in-south-africa-by-market-cap/#google_vignette

References

Aaron L (2008) Writing a literature review article. Radiol Technol 80(2):185–186

Ali SM, Hasan ZJ, Hamdan A, Al-Mekhlaf M (2022) Artificial intelligence (AI) in the education of accounting and auditing profession. In: International conference on business and technology. Springer International Publishing, Cham, pp 656–664

Andreoni A, Avenyo E (2021) South Africa is failing to ride the digital revolution wave. What it needs to do, available at: https://theconversation.com/south-africa-is-failing-to-ride-the-digital-revolution-wave-what-it-needs-to-do-171515. Accessed 31 Jan 2022

Asatiani A, Malo P, Nagbøl PR, Penttinen E, Rinta-Kahila T, Salovaara A (2021) Sociotechnical envelopment of artificial intelligence: an approach to organizational deployment of inscrutable artificial intelligence systems. J Assoc Inf Syst 22(2):325–352

Bharadiya JP (2023) Machine learning and AI in business intelligence: trends and opportunities. Int J Comput (IJC) 48(1):123–134

Bonney K, Breaux C, Buffington C, Dinlersoz E, Foster LS, Goldschlag N et al (2024) Tracking firm use of AI in real time: a snapshot from the business trends and outlook survey, vol No. w32319. National Bureau of Economic Research

Boobier T (2020) AI and the future of banking. John Wiley & Sons

Capitec Bank (2024) Integrated Annual Report 2024. Accessed: https://www.capitecbank.co.za/globalassets/pages/investor-relations/financial-results/2024/annual-report/integrated_annual_report_2024.pdf [Available: 10/10/2024]

Cascio WF, Montealegre R (2016) How technology is changing work and organizations. Annu Rev Organ Psych Organ Behav 3(1):349–375

Cave S, ÓhÉigeartaigh SS (2018, December) An AI race for strategic advantage: rhetoric and risks. In: Proceedings of the 2018 AAAI/ACM Conference on AI, Ethics, and Society, pp 36–40

Czarnitzki D, Fernández GP, Rammer C (2023) Artificial intelligence and firm-level productivity. J Econ Behav Organ 211:188–205

Devine RA, Kiggundu MN (2019) Entrepreneurship in Africa: identifying the frontier of impactful research. In: Entrepreneurship in Africa. Routledge, pp 115–146

Du S, Xie C (2021) Paradoxes of artificial intelligence in consumer markets: ethical challenges and opportunities. J Bus Res 129:961–974

Fryer D (2020) Digital transformation impact on businesses within South Africa. Available at: https://www.bbrief.co.za/2020/08/17/digital-transformation-impact-on-businesses-within-south-africa/. Accessed 31 Jan 2022

Gaffley G, Pelser TG (2021) Developing a digital transformation model to enhance the strategy development process for leadership in the South African manufacturing sector. South Afr J Bus Manage 52(1):a2357. https://doi.org/10.4102/sajbm.v52i1.2357

Gikunda K (2023) Empowering Africa: an in-depth exploration of the adoption of artificial intelligence across the continent. arXiv preprint arXiv:2401.09457

Gold Fields (2023) Annual Financial Report 2023. Accessed: https://www.goldfields.com/pdf/investors/integrated-annual-reports/2023/afs-2023.pdf [Available: 10/10/2024]

IFC (2022) Unlocking the Potential of Africa's SME's Using Emerging Technologies in Africa Accessed: https://www.nepad.org/blog/unlocking-potential-of-africas-smes-using-emerging-technologies-africa [Available: 20/10/2024]

Jegede O (2021) South Africa's capacity to deploy Fourth Industrial Revolution technologies post-COVID-19. United Nations Industrial Development Organisation. https://www.unido.org/stories/south-africas-capacity-deploy-fourth-industrial-revolution-technologies-post-covid-19#story-start

Magwentshu N, Rajagopaul A, Chui M, Singh A (2019) The future of work in South Africa. McKinsey and Company: New York, NY, USA

Makarius EE, Mukherjee D, Fox JD, Fox AK (2020) Rising with the machines: a sociotechnical framework for bringing artificial intelligence into the organization. J Bus Res 120:262–273

McGrath QP (2022) An enterprise risk management framework to design pro-ethical AI solutions, Doctoral dissertation. University of South Florida

Naspers (2024) 2024 Integrated Annual Report. Accessed: https://www.naspersreport2024.com/pdf/Naspers-integrated-annual-report.pdf Available: [10/10/2024]

Nikolova I (2019) External debt and debt crises in European economies. In: Conference Proceedings "Bulgaria and Romania: Country Members of the EU, Part of the Global Economy

Parker H, Appel SE (2021) On the path to artificial intelligence: the effects of a robotics solution in a financial services firm. South Afr J Ind Eng 32(2):37–47

Rakipi R, De Santis F, D'Onza G (2021) Correlates of the internal audit function's use of data analytics in the big data era: global evidence. J Int Account Audit Tax 42:100357

Ribeiro J, Lima R, Eckhardt T, Paiva S (2021) Robotic process automation and artificial intelligence in industry 4.0–a literature review. Procedia Computer

Schoeman W, Moore R, Seedat Y, Chen JYJ (2021) Artificial intelligence: is South Africa ready?

Seeber I, Bittner E, Briggs RO, De Vreede T, De Vreede GJ, Elkins A et al (2020) Machines as teammates: a research agenda on AI in team collaboration. Inform Manage 57(2):103174

Travis D (2016) Desk Research: the what, why and how. Accessed 16 Feb 2022 https://www.user-focus.co.uk/articles/desk-resaerch-the-what-why-and-how.html

Uwagaba J, Omotosho TD, George GO (2023) Exploring the barriers to artificial intelligence adoption in Sub-Saharan Africa's small and medium enterprises and the potential for increased productivity. World Wide Journal of Multidisciplinary Research and Development

Wamba-Taguimdje SL, Wamba SF, Kamdjoug JRK, Wanko CET (2020) Influence of artificial intelligence (AI) on firm performance: the business value of AI-based transformation projects. Bus Process Manag J 26(7):1893–1924

Yu H, Yang X, Zheng S, Sun C (2018) Active learning from imbalanced data: A solution of online weighted extreme learning machine. IEEE Transact Neural Netw Learn Systems 30(4):1088–1103

Zhou G (2021) Research on the development of CPA audit from the perspective of artificial intelligence. In: E3S web of conferences, vol 251. EDP Sciences, p 01056

Financial Time Series Forecasting in the Artificial Intelligence Domain: Learning Through the Lens of Time

Milan De Wet and Botha Ilse

Abstract Future events and outcomes could have a significant impact on our decision-making today. The ability to accurately forecast future outcomes has been shown to add value to many economic agents, such as policymakers, market participants and financial managers. Given the value of accurate forecasts, the development and testing of forecasting tools in the literature are vast. In this light, identifying optimal models to forecast financial and economic variables has been a point of great consideration in literature. Decades ago, a central challenge in forecasting was a lack of data availability. Today, a key challenge is the significant volume of data available and the structuring of models that could accurately work with big data. The Big Data revolution has transformed the modern world and is an important data mining topic that spans across fields. Data mining forms the basis for AI and machine learning (ML) and works together to answer questions, prove hypotheses and give insight into the behaviour of time series. Time series forecasting is part of ML and it has evolved over time from simple linear methods to non-linear methods and complex deep learning (DL) methods, showing a shift from supervised to unsupervised learning. The main aim of this chapter is to establish the evolution and future of time series forecasting through the lens of AI. The findings of this research show that due to the data revolution, challenges and opportunities exist for research, education, current research fields and new research fields. Therefore, looking at the future—the lens we use should focus on a multidisciplinary approach to solving complex problems in time series forecasting.

Keywords Artificial intelligence · Forecasting · Bibliometrics · Time-series analysis · Big data

M. De Wet (✉) · B. Ilse
Department of Accountancy, University of Johannesburg, Johannesburg, South Africa
e-mail: miland@uj.ac.za; ilseb@uj.ac.za

© The Author(s), under exclusive license to Springer Nature
Switzerland AG 2025
M. Adelowotan, C. A. Leke (eds.), *Artificial Intelligence in Accounting, Auditing and Finance*, Contributions to Finance and Accounting,
https://doi.org/10.1007/978-3-031-87368-3_11

1 Introduction

Humans are curious about the future and therefore we are interested in making predictions. We are interested in the future if we draw value from such a prediction.
Time is the determining factor for forecasting or prediction, since we can only forecast the future if time passes. Time never stops and this is the reason why forecasting exists.

This chapter will focus on the evolution and future of time series analysis and
forecasting through the lens of artificial intelligence (AI). A time series is a data
series that varies over time. Examples of this are: the daily exchange rate, weekly
sales, the monthly inflation rate, quarterly tourist arrivals or annual GDP growth
rates. Time series analysis and time series forecasting are terms that are used interchangeably and they address the three main objectives (Fig. 1) of a time series
problem: firstly, to analyse data in order to identify patterns; and, secondly, to make
forecasts from these identified patterns. Lastly, we predict future trends based on
past behaviour, and these forecasts have value in business, finance and economics,
which need reliable information on the current economic state and the predicted
future state to inform decision-making.

There are two main approaches to forecasting, namely qualitative and quantitative forecasting methods. The qualitative approach focuses on judgmental

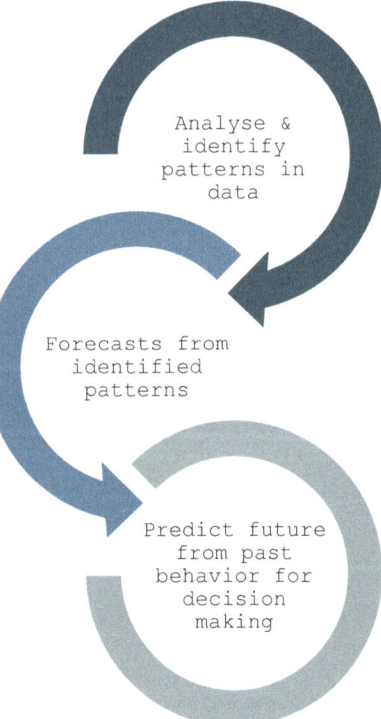

Fig. 1 Objectives of time
series forecasting. Source:
self-constructed

Analyse &
identify
patterns in
data

Forecasts from
identified
patterns

Predict future
from past
behavior for
decision
making

forecasting, which involves a subjective opinion of an expert about the future. The quantitative approach is an objective assessment where past behaviour informs the present and the future. The most widely spread quantitative methods are various time series models. A large number of models are used to forecast time series, ranging from simple regression and exponential smoothing models to complex combined models (Zharov et al. 2016).

A major advance in the forecasting field which distinguishes it from other fields is that there are a vast number of empirical studies that focus on theoretical or academic problems, as well as addressing problems that practitioners face. Econometric theory is closely linked to empirical problems in time series econometrics and is developed by these practical empirical problems (Stock and Watson 2017; Makridakis et al. 2018). This is evident if we look at how time series methods have evolved and adapted to theoretical and practical challenges that have transpired over time. Time series econometrics has improved our ability to address these real-world problems (Stock and Watson 2017).

2   The Evolution of Time Series Forecasting

Analysis and forecasting of time series data can be applied to any time series that has specific seasonal or trend changes with time. Consequently, there are many application fields, such as business finance, stock markets, exchange rates, weather, supply chain, electricity demand, consumer demand, tourism demand, business cycles and macroeconomic monitoring, to name a few (Hassani and Silva 2015; Mahalakshmi et al. 2016; Stock and Watson 2017).

Time series forecasting has developed over time, and a vast number of papers are published in the broader fields of business, finance and economics. These papers usually involve a comparison of forecasting accuracy between certain models or methods against a benchmark model. Certain fields in time series forecasting have certain preferred benchmark models and types of forecasting models, due to the underlying data-generating process (DGP) of the data at hand. Time series data have certain components (Fig. 2) that drive the DGP, such as seasonality (tourism), cyclicality (business cycle indicators), trends or volatile behaviour (exchange rates).

Time series models are developed to specifically address these components present in a time series. The models that are used for forecasting also depend on whether the objective of forecasting is such as to propagate the history into the future using only one variable or multiple variables, whether you are interested in a long- or short-term forecast, or whether you are interested in a causal relationship in order to make a forecast.

Figure 3 shows how time series analysis has evolved from 1920 over the decades until today. Early in the nineteenth century, attempts to study time series assumed a deterministic world. In 1921, Yule introduced the first autoregressive (AR) concept and predicted the sequence of sunspots using a linear model (Rezaee et al. 2018). The theoretical developments in time series analysis on the notion of stochastic

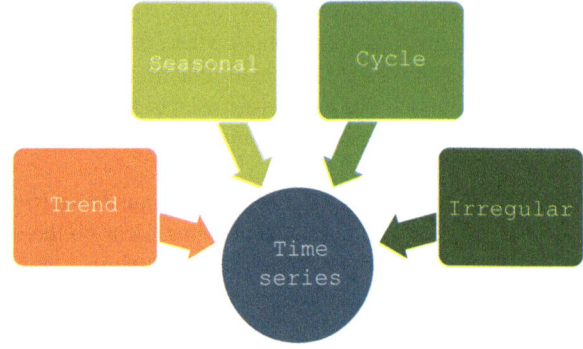

Fig. 2 Time series components. Source: self-constructed

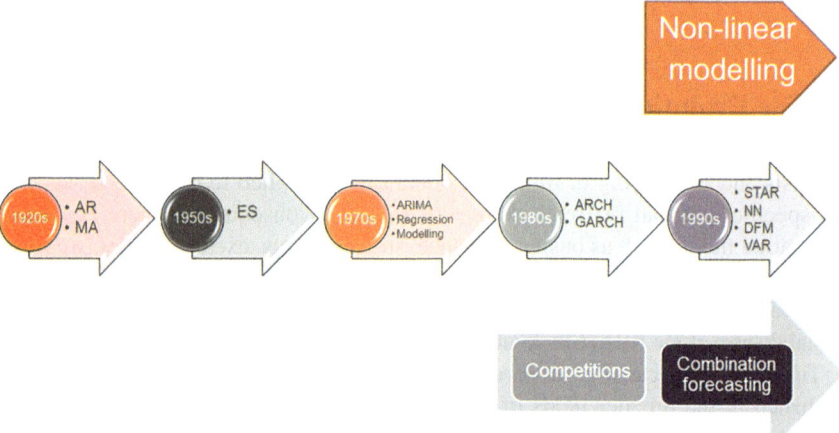

Fig. 3 The evolution of time series analysis. Source: self-constructed

processes were launched in 1927 by Yule (Tsay 2000; De Gooijer and Hyndman 2006). This sparked the development of several time series methods, such as the concept of AR and moving average (MA) models. Exponential smoothing methods, which originated in the 1950s and 1960s were widely used in business and industry. These methods did not have a well-developed statistical foundation and further developments by Box and Jenkins in the early 1970s showed that exponential smoothing models are special cases of autoregressive integrated moving average (ARIMA) models (De Gooijer and Hyndman 2006).

ARIMA was popularised due to the ease of computing when computers became widely available. The first generalisation of these models was the multivariate ARIMA models and even today these Box–Jenkins models are the most commonly used ones. Many techniques used for forecasting and seasonal adjustment can be traced back to these models. This field, which was then dominated by practitioners, evolved academically and regression and econometric models developed the body of knowledge (Makridakis et al. 2018).

Other developments that originated from the Box–Jenkins models are the non-linear generalisations, namely the autoregressive conditional heteroscedastic (ARCH) and generalised regressive conditional heteroscedastic (GARCH) models. A key feature of financial time series is that there are periods of high (low) volatility that tend to be followed by high (low) volatility, termed "volatility clustering" in econometrics and finance. The family of ARCH models was introduced by Engle (1982) to address this feature. These models are useful in financial time series and allow for the parameterisation and prediction of non-constant variance. C. W. J Granger and R. F. Engle received the Nobel Memorial Prize in Economic Sciences in 2003 for the ARCH and error correction models (De Gooijer and Hyndman 2006).

Compared to the study of linear time series, the development of non-linear time series analysis and forecasting was neglected for a long time. This can be attributed to the complexity of these models and computational difficulties. During the late 1970s and early 1980s, it became evident that linear models were insufficient in many real-world applications. In the early 1990s, Granger and Teräsvirta advanced new developments in non-linear forecasting models for economic and financial time series. These models impose time-varying parameters or parameters whose values change when the process switches between different regimes, such as the SETAR, STAR and Markov switching models (De Gooijer and Hyndman 2006; Zharov et al. 2016). Another non-linear model that has gained popularity is the artificial neural network (ANN), which has been applied to many areas of statistics, one of which is time series forecasting. Although adaptable, consistent and trainable, a general problem with non-linear models is their complexity (Wang et al. 2016).

During the mid-1990s, vector autoregressions (VARs) became popular macro-econometric models to use; however, the need to increase the number of variables to improve forecasting accuracy remained a challenge. With the unrestricted VAR, the number of parameters increases with the square of the number of variables. Time series methods needed to be developed to circumvent this propagation of parameters when large numbers of variables are used—the need for high-dimension modelling. Dynamic factor models (DFMs) addressed this challenge (Stock and Watson 2017).

A given observable variable in a DFM can be written as the sum of a common component and an idiosyncratic component. This common component depends on latent (unobserved) factors (common variables). The idiosyncratic component is uncorrelated with the common component and has a low correlation with the other idiosyncratic components. In a DFM, a small number of latent factors explain the co-movement of a large number of variables. When the number of variables increases, the computational burden does not increase, but the precision of the estimation of the factor improves. The "curse of dimensionality" therefore becomes a blessing. Research over the past 20 years has established that DFMs are a leading method for the joint modelling of large numbers of time series (Stock and Watson 2017).

Another method available for high-dimensional modeling is the Global VAR. This model allows for interdependencies on different levels while reducing the dimensionality of the VAR parameters, whereby the domestic variables depend on foreign variables through a small number of weighted averages of global variables (Stock and Watson 2017).

Forecasters often compare different models with similar predictive power and it is difficult to single out one superior model. Some models are accurate in certain market conditions, but due to the uncertainty of the future, it is difficult to tell which conditions will prevail. Individual models might not be able to track all these conditions hence the rise of combination or hybrid models. The combination of forecasts, mixing or pooling quantitative forecasts from different time series methods, or judgmental forecasts, has been studied for the past three decades (De Gooijer and Hyndman 2006; Timmermann 2018). These combination forecasts have proven to outperform single models (Jiao and Chen 2018; Kim and Swanson 2018). These models have the ability to diversify uncertainty. Usually, similar models have been combined (a combination of traditional forecasting models or a combination of different neural nets), but recent literature shows that accuracy improves if different models are combined to address different components of a time series (Wang et al. 2013). Real-world time series problems are complex and are seldom purely linear or non-linear; they often contain both linear and non-linear components. In such a case, a pure linear or non-linear model will not be adequate in modelling and forecasting the time series. These hybrid models integrate the features and strengths of different models to overcome individual weaknesses in models (Zhang 2003; Bahrammirzaee 2010; Hajizadeh et al. 2012).

3 Forecasting Competitions

Forecasting competitions have become very popular in time series literature. The latest forecast competition was the M6 which took place from March 2022 to February 2023, by the pioneer of forecasting competitions and world leader in forecasting, Prof Spyros Makridakis (Professor at the University of Nicosia and Director of the Institute for the Future). These competitions started in the 1980s and were called M-competitions. These competitions involved large-scale empirical forecast evaluations of newly proposed methods against existing methods, and played an integral part in the development of new methods in time series forecasting that have proved to work in practice (Hyndman 2019). The first few competitions, before the 1980s, were by individual researchers comparing the accuracy of several methods applied to multiple time series. Full-scale competitions only became feasible after the computer became widely available. In their 1979 paper, Spyros Makridakis and Michèle Hibon used 111-time series and compared several forecasting methods. The research community did not react well to this, and in response, they followed up with a new competition involving the 1001 series. This time any forecaster could submit forecasts, marking the first true forecasting competition. The results confirm their previous results, namely that complex methods do not necessarily outperform simple methods; combination forecasts outperform individual forecasts most of the time; and, that performance of the methods depends on the accuracy measure and the forecast horizon. This paper was seminal in forecasting research since the focus in research shifted to the importance of producing good forecasts rather than getting caught up in the mathematical properties of the model; it cautioned researchers on overfitting and it was also the start of automated forecasting methods (Hyndman 2019). The M2 competition was next, in 1993, with only 29 time series, but it contained a rich data set run in real time. The M3 competition in 1998 was held by Makridakis and Hibon to take account of new methods since their first competition, involving 3003 time series from business, demography, finance and economics on an annual, quarterly or monthly basis (Hyndman 2019). The most recent competition in this M-series of competitions required participants to construct quantile predictions for 100 assets over the course of 1 year. The frequency of the data ranged from hourly, daily and weekly data to monthly, quarterly and annual data. The emphasis for this competition was born from concerns about the M3 competition results; competitors had to prove that their results could be reproduced and were required to submit their code. The aim of this competition was to evaluate the performance of machine learning (ML) and deep learning (DL) methods as a forecasting tool in response to the increasing number of papers and claims that these methods offer superior results for time series forecasting. Findings show that simple time series forecasting methods outperform more sophisticated methods, including ANN models, confirming the results from previous M-competitions (Makridakis et al. 2018). The authors were puzzled that ML methods perform so poorly in practice.

ML methods and DL methods have the potential of better learning time series data than classical statistical methods and, due to their learning ability, should do better than simple benchmarks, such as exponential smoothing (Makridakis et al. 2018). Recommendations from these competitions are that ML theorists need to improve the accuracy of their methods. The problem might lie in the fact that academic ML forecasting literature claims forecast accuracy without comparison with simple statistical methods or naïve benchmarks. This creates the expectation that ML methods provide accurate forecasts without empirical proof. Additionally, disclosure on how the forecasts of ML methods are generated, the black box where these are generated, is not acceptable for practitioners, who need to know how forecasts are generated, influenced or adjusted. Additionally, ML methods must also be able to provide confidence intervals. Uncertainty has not been addressed in the ML field, leaving a gap that must be filled, since estimating uncertainty in forecasts, the confidence interval, is as important as the forecasts themselves. The authors note that the type of series, as well as their length, may be factors determining the accuracy of the various methods reported in this paper. Another consideration is that the lengths of business series are relatively short compared to those that ML methods are typically using, which may also affect performance as proper training cannot take place when a time series is short.

Although the forecasting accuracy of ML models is lower than traditional forecasting methods, the potential in ML models exists, and accuracy needs to be improved, as is the case with all new techniques. This is evident in time series forecasting literature where complex forecasting methods have improved their accuracy considerably over time. Makridakis et al. (2018) note that using DL methods for forecasting is different to using it for games or image and speech recognition and may require different, specialised algorithms in order to be successful. The reason is that future time series patterns are never identical to the past, and training of DL methods should address this.

4　Time Series Forecasting in the Context of AI

The fourth industrial revolution brought about a new wave of terms, such as data science, AI and data mining, with time series related terms such as predictive analytics, machine learning (supervised and unsupervised) and structured and unstructured data (Big Data). Figure 4 is a summary of how the terms relate to each other.

Data science is an interdisciplinary field to extract insight from data and it is mainly concerned with prediction, summation, data manipulation and visualisation (Varian 2014). Data mining can be considered a superset of many different methods to analyse structured or unstructured data. Data mining applies methods to identify

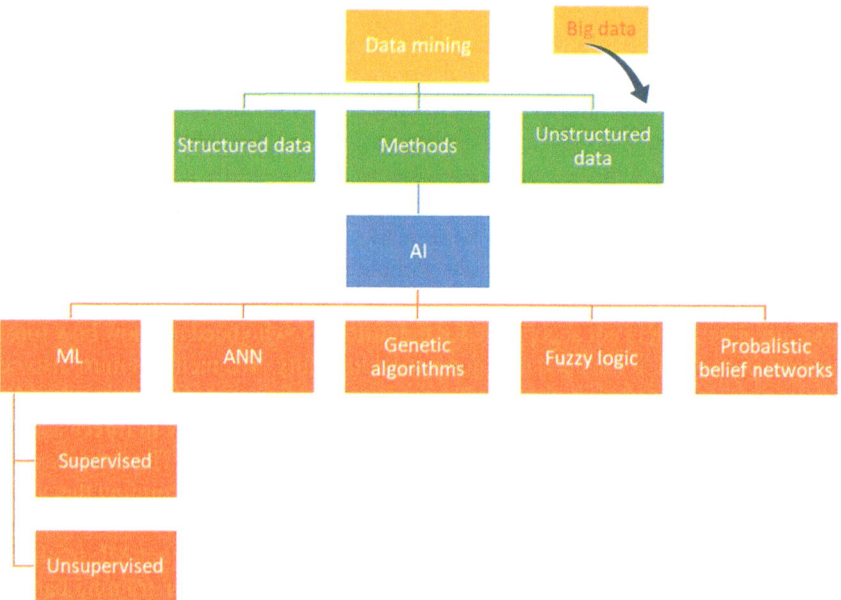

Fig. 4 Data Science and related terms

previously unknown patterns from data. Data mining also includes data storage and data manipulation (Mahalakshmi et al. 2016).

AI can be defined as a revolutionary technology that learns on its own from analysing and discovering patterns in large amounts of data. It consists of a group of data-driven methodologies, and the components of AI can be classified into artificial neural networks, genetic algorithms, fuzzy logic, probabilistic belief networks and ML (Binner et al. 2004).

ML is a component of AI (Fig. 5) and is closely related to data mining, but it is primarily focused on predictions, while data mining is concerned with summation of data and identifying patterns (Varian 2014). ML is central to many approaches to AI and is primarily analytical or statistical. Basic ML is predictive analytics using supervised learning based on data for which the values of the outcome variable are known; a typical example here is the regression-based ML model (Fig. 5). ML also includes model types like artificial neural networks and deep learning (DL), which are also statistical in nature, but are categorised as unsupervised learning (Davenport 2018) (Fig. 5). These methods identify patterns from large amounts of data and automatically learn from these patterns. ANNs and DL are the dominant ML techniques in this area (Krollner et al. 2010). AI has developed rapidly over the last decade including, inter alia, autonomous vehicles, intelligent robots, image and speech recognition, automatic translation and gaming, to name a few. AI has also been applied to forecasting using ML, and especially ANNs, to improve time series forecasts (Makridakis et al. 2018). AI has caused a paradigm shift in forecasting moving from supervised to unsupervised learning, due to Big Data. This means there was a shift from computer-assisted model- and assumption-based to data-driven and fully-automated forecasting (Faloutsos et al. 2018).

The first significant academic references to Big Data in computer science were by Weiss and Indurkhya (1998) in computer science, and Diebold (2000) in statistics and econometrics (Diebold 2012). The reference to Big Data in those first citations pertained to bigger data sets than normal, but since then it has evolved to include a range of characteristics (Leary 2013). Big Data spans and differs across fields such as computer science, statistics and econometrics and has several broad forms, such as photographic, binary and numerical. Numerical data has three main

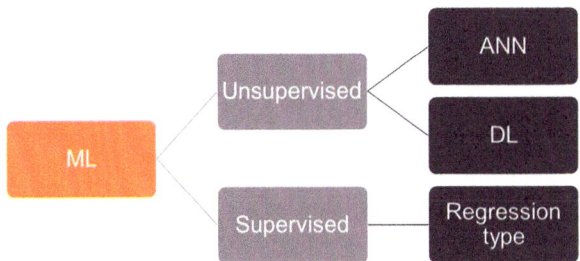

Fig. 5 The components of machine learning. Source: self-constructed

forms, namely a cross-section of observations at a single point in time, a time series of observations and a panel (Doornik and Hendry 2015).

Big Data can therefore be defined as a complex heterogeneous data set including huge-volume, high-velocity and high-variety data with potential value that can be processed electronically to inform decision-making (Rezaee et al. 2018). The Big Data revolution has transformed the modern world and is an important data mining topic currently. Data mining methods are also key in modelling the complex relationships inherent in Big Data (Hassani and Silva 2015; Mahalakshmi et al. 2016). This brings about an opportunity, as Big Data forecasting has the ability to improve organisational performance, which can mitigate risk.

There is a strong connection between Big Data and predictive analytics, even though traditional forecasting tools cannot handle the unstructured nature and size of these data sets (Hassani and Silva 2015). It is important to structure unstructured data and reduce the dimensionality, in order to capture the dynamic changes. This is a common challenge in empirical research that traditional econometric methods should address (Einav and Levin 2014). Factor modelling, a statistical dimension reduction technique, is a possible answer to this challenge and is a popular technique for Big Data forecasting. DFMs, an extension of factor models, are used extensively in Big Data forecasting; other econometric extensions are the factor-augmented error correction model (FECM), factor-augmented vector autoregression (FAVAR), the multivariate factor-augmented Bayesian shrinkage model, principle component analysis (PCA), independent PCA (ICA), sparse PCA (SPCA) and Kalman filtering for large VAR and DFM models. All these factor estimation methods have been developed in light of Big Data forecasting (Hassani and Silva 2015). ANNs and Bayesian models are also popular (Hassani and Silva 2015; Stock and Watson 2017). Furthermore, hybrid forecasting methods with dimension reduction for specification and estimation of factors with various types of ML and shrinkage methods are showing potential in Big Data forecasting (Kim and Swanson 2018).

The body of knowledge on the modelling and forecasting of time series data with econometric models is established and well understood. However, given the relative novelty of time series modelling with AI tools and Big Data within the time series context, the establishment of the body of knowledge on this is in progress. In order to aid in understanding the body of knowledge on time series modelling within the AI and Big Data space, this chapter presents a bibliometric analysis of this specific body of knowledge.

5   Methodology

In this chapter, a bibliometric analysis is implemented to offer a rigorous methodological examination of the body of knowledge on time series modelling within the AI and Big Data space. We have three objectives with the bibliometric analysis. The first objective is to determine how the production levels and number of citations within the field develop over time. The second objective is to identify the studies in the field with the highest impact. The third objective is to identify the important topics and themes in the field and how it evolves over time.

This study only considered studies published in journals that are indexed by Scopus. Therefore, the Scopus database was used to source details of all the articles related to the search terms of the study. The study excluded papers published in conference proceedings and only considered journal articles. No particular time frame is specified for this study; however, the first study that falls within the search criteria of this chapter was published in 1998. Therefore, the time horizon of the study spans from 1998 to 2024. In this study, the following search syntax was used based on Keywords:

(("modeling" OR "modelling" OR "analysis" OR "estimating" OR "estimate" OR "forecasting" OR "analysing" OR "analyzing" OR "analyse" OR "analyze") AND ("Time-series" OR "Time series" OR "Timeseries") AND ("Artificial Intelligence" OR "AI" OR "machine learning" OR "ML" OR "big data" OR "Neural Networks" OR "ANN" OR "Fuzzy Logic" OR "Genetic Algorithms" OR "Probabilistic Belief Networks") and ("Finance" or "Financial"))

In summary, this search syntax extracted all the articles that relate to time series modelling within the AI and Big Data context in the field of finance. This is based on the keywords of articles. The study made use of Biblioshiny within the RStudio package.

6 Findings

Figure 6 shows the annual production over time. This shows that there has been a steady increase in the number of articles published per annum in the field. The increase in published articles is particularly noticeable from 2018 onwards. This indicates that research interest in the field of time series modelling within the AI and Big Data context in the field of finance is growing. The productivity growth in this field is expected, given the growing popularity and awareness of AI and Big Data. It is, however, interesting to note how productivity in the field had a relative decline during the COVID pandemic (2020 to 2022).

Figure 7 shows the annual citations per year. From this figure, it is clear that citations increased considerably from 2014 to 2018, reflecting the spike in interest during this time. However, despite the continuous increase in productivity in this field from 2022 to 2024, reflected in Fig. 6, annual citations have reduced considerably. This indicates that the impact of these papers has reduced over the past 2 years. In turn, this could indicate that the body of knowledge is slightly saturated, requiring a new stream of innovative literature.

The Impact of journals in the field, measured by the H index, is reflected in Fig. 8. This shows that *Expert Systems with Applications*, *IEEE Access*, *Neurocomputing*, *Applied Soft Computing* and *Soft Computing* are the journals publishing articles with the highest impact in the field.

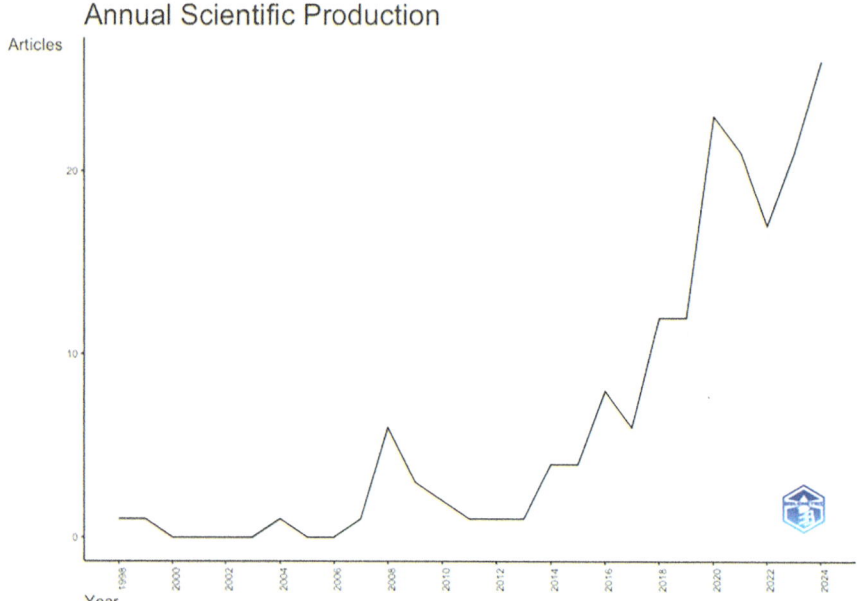

Fig. 6 Annual production over time. Source: self-constructed in RStudio

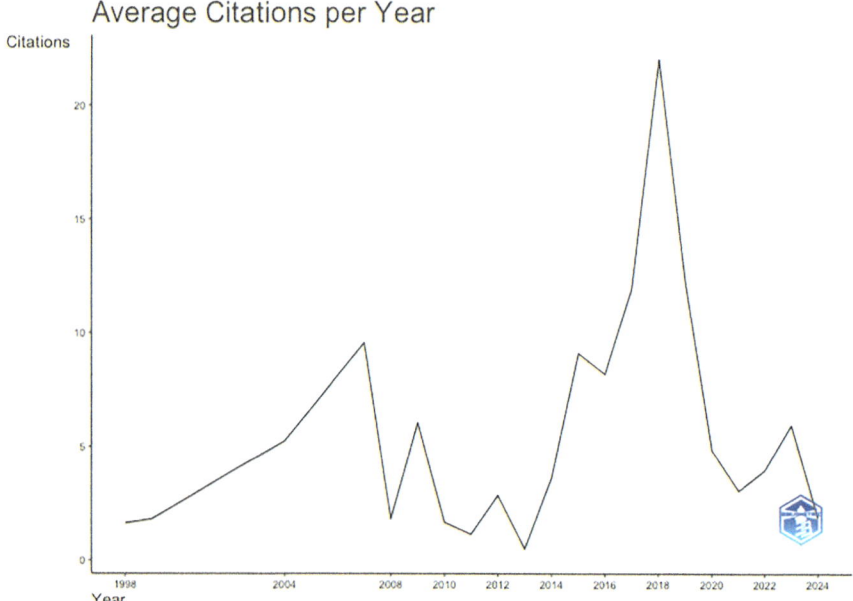

Fig. 7 Annual citations per year. Source: self-constructed in RStudio

Fig. 8 Impact of journals in the field by H index. Source: self-constructed in RStudio

Fig. 9 Word Cloud. Source: self-constructed in RStudio

A word cloud is presented in Fig. 9, showing the most prominent keywords within this field. The most prominent word in this study is "forecasting" followed by the phrase "time series analysis". These keywords used to search the articles in this study are expected to be prominent in this word cloud. It is interesting though that forecasting is the most prominent keyword amongst these articles, showing that in the field of Finance, forecasting financial variables using AI and Big Data is of primary interest. From the AI and Big Data side of the search, "Machine Learning" and "learning systems" appear to be popular AI approaches to analyse and model financial time series, followed by "Deep Learning". It is interesting and surprising to note that "Big Data" occurs very seldom as a keyword. This could potentially point to a research gap in this field that could be filled by future research.

Variables and concepts that are prominent from a finance perspective are "Electronic Trading", "Investments" and to a lesser extent, "Costs". This shows that these are the areas of finance that researchers in this field are particularly interested in. Based on keywords, there are many financial concepts with limited explicit exploration, notably, the universe of financial risks within a company and financial ratios. Further research should be done on specific financial concepts and variables. Figure 10 reflects the trending topics from 2007 to 2024.

Here we only focus on the terms related to modelling and analysis techniques. Terms that used to be prominent in this literature, but lost prominence are "computer simulation", "statistical models", "Mathematical analysis", "Mathematical computing" and "backpropagation". From this, it could be argued that maths and stats play a key role in the inauguration of AI, but once AI models are formed, the consideration of mathematical concepts in this field reduces. The reduced consideration of backpropagation is also interesting, provided that backpropagation is the process where errors of previous iterations are considered, and the weightings of neural networks are adjusted to reduce future errors (Shen et al. 2015). The reduced

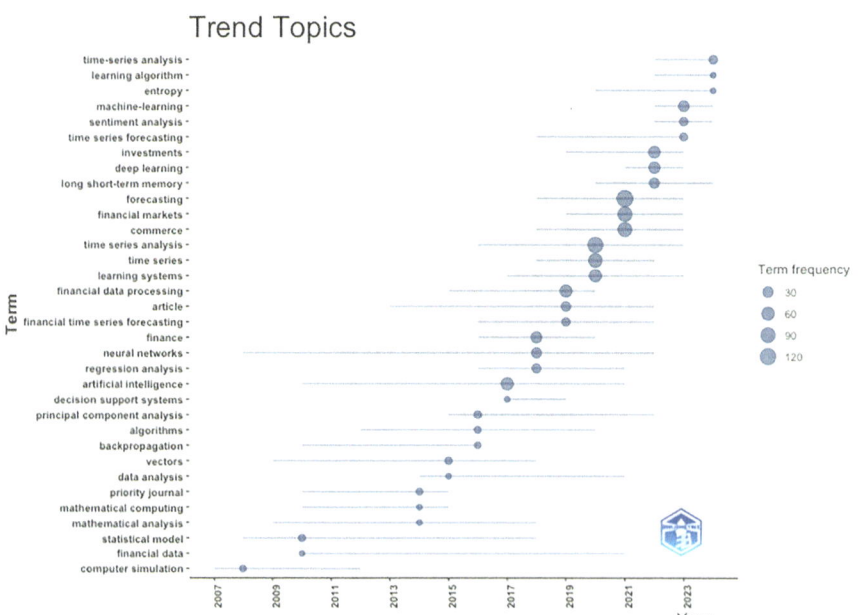

Fig. 10 Trending topics. Source: self-constructed in RStudio

focus on backpropagation could indicate that error levels of AI models have been sufficiently reduced.

Terms that have increased in prominence in recent years are "learning algorithms", "entropy", "machine learning", "deep learning", "long short-term memory" and "sentiment analysis". Of particular interest is the increase in the popularity of entropy, which relates to machine learning and is a measure of randomness in the analysis process. The rule of thumb is, the more random the process, the less usable the resulting information is (Picasso et al. 2019). This is relevant to the field of forecasting and the debate between econometric and AI forecasting. Where the process of econometric modelling is very transparent and therefore, the outputs are easily linked to the inputs and modelling process. This, in turn, increases the ability of the outputs. The increased focus on this in the literature considered in this study speaks to the importance of non-randomness to the usability of information. Given the long-term dependencies in financial data, the increased focus on "long short-term memory" in the field of financial time series modelling is also interesting. This is because "long short-term memory" is an RNN that addresses long-term dependencies in sequential data (Picasso et al. 2019). This shows that past modelling of financial data might have suffered from long-term dependencies.

The articles with the highest impact in the field, measured by citations, are reflected in Fig. 11. This shows that, to date, the following five papers have had the highest impact: Fischer and Krauss (2018), Henrique et al. (2019), Singh and Srivastava (2017), Shen et al. (2015) and Picasso et al. (2019). The paper by Fischer

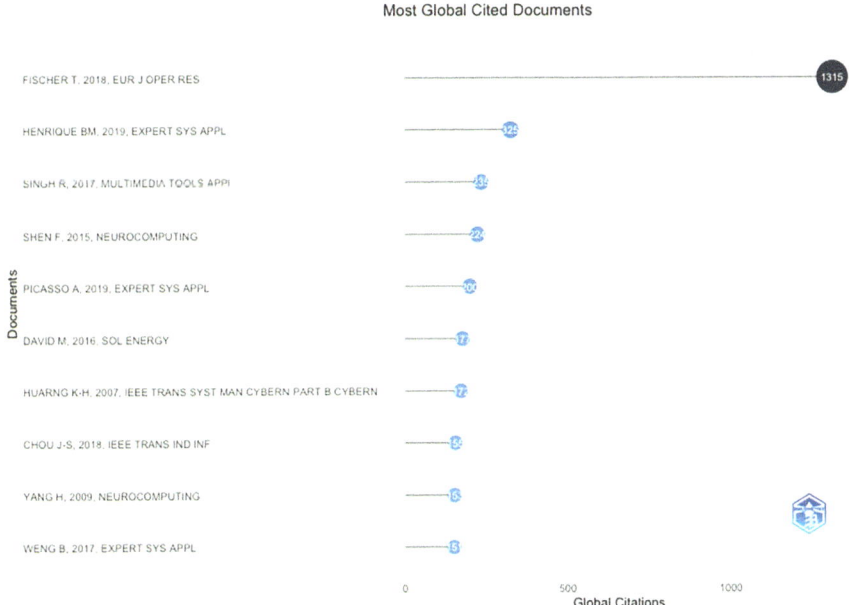

Fig. 11 Documents with the highest impact. Source: self-constructed in RStudio

and Krauss (2018) focuses on predicting financial markets with long short-term memory networks. They found that Long short-term memory networks outperform memory-free classification methods in predicting share price movements. This confirms the long-term dependencies in financial market data.

Henrique et al. (2019) conducted a literature review on machine learning techniques in forecasting financial markets. This study shows that the majority of AI forecasting models utilise support vector machines. Furthermore, the study shows that the majority of models utilise financial data from the USA to calibrate the models. This shows that there is a need to expand the literature on AI modelling in finance beyond the USA, specifically to emerging markets. The study by Singh and Srivastava (2017) uses Deep Learning in combination with Dimensional Principal Component Analysis to predict large-cap US stocks. They found that Deep Learning in combination with Dimensional Principal Component Analysis outperforms both Recurrent Neural Network and the Radial Basis Function Neural Network by approximately 16%.

The study by Shen et al. (2015) makes use of Continuous Restricted Boltzmann machines within a deep belief network to forecast exchange rates and found that this approach predicts exchange rates more accurately than traditional AI methods. The study by Picasso et al. (2019) aimed to construct a US-based stock portfolio that outperforms the broad-based US stock index by means of using machine learning techniques to combine technical and fundamental analysis. They constructed a synthetic portfolio that rendered an annualised return of 80%.

7   Challenges and the Way Forward (Education, Practice and Research)

The advanced skills required to work with Big Data present a major challenge since there is a shortage of data scientists. Researchers are highly proficient in using traditional statistical techniques to obtain accurate forecasts, but the incompatibility of traditional statistical techniques with unstructured and large data sets is impeding the effectiveness and application of forecasts from Big Data. In order to overcome this problem, it is important that curricula be developed to incorporate the skills necessary to analyse Big Data in order for future statisticians or econometricians to be well-equipped with the required skills (Hassani and Silva 2015).

To overcome the constraints imposed by skills in other disciplines, modules should also be incorporated into various programmes to develop the skills required to understand and analyse Big Data, using novel techniques (Hassani and Silva 2015). The application of Big Data and time series models in accounting and auditing is still in its infancy, but due to the availability of Big Data, the opportunity is promising (Rezaee et al. 2018). Nowadays, quality financial and non-financial information is very important and this requires the use of technology to improve financial reporting and audit processes. Business analytics, along with access to detailed industry information, aids businesses in identifying challenges and opportunities that can create business value (Bhimani and Willcocks 2014). According to Faloutsos et al. (2018), time series forecasting is central to the automation and optimisation of business processes such as supply chain, cloud computing and workforce scheduling. Big Data analytics can identify patterns and detect abnormalities and irregularities in very large data sets with uncountable transactions. Big Data time series analysis and data analytics should be incorporated into business and accounting programmes. The American Accounting Association (AAA) has promoted the integration of Big Data education in higher education over the past few years (Rezaee et al. 2018).

In terms of DFMs, opportunities exist for drawing useful information from higher factors which are usually excluded, or perhaps to exploit non-linear structure in these factors that could be revealed by modern ML methods. To explore this additional information in large datasets new methods should be developed, guided by theory (Song et al. 2019). We have seen rapid developments in methods for time series data over the past 20 years. These new methods saw the light due to improved computational capacity, improved data availability and new understanding in econometric and statistical theory. The driver behind these developments is the need for policymakers and private-sector decision-makers to understand the uncertain future. This drive will not change and time series econometricians have a challenge lying ahead, however, similar challenges stood before us 20 years ago (Stock and Watson 2017).

Similar to statistical methods, the objective of ML methods is to improve forecast accuracy by minimising the sum of squared errors. The difference lies in the fact that ML methods use non-linear algorithms, while statistical methods use mostly linear processes to minimise the loss function. Some ML methods are computationally challenging and complex, requiring computer programming skills, consequently meaning that ML is at the intersection of statistics and computer science (Makridakis et al. 2018).

Additionally, statistical software is not able to handle Big Data forecasting and computing capabilities and the structure of current statistical software will require improvements in order to be able to analyse Big Data sets. To work with Big Data sets, knowledge of the tools of computer scientist, such as Python, R and SQL, is key (Einav and Levin 2014; Hassani and Silva 2015).

Not only does time series forecasting have a wide application field, but the research landscape is also quite wide, with research experts in statistics, econometrics, data mining and data bases—each with a unique focus. In statistics and econometrics, forecasting methods have been developed to forecast time series with an array of models to fit a time series pattern. Then again, data mining and database researchers focus on finding patterns in Big Data time series. DL is dominant in ML applications (Fig. 4) and has gained interest in the field of time series forecasting, which has the potential to improve forecasting performance (Faloutsos et al. 2018). Opportunities exist for productive collaboration between econometricians and ML theorists. Econometricians, statisticians and data mining specialists are concerned with the insights from data, and ML specialists are concerned with developing high-performing computer systems to produce useful forecasts—a powerful combination (Varian 2014).

8 Conclusion

Time series forecasting is part of ML and it has evolved over time from simple linear methods to non-linear methods and complex deep learning methods, showing a shift from supervised to unsupervised learning.

Forecasting competitions over the years have facilitated the development of the time series forecasting field, and the latest competition highlighted the shortcomings of unsupervised ML and DL methods for time series forecasting. However, unsupervised ML methods and DL methods have the potential to increase forecasting accuracy over time since these methods have a better learning ability than classical statistical methods. Forecast accuracy should be established by comparing these models' ability to simple statistical methods or naïve benchmarks. Combining various methods addressing different components of a time series has proven to improve forecast accuracy, equally, the combination of supervised and unsupervised learning has shown a similar trend.

The Big Data revolution has transformed the modern world and is an important data mining topic that spans across fields. Data mining forms the basis for AI and ML. Although ML is a component of AI, these three notions are intertwined and work together to answer questions, prove hypotheses and give insight into the behaviour of time series. An interdependent relationship exists by which a combination of methods can be used to produce more accurate results.

Due to this data revolution, challenges and opportunities exist for research, education, current research fields and new research fields. A new skill set is necessary due to the availability of data in certain fields, and the advances in computational power, technology and DL empower researchers to handle bigger time series data sets with better speed and accuracy. Various approaches give the flexibility to choose the best method according to the characteristics of the data.

The challenges that researchers face are: how to build time series models that significantly learn to forecast from Big Data sets; and, how to improve forecasting with learning models when we have limited observations. It is also important to determine the implications for building forecasting systems that can handle large data volumes. Subjects such as the black box in learning models, confidence intervals and uncertainty of forecasts should be considered.

As the forecasting field has evolved, two findings have changed the field fundamentally and have stood steadfast through the test of time. These findings are, firstly, that the best methods or models to fit a time series do not necessarily result in more accurate *ex ante* forecasts and, secondly, that *ex ante* forecasts of simple models are found to be at least as accurate as the complex ones. Researchers should therefore take cognisance of this with the new wave of developments in time series forecasting we are facing.

Furthermore, these developments also brought forth the combination of different fields or disciplines and expertise. Therefore, looking at the future—the lens we use should focus on a multidisciplinary approach to solving complex problems in time series forecasting.

References

Bahrammirzaee A (2010) A comparative survey of artificial intelligence applications in finance: artificial neural networks, expert system and hybrid intelligent systems. Neural Comput & Applic:1165–1195. https://doi.org/10.1007/s00521-010-0362-z

Bhimani A, Willcocks L (2014) Digitisation, "Big Data" and the transformation of accounting information digitisation. Account Bus Res 44(4):469–490. https://doi.org/10.1080/0001478 8.2014.910051

Binner JM, Kendall G, Chen S (2004) Applications of aritificial intelligence in finance and economics. Advances in Econometrics, Vol. 19. Elsevier

Davenport TH (2018) From analytics to artificial intelligence. J Bus Anal Taylor & Francis 1(2):73–80. https://doi.org/10.1080/2573234X.2018.1543535

De Gooijer JG, Hyndman RJ (2006) 25 years of time series forecasting. Int J Forecast 22(3):443–473. https://doi.org/10.1016/j.ijforecast.2006.01.001

Diebold FX (2012) PIER Working Paper 12-037 On the Origin (s) and Development of the Term "Big Data"

Doornik JA, Hendry DF (2015) Statistical model selection with "Big Data". Cogent Econ Finance 169:1–15. https://doi.org/10.1080/23322039.2015.1045216

Einav L, Levin J (2014) The data revolution and economic analysis. Innov Policy Econ 14:1–24

Faloutsos C et al (2018) Forecasting big time series. In: Proceedings of the VLDB Endowment, pp 2102–2105. https://doi.org/10.14778/3229863.3229878

Fischer T, Krauss C (2018) Deep learning with long short-term memory networks for financial market predictions. Eur J Oper Res 2(270):654–669. https://doi.org/10.1016/j.ejor.2017.11.054

Hajizadeh E et al (2012) A hybrid modeling approach for forecasting the volatility of S & P 500 index return. Exp Syst Appl Elsevier Ltd 39(1):431–436. https://doi.org/10.1016/j.eswa.2011.07.033

Hassani, H. and Silva, F. S. (2015) 'Forecasting with big data: a review', Annals of data science. Springer: Berlin, Heidelberg, 2(1), pp. 5–19. doi: https://doi.org/10.1007/s40745-015-0029-9

Henrique BM, Sobreiro VA, Kimura H (2019) Literature review: machine learning techniques applied to financial market prediction. Expert Syst Appl 124:226–251. https://doi.org/10.1016/j.eswa.2019.01.012

Hyndman RJ (2019) A brief history of forecasting competitions. Monash Econometrics and Business Statistics Working Papers

Jiao EX, Chen JL (2018) Tourism forecasting: a review of methodological developments over the last decade. Tour Econ 25(3):469–492. https://doi.org/10.1177/1354816618812588

Kim HH, Swanson NR (2018) Mining big data using parsimonious factor, machine learning, variable selection and shrinkage methods. Int J Forecast 34(2):339–354

Krollner B, Vanstone B, Finnie G (2010) Financial time series forecasting with machine learning techniques: a survey. European Symposium on Artificial Neural Networks: Computational and Machine Learning, pp 25–30. Available at: http://epublications.bond.edu.au/infotech_pubs/110%5Cn http://epublications.bond.edu.au/infotech_pubs/110/

Leary DEO (2013) "Big data", the "internet of things" and the "internet of signs". Intell Syst Account Finance Manage 20:53–65. https://doi.org/10.1002/isaf

Mahalakshmi G, Sridevi S, Rajaram S (2016) A survey on forecasting of time series data. In: 2016 International Conference on Computing Technologies and Intelligent Data Engineering,

ICCTIDE 2016 Institute of Electrical and Electronics Engineers Inc. https://doi.org/10.1109/ICCTIDE.2016.7725358

Makridakis S, Spiliotis E, Assimakopoulos V (2018) Statistical and machine learning forecasting methods: concerns and ways forward. PLoS One 13(3):1–26. https://doi.org/10.1371/journal.pone.0194889

Picasso A, Merello S, Ma Y, Oneto L, Cambria E (2019) Technical analysis and sentiment embeddings for market trend prediction. Expert Syst Appl 135:60–70. https://doi.org/10.1016/j.eswa.2019.06.014

Rezaee Z, Dorestani A, Aliabadi S (2018) Application of time series analyses in big data: practical, research, and education implications. Ssrn 15(1):183–197. https://doi.org/10.2139/ssrn.3148726

Shen F, Chao J, Zhao J (2015) Forecasting exchange rate using deep belief networks and conjugate gradient method. Neurocomputing 167:243–253. https://doi.org/10.1016/j.neucom.2015.04.071

Singh R, Srivastava S (2017) Stock prediction using deep learning. Multimed Tools Appl 18(76):18569–18584. https://doi.org/10.1007/s11042-016-4159-7

Song H, Qiu RTR, Park J (2019) A review of research on tourism demand forecasting. Ann Tour Res Elsevier 75:338–362. https://doi.org/10.1016/j.annals.2018.12.001

Stock JH, Watson MW (2017) Twenty years of time series econometrics in ten pictures. J Econ Perspect 31(2):59–86. https://doi.org/10.1257/jep.31.2.59

Timmermann A (2018) Forecasting methods in finance. Annu Rev Financ Econ 10(1):449–479. https://doi.org/10.1146/annurev-financial-110217-022713

Tsay RS (2000) Time series and forecasting : brief history and future association. J Am Stat Assoc 95(450):638–643

Varian HR (2014) Big data : new tricks for econometrics. J Econ Perspect 28(2):3–28

Wang J et al (2016) Elman recurrent random neural networks. Comput Intell Neurosci 2016

Wang L et al (2013) An ARIMA-ANN hybrid model for time series forecasting. Syst Res Behav Sci 30(May):244–259. https://doi.org/10.1002/sres

Weiss SM, Indurkhya N (1998) Predictive data mining: a practical guide. Morgan Kaufmann

Zhang GP (2003) Time series forecasting using a hybrid ARIMA and neural network model. Neurocomputing 50:159–175

Zharov AN et al (2016) Theoretical foundations of using econometric methods of time series forecasting. Glob J Pure Appl Math 12(1):157–166

Conclusion: The Currency of Our Remade World

Collins Achepsah Leke and Michael Adelowotan

Abstract This concluding chapter synthesises the transformative impact of artificial intelligence on accounting, auditing, and financial services, with particular emphasis on the fundamental role of data as a strategic asset. The chapter examines how the convergence of AI, underpinned by sophisticated data infrastructure, is reshaping professional roles and organisational capabilities in the financial sector. Through analysis of current research and industry practices, we demonstrate how effective data management and governance have become critical success factors in modern financial services.

The discussion encompasses the technical, operational, and strategic challenges organisations face in building robust data infrastructure, implementing AI solutions, and ensuring regulatory compliance. Special attention is given to the evolution of professional roles, as traditional financial functions transform into data-driven, advisory positions requiring new combinations of technical and business skills. The chapter also explores emerging trends in quantum computing, edge processing, and artificial general intelligence, highlighting their potential impact on future financial services.

Key findings indicate that organisations successful in this transformation demonstrate superior profitability and operational efficiency, while emphasising the critical balance between automation and human judgment. The conclusion presents a framework for understanding and navigating the future of financial services, where data quality, ethical considerations, and continuous professional development emerge as crucial elements for success in an AI-driven financial landscape.

Keywords Artificial intelligence · Data infrastructure · Financial services · Professional evolution · Data governance · Emerging technologies

C. A. Leke (✉) · M. Adelowotan
Department of Accountancy, University of Johannesburg, Johannesburg, South Africa
e-mail: collinsl@uj.ac.za; madelowotan@uj.ac.za

© The Author(s), under exclusive license to Springer Nature
Switzerland AG 2025
M. Adelowotan, C. A. Leke (eds.), *Artificial Intelligence in Accounting, Auditing and Finance*, Contributions to Finance and Accounting,
https://doi.org/10.1007/978-3-031-87368-3_12

As we conclude our comprehensive exploration of artificial intelligence in accounting, auditing, and finance, it becomes increasingly clear that we stand at a pivotal moment in the evolution of financial services. The Fourth Industrial Revolution (4IR) technologies, powered by the exponential growth in data availability and processing capabilities, are fundamentally reshaping how financial information is collected, analysed, and utilised (Francisco and Linnér 2023). This transformation is not merely technological but represents a paradigm shift in how we understand and manage financial systems.

1 The Centrality of Data in Modern Financial Services: Data as the New Currency

The phrase "data is the new oil" has become somewhat cliché, but in financial services, data has emerged as something even more fundamental—it has become the new currency itself (MacPherson and Ramsay 2023). The value of financial institutions and their services increasingly depends on their ability to:

- Collect and process vast amounts of structured and unstructured data (Deekshith 2023)
- Extract meaningful insights from complex data sets (Chui et al. 2023)
- Ensure data quality, security, and compliance (Marelli and Testa 2018), and,
- Leverage data for competitive advantage (Khan et al. 2024)

Research by Glasser (2013) and Adeoye et al. (2024) indicates that financial institutions that effectively leverage their data assets demonstrate 23% higher profitability than their peers, highlighting the critical importance of data management capabilities.

2 The Data Infrastructure Challenge

The foundation of successful AI implementation in financial services rests on robust data infrastructure. Organisations must address several critical challenges, like:

1. Data Quality and Standardisation

   - Ensuring consistency across diverse data sources (Shi et al. 2019)
   - Implementing effective data governance frameworks (Ladley 2019) and
   - Maintaining data accuracy and reliability (Lu et al. 2023)

2. Data Integration and Accessibility

   - Breaking down data silos (Valleru et al. 2022)
   - Creating unified data platforms (Mijić and Varga 2018) and
   - Enabling real-time data access and processing (Sharma and Wang 2017)

3. Data Security and Privacy
   - Implementing robust cybersecurity measures (Abrahams et al. 2024)
   - Ensuring compliance with privacy regulations (Manda 2022) and
   - Managing data sovereignty requirements (Hellmeier et al. 2023)

3   The Convergence of 4IR Technologies and Financial Services: The Synergistic Effect

The true power of 4IR technologies lies in their convergence. Our analysis throughout this book has demonstrated how the use of AI, in certain instances combined with other technologies like blockchain, IoT, and cloud computing, creates transformative capabilities like:

1. Enhanced decision-making which would involve real-time data analytics, predictive modelling and forecasting, and risk assessment and management.
2. Automated processes entailing intelligent process automation, smart contracts and blockchain integration, and machine learning-driven workflows.
3. Improved customers experience due to personalised financial services, AI-powered customer support, and enhanced security and fraud prevention.

4   Impact on Professional Roles

The convergence of these technologies is reshaping professional roles in accounting, auditing, and finance. Some of these are as follows:

1. Accountants would evolve from data processors to strategic advisors, would focus on data interpretation and analysis, and would oversee the integration of technology and financial expertise.
2. Auditors would shift to continuous auditing models as opposed to traditional methods, would benefit from enhanced fraud detection capabilities, and would have access to real-time risk assessment.
3. Financial Analysts would possess advanced data analytics skills, would benefit from the integration of alternative data sources resulting in accurate and relevant suggestions, and would be beneficiaries of advanced predictive modelling expertise.

5   The Future of Data-Driven Financial Services: Emerging Trends

Looking ahead, several key trends will shape the future of financial services, like:

1. Quantum Computing and Financial Data whereby there would be enhanced cryptographic security, complex portfolio optimisation, and advanced risk modelling.
2. Edge Computing and Real-Time Processing because of distributed data processing, enhanced mobile banking capabilities, and IoT integration in financial services.
3. Artificial General Intelligence (AGI) leading to advanced decision-making capabilities, enhanced pattern recognition, and automated complex analysis.

6   Challenges and Opportunities

The road ahead presents both challenges and opportunities, some of these being:

1. Technical challenges that would entail data quality and standardisation, system integration and interoperability, and processing power and efficiency.
2. Regulatory considerations that would comprise the likes of data privacy and protection, financial regulations compliance, and cross-border data flows.
3. Professional development with skill gap bridging, continuous learning requirements, and technical and soft skills balance all coming to the fore.

7   Final Thoughts

As we conclude this comprehensive examination of AI in accounting, auditing, and finance, several key insights emerge, for instance:

1. The fundamental role of data quality and governance in successful AI implementation
2. The critical importance of integrating 4IR technologies effectively
3. The need for continuous professional development and adaptation
4. The balance between automation and human judgment and
5. The ethical considerations in AI-driven financial services

The future of financial services will belong to those organisations and professionals who can effectively harness the power of data and AI, maintain ethical standards and transparency, adapt to rapid technological change, balance innovation with risk management, and prioritise security and privacy. This transformation represents not just a technological evolution, but a fundamental reimagining of how financial services operate and create value. As we move forward, the successful integration of AI and data-driven technologies will require a delicate balance between innovation and responsibility, automation and human judgment, efficiency and security.

The journey ahead is both challenging and exciting. Those who embrace these changes while maintaining a focus on ethical considerations and professional standards will be best positioned to thrive in this new era of financial services. As we close this book, we encourage readers to view these developments not as threats but as opportunities to enhance and elevate their professional capabilities and the value they provide to their organisations and clients.

References

Abrahams TO, Ewuga SK, Dawodu SO, Adegbite AO, Hassan AO (2024) A review of cybersecurity strategies in modern organizations: examining the evolution and effectiveness of cybersecurity measures for data protection. Comput Sci IT Res J 5(1):1–25

Adeoye OB, Addy WA, Ajayi-Nifise AO, Odeyemi O, Okoye CC, Ofodile OC (2024) Leveraging AI and data analytics for enhancing financial inclusion in developing economies. Finance Account Res J 6(3):288–303

Chui M, Issler M, Roberts R, Yee L (2023) Technology trends outlook 2023

Deekshith A (2023) Scalable machine learning: techniques for managing data volume and velocity in AI applications. Int Sci J Res 5(5)

Francisco M, Linnér BO (2023) AI and the governance of sustainable development. An idea analysis of the European Union, the United Nations, and the world economic forum. Environ Sci Pol 150:103590

Glasser TD (2013) Leveraging data for financial stability monitoring. J Bank Regul 14(3):195–208

Hellmeier M, Pampus J, Qarawlus H, Howar F (2023) Implementing data sovereignty: requirements & challenges from practice. In: Proceedings of the 18th international conference on availability, reliability and security, pp 1–9

Khan R, Usman M, Moinuddin M (2024) The big data revolution: leveraging vast information for competitive advantage. Revista Espanola de Documentacion Cientifica 18(02):65–94

Ladley J (2019) Data governance: how to design, deploy, and sustain an effective data governance program. Academic Press

Lu YJ, Lee WC, Wang CH (2023) Using data mining technology to explore causes of inaccurate reliability data and suggestions for maintenance management. J Loss Prev Process Ind 83:105063

MacPherson A, Ramsay J (2023) Are intelligence agencies opening up? A proposed research agenda. J Homel Secur Educ 16:1–15

Manda JK (2022) Data privacy and GDPR compliance in telecom: ensuring compliance with data privacy regulations like GDPR in telecom data handling and customer information management. MZ Comput J 3(1)

Marelli L, Testa G (2018) Scrutinizing the EU general data protection regulation. Science 360(6388):496–498

Mijić D, Varga E (2018) Unified IoT platform architecture platforms as major iot building blocks. In: 2018 international conference on computing and network communications (CoCoNet). IEEE, pp 6–13

Sharma SK, Wang X (2017) Live data analytics with collaborative edge and cloud processing in wireless IoT networks. IEEE Access 5:4621–4635

Shi P, Cui Y, Xu K, Zhang M, Ding L (2019) Data consistency theory and case study for scientific big data. Information 10(4):137
Valleru V, Alapati NKK, Visa I (2022) Breaking down data silos: innovations in cloud data integration. Adv Comput Sci 5(1)

The manufacturer's authorised representative in the EU is Springer
Nature Customer Service Centre GmbH, Europaplatz 3, 69115 Heidelberg,
Germany. If you have any concerns regarding our products, please
contact ProductSafety@springernature.com

Printed and bound by CPI Group (UK) Ltd, Croydon, CR0 4YY
24/04/2026
02096316-0003